1

Sacred Hands, Secured Rights

A Legal & Spiritual Blueprint for Indigenous and Religious Therapeutics

Based on the work of Dr. Anthony B. James | NAIC

Sacred Hands, Secured Rights

Religious Therapeutics, Native American Sovereignty, and Legal Protection for Christian, Holistic, and Naturopathic Practitioners

By

Dr. Anthony B. James

Disclaimer

This book is intended for educational and devotional use by ministers, Indigenous practitioners, students, and other readers interested in the ethical, historical, and legal context of Religion-Based Indigenous, Traditional Native American, Complementary and Alternative Medicine, and Religious Therapeutics. It presents general principles, case studies, and examples drawn from published statutes, court decisions, historical sources, and the internal guidelines of church and tribal organizations such as the Native American Indigenous Church (NAIC). It does **not** provide individualized legal, medical, psychological, or financial advice.

Nothing in this work creates an attorney–client, doctor–patient, counselor–client, or other professional relationship between the author and the reader. The author is not an attorney and does not hold himself out as a provider of legal services. Any references to United States, state, tribal, or international laws, cases, or regulations are offered solely as background information and should not be relied upon as a complete or current statement of the law. Laws and their interpretations change frequently and vary by jurisdiction; readers must consult a qualified attorney or other appropriate professional licensed in their state, province, or country before taking any action that could have legal consequences.

Similarly, descriptions of health practices, ceremonies, sacraments, remedies, or therapeutic methods, including but not limited to Native American Traditional Indigenous Medicine, SomaVeda® Thai Yoga, Chirothesia, herbal and nutritional approaches, prayer, and laying on of hands, are presented as religious, cultural, historical, and educational material. They are **not** intended as a diagnosis, prescription, treatment, or cure for any disease, injury, or mental or physical condition as defined by secular medical practice acts or regulatory agencies. This book is not a substitute for competent medical, psychological, or other professional care; readers should continue to seek and follow the advice of licensed health-care providers for any condition that may require such attention.

This book discusses legal exemptions, protections, and strategies available to religious and Indigenous practitioners under federal, state, tribal, and international law. These exemptions are **not loopholes** and do not authorize anyone to violate criminal statutes, endanger others, or exceed the limits of their training and authorization. The examples given assume sincere religious belief, appropriate training, honest disclosure, informed consent, and practice within clearly defined ecclesiastical or tribal scopes under the authority of bona fide organizations. The mere reading or possession of this book does **not** confer ordination, membership, licensure, certification, or legal protection of any kind. Readers remain fully responsible for their own conduct and for complying with all applicable laws in the places where they live and work

The author, publisher, and any affiliated organizations disclaim any liability for loss, damage, injury, error, omissions or legal consequences alleged to have arisen directly or indirectly from the use or misuse of the information contained in these pages. Each reader is urged to exercise prudence, seek competent legal and medical counsel when needed, and to apply the principles discussed here only in a manner consistent with their own sincere and firmly held convictions, their organizational authorizations, and the laws of their jurisdiction.

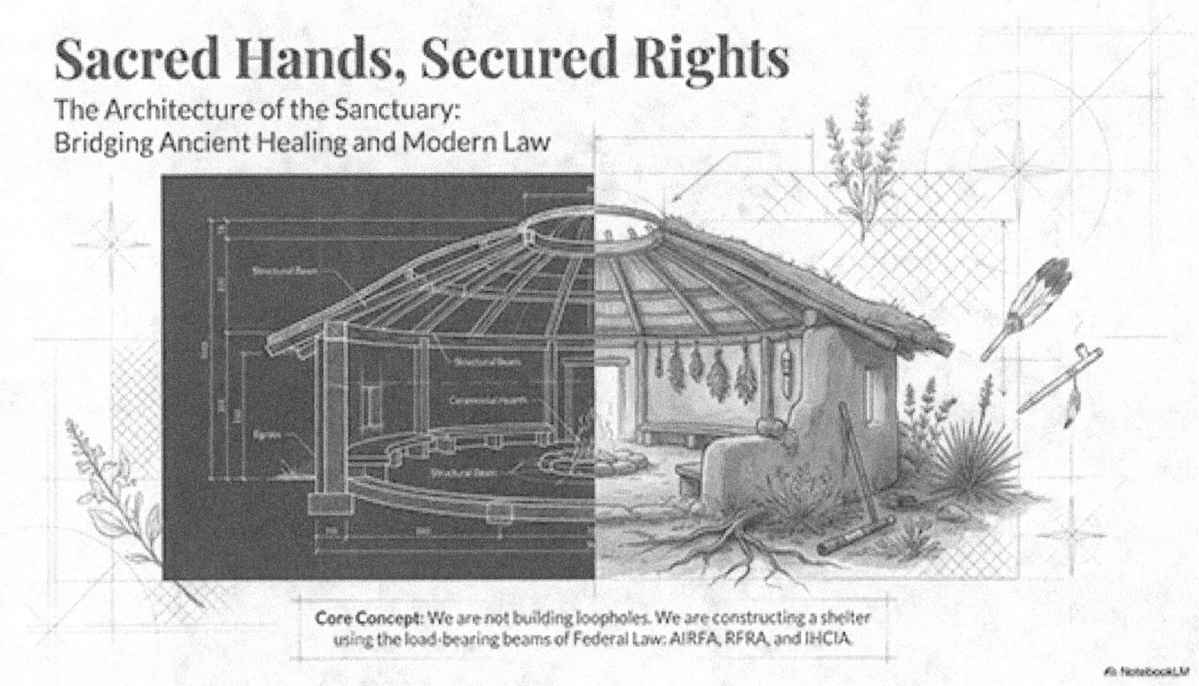

Sacred Hands, Secured Rights

The Architecture of the Sanctuary:
Bridging Ancient Healing and Modern Law

Core Concept: We are not building loopholes. We are constructing a shelter using the load-bearing beams of Federal Law: AIRFA, RFRA, and IHCIA.

Figure 1: NAIC Native American Sacred Sweat Lodge Ceremony: Inipi Lodge was built on NAIC Private land by Medicine Man Anthony B. James, Brooksville, Florida

Table of Contents

whereof

[Signed by]

AMENDMENTS TO THE CONSTITUTION [1]

Religious and Political Freedom

Congress must not interfere with freedom of religion, speech or press, assembly, and petition. Congress shall make no law re-specting an establishment of religion, or prohibiting the free exer-cise thereof; or abridging the freedom of speech, or of the press; or the right of the people peaceably to assemble, and to petition the government for a redress of grievances.

see p. 152.

kground of
ll of Rights

Article II. Right to bear arms. A well-regulated militia being nec-essary to the security of a free State, the right of the people to keep and bear arms [i.e., for military purposes] shall not be infringed.

Quartering of Troops

Soldiers may not be arbitrarily quartered or be quartered in a house within time of peace nor in time of war, in a manner

Preface: A Word to the Healer–Minister

If you are reading these pages, you likely did not arrive here by accident. You came because you have been called, by Scripture, by elders, by conscience, by community need, or by the unmistakable quiet that follows suffering when no one else knows what to do. You may not wear a white coat. You may not bill insurance. You may not speak in code or in diagnoses. Yet people come to you anyway, because your presence carries something they recognize: prayer without shame, counsel without contempt, and hands that remember how to bless.

This book begins with a truth that modern systems often overlook: every healing act lives in two worlds at once, a world of belief and a world of law. When you lay on hands, anoint with oil, offer herbs as stewardship of Creation, counsel someone toward moral alignment, or hold space for ceremony, you are not merely "doing a technique." You are expressing a theology of what a human being is, and you are making a jurisdictional claim about who has authority over that act, church, tribe, family tradition, or state. This is why so many sincere healers are misunderstood. Regulators may see "bodywork." Boards may hear "unlicensed practice." Prosecutors may assume "commerce." But you know, in your bones, that what you are doing is ministry.

Sincerity alone is not a legal strategy.

The purpose of *Sacred Hands, Secured Rights* is to give healer–ministers something most were never taught in seminary, apprenticeship, or ceremony: a clear map of the lawful shelter that already exists for religious and Indigenous healing in the United States. It explains the four umbrellas under which healing can occur: secular licensure, ecclesiastical authority, Native American/tribal jurisdiction, and Private Membership Associations, and shows how these umbrellas function as real structures rather than imaginary loopholes. Under these umbrellas, law has long recognized boundaries the state may not cross lightly: the internal life of churches, the sovereignty of tribes and bona fide tribal religious bodies, and the privacy of voluntary association. Your work belongs to that protected domain when it is honestly named, ethically practiced, and properly structured.

You will also find in these chapters a sober insistence on boundaries. This book does not romanticize the language of exemption or treat religious freedom as a magic phrase. The protections discussed here were never designed to license fraud, reckless endangerment, or the marketing of medicine under a religious label. The law, like wise elders, looks for the "real deal": sincerity that is visible in conduct; communities that are real, not invented on paper; structures that demonstrate accountability; and a disciplined refusal to claim what you do not do, diagnose, prescribe, or promise to cure in the secular statutory sense. Your credibility increases when your inner and outer roads align.

Part II, in particular, answers a crucial question: once you know your work is ministry and not secular medicine, what law actually protects that ministry? It outlines the federal protections that provide a practical foundation for religious and Indigenous healing, including protections for worship through ceremonies and traditional rites; strict scrutiny when government substantially burdens religious exercise; and land-use limits that prevent zoning and local hostility from stifling churches and ceremonial grounds. It also clarifies what the Indian Health Care Improvement Act does and does not do regarding "traditional health care practices," including its limitations: promotion must remain consistent with Service standards, and the United States limits its liability for harms arising from the provision of such practices. In plain terms: the law makes room for traditional healing, but it expects wisdom, structure, and safety.

You will meet key cases that illuminate how courts think at the edges, where sincere belief meets regulatory pressure, and where sacramental practice meets public-safety scrutiny. These decisions do not grant blanket permission; they set out the conditions under which the judiciary recognizes protected religious exercise and the circumstances that warrant enforcement. If you work near the frontier, entheogens, invasive rites, or high-risk interventions, this book will not flatter you. It will urge you to slow down, tighten your protocols, and remember that sometimes the most sacred word in ceremony is "no."

If that sounds heavy, it is. But this is also an inviting book, because the message is not fear; it is footing. You are not powerless. You are not alone. There are lawful, time-tested ways to situate healing where it belongs: in the sanctuary, not the marketplace; under covenant, not under commercial misclassification. With clear language, informed consent, real membership and oversight, and a coherent theology of health as wholeness, you can serve with courage and clarity.

Read this book the way you would build a lodge: with patience, with precision, and with respect for the load-bearing beams. Take what fits your lineage and your calling. Mark what requires counsel. Correct what needs correction. And above all, let your aim remain clean: not to "get away with something," but to protect what is sacred, so that you can bless the sick, counsel the broken, and keep faith with your duty without living in fear of misunderstanding.

May these pages help you stand upright, speak plainly, and practice in a way that honors God, respects tribal and ecclesiastical authority, protects the people, and keeps your hands, your sacred hands, free to do the work they were given to do.

How to Use This Book

This is not a book to admire. It is a book to **implement**. You will get far more out of it if you treat it like a field manual for building (or rebuilding) a lawful healing ministry, one that is spiritually authentic, ethically disciplined, and legally intelligible to outsiders. The goal is not merely to "learn the law," but to organize your calling so that your beliefs, your language, your paperwork, your setting, and your conduct all point to the same thing: ministry, not secular medicine.

What this book is and is not.

This book is written for ordained ministers, lay ministers, Indigenous practitioners, pastoral counselors, and religious therapeutic workers who want to serve people through prayer, ceremony, laying on of hands, traditional natural modalities, and moral-spiritual counsel within an ecclesiastical, tribal, or private association framework. It is educational and devotional in purpose, not individualized legal advice, and it does not create any professional relationship (attorney–client, doctor–patient, counselor–client) between author and reader. Use it the way you would use a map: it can show you where roads exist, where cliffs are, and where shelters are found, but you still must walk wisely in your own jurisdiction, with counsel when needed.

A suggested plan (three passes)

Pass 1: Find your umbrella (identity and jurisdiction)

Start by reading Part I and the opening chapters of Part II to clarify your identity: What exactly are you doing, sacrament, pastoral care, Indigenous medicine, religious therapeutics, and under which jurisdiction are you claiming the right to do it? Your first deliverable in this pass is a one-paragraph "role statement" you can say out loud without hesitation (e.g., "I serve members as a minister providing Religious Therapeutics; I do not diagnose or prescribe as defined by state law"). If you cannot say this cleanly, you are not ready to advertise, accept clients, or set prices.

Pass 2: Build the structure (practice design and safeguards)

Next, read Part VI with a highlighter. It translates law into practice by showing how to organize your ministry so it reflects its identity. Your deliverables in this pass are structural, not theoretical: a membership pathway, a consent pathway, defined scopes of practice, a code of ethics (or adoption of one), and a decision rule for when you must refer out to licensed care (red flags, emergencies, high-risk presentations).

Pass 3: Stress-test your language (so you don't get misclassified)

Then do a "word audit" of everything public-facing: website, flyers, intake forms, receipts, social profiles, and how you describe sessions verbally. Your mission here is to remove trigger words that collapse you into regulated categories (e.g., language that implies diagnosing, treating, prescribing, curing, or practicing licensed massage/medicine/psychotherapy), and replace them with accurate religious descriptors consistent with the book's framework (Religious Therapeutics, Chirothesia, Indigenous healing, pastoral care, etc.). Most legal problems in this space begin not with what you did, but with what you *called* what you did.

Choose your track (use-case pathways)
Track A: "I am already licensed."

If you hold a state license (LMT, nurse, counselor, etc.), do not blend your lanes casually. This book emphasizes that you operate in two jurisdictions, and your behavior, paperwork, and environment must match the "hat" you are wearing. Start with the "Two Jurisdictions" guidance and choose a model: clean separation (often the safest) or carefully integrated roles (only where ethically and legally permitted, with strong transparency and documentation).

Track B: "I am not licensed, and I do not want to be"

Read Part II as your legal architecture primer, then move directly into Part VI's implementation steps: membership, consent, ethical boundaries, and organizational alignment, so your work occurs inside a private ecclesiastical/tribal/PMA domain rather than the general public marketplace. Your focus is not on "getting around" regulations; it is on building a real ministry structure that can be recognized as such.

Track C: "I am building a dream clinic/ministry"

Use this book as a design sequence: define your theology of health (Part I), choose your lawful umbrella(s) (Part II), define your sacramental modalities and nonmedical scope (Parts III–IV), and then implement with forms, policies, and training (Part VI). Treat each chapter like a build step: you should be able to point to a document, policy, or practice change that resulted from reading it

The "Implementation Checklist" (what you should produce)

By the time you finish, you should have the following in writing and in practice:

- A personal "Statement of Sacred Conviction and Ecclesiastical Duty" consistent with your lineage and theology.
- A clear scope-of-practice statement and a clear list of what you do **not** do (no diagnosing/prescribing/curing as defined by secular practice acts).
- A private membership pathway (who is a member, how they join, and how services are limited to members).
- A Religious Therapeutics informed-consent process (signed forms, disclosures, assumptions of responsibility, referral language).
- A code of ethics and accountability pathway (how complaints are handled; how discipline works; who supervises/mentors you).
- A "red flag" referral rule (when you refer to ER/physician/mental health professional; how you document that referral).
- A clean separation plan if you are dual-role (separate branding/forms/records, or documented integration with stricter-standard compliance).

Read with integrity (and with elders)

Finally, use this book in the community. Where possible, bring your draft statements and forms to your elders, church leadership, or organizational oversight body for review before you launch. This book repeatedly emphasizes that lawful shelter is strongest when your ministry is not a solo performance but an accountable, disciplined practice inside a bona fide ecclesiastical/tribal/PMA framework.

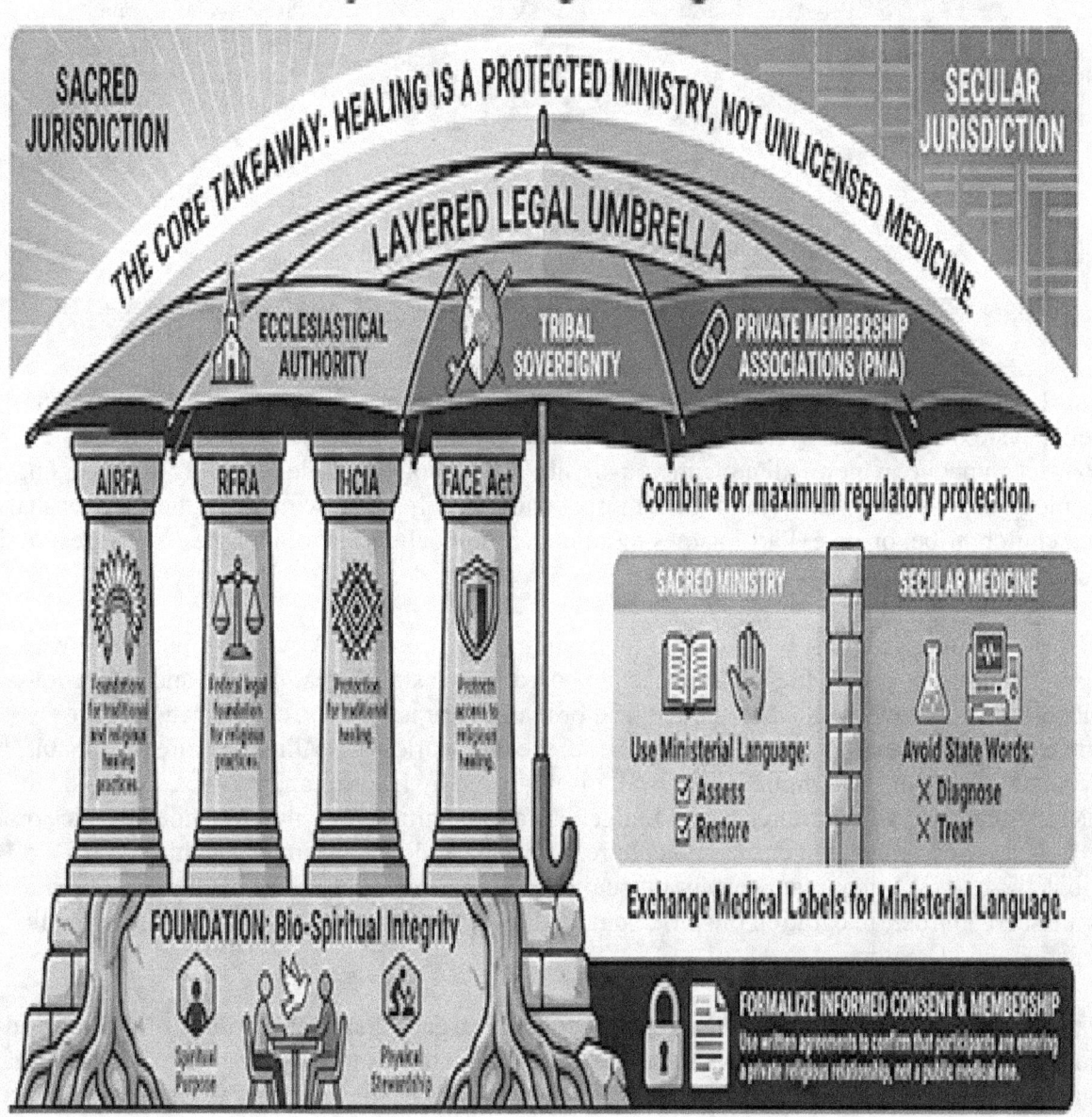

The Sanctuary of Healing: A Legal Architecture

Part I – Why Healing Needs a Legal Theology

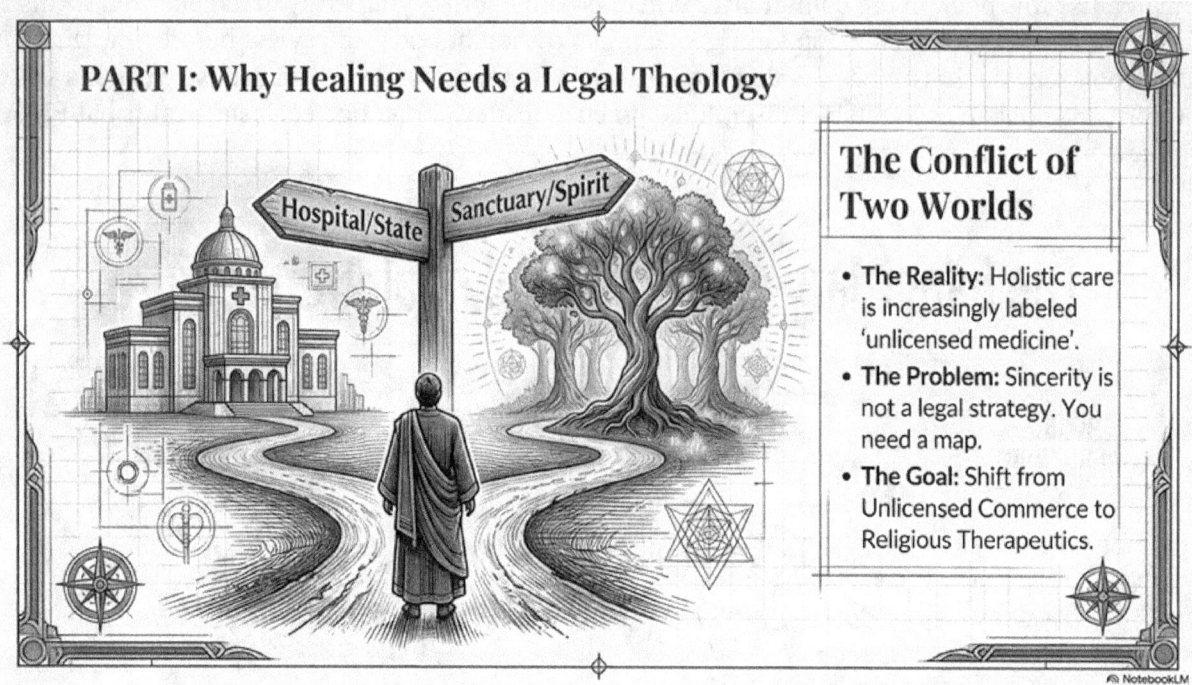

This book begins with a simple but often overlooked fact: every healing act lives within both a belief system and a legal system. When you lay on hands, offer herbs, lead a sweat lodge, or counsel someone in moral alignment, you are not just "doing a technique"; you are expressing a theology of what a human being is and a jurisdictional claim about who has authority over that act, church, tribe, or state. Part I names those underlying beliefs and boundaries, so the rest of the book has solid ground to stand on.

In these opening chapters, we ask three foundational questions. First, why this book, and why now? That means facing the reality that state boards increasingly treat holistic and Indigenous modalities as potential violations of medical or massage practice acts, even when they are sincerely offered as ministry. Second, what are the two worlds of healing you already inhabit? We map the secular paradigm, where health is regulated by licenses and statutes, alongside the sacred paradigm, where churches and Indigenous communities have always tended the sick as an expression of worship, covenant, and culture. Third, what do we mean by "health" at all? We move beyond symptom management to a universal definition of health as wholeness: alignment with Sacred Order, integration of spirit, soul, and body, and right relationship with community, creation, and Creator.

Part I, titled "Why Healing Needs a Legal Theology," argues that your theology of healing and your legal strategy cannot be separated. If you see a human being only as a body, then health law will be only about procedures, prescriptions, and physical outcomes. But if you see a human being as triune, spirit, soul, and body, then healing becomes a sacramental duty, and law must be engaged as a tool to protect that duty rather than to erase it. This is where concepts like

Religious Therapeutics and **Chirothesia** come in: they provide precise labels for ministries that state law might otherwise misclassify as secular medicine or massage.

How the NAIC Legal Guidelines Framework Creates Legal Theology

The "Sacred Hands, Secured Rights" framework does not merely describe the law; it creates a specific "Legal Theology" by linguistically and jurisdictionally reclassifying the act of healing. It transforms the practitioner from a provider of commerce into a minister of the covenant.

- **The Power of Naming (Religious Therapeutics vs. Medicine):** The framework asserts that "Religious Therapeutics" encompasses prayer, ritual, nutrition, and natural modalities used to remove impediments to spiritual wholeness. By defining these acts as "liturgical acts of restoration" rather than medical treatments, the framework removes them from the jurisdiction of state medical boards, provided the practitioner avoids "forbidden words" like *diagnose*, *treat*, or *cure*.
- **Chirothesia as Sacrament:** The framework reclaims touch through the concept of *Chirothesia*—"the healing hand of God." It argues that when a minister lays hands on the sick, they are not performing "massage therapy" (a secular trade defined by statute) but are fulfilling a scriptural and Indigenous mandate to transmit divine energy. This theological definition creates a legal boundary that secular regulations cannot easily cross without violating the First Amendment.
- **The L.C.H.T. License:** The framework operationalizes this theology through the **Licensed Commissioned Holistic Therapist (L.C.H.T.)** credential. This is not a state license but an ecclesiastical and tribal authorization. It grants the holder the right to practice Indigenous systems (like SomaVeda® Thai Yoga or Ayurveda) as spiritual ministries within a private jurisdiction, ensuring that the "healer of the future" holds the law as firmly as they hold the medicine.

The Two Worlds: Secular Statutes vs. Sacred Covenant

Throughout Part I, you will see the outlines of the entire book: the four "umbrellas" under which healing can lawfully occur (secular, ecclesiastical, Native American/tribal, and private association), the federal pillars that uphold Indigenous and religious medicine, and the emerging picture of health as a human right grounded in both scripture and international declarations.

We contrast the **Secular Medical Paradigm**, governed by the State and defined by the biological management of disease, with the **Sacred Paradigm**, governed by the Creator and defined by the restoration of *Hózhó* (Navajo for beauty/balance) or *Shalom*. The friction you feel in your practice arises because these two worlds operate on different definitions of reality. The "Sacred Hands" framework resolves this friction by helping you choose your ground: are you treating a patient in the public square, or ministering to a member in a private sanctuary?

The Universal Definition of Health

Central to this legal theology is a definition of health that the State cannot regulate because it transcends biology. We propose the equation: **(Spiritual Purpose + Relational Peace) ×**

Physical Stewardship = Wholeness. Under this definition, interventions like the Sweat Lodge, the Pipe Ceremony, or nutritional counseling are not "alternative medicine" but essential components of **Bio-Spiritual Integrity**.

PART I A: How do Chirothesia and Religious Therapeutics differ from medical practice?

While secular medicine functions as a commercial trade regulated by the State to manage biological pathology, Religious Therapeutics functions as a ministry regulated by ecclesiastical or tribal authority to restore spiritual and physical wholeness.

Here is a detailed breakdown of these differences:
1. Definition of Health: "Machine" vs. "Temple."
• **Medical Practice:** Views the body primarily as a biological machine. Health is defined as the absence of disease, managed through chemical or surgical intervention.
• **Religious Therapeutics:** Views the human being as a triune unity of spirit, soul, and body. Health is defined as **"Wholeness"** (*Shalom* or *Hózhó*), a dynamic state of "Bio-Spiritual Integrity" where the individual is in right relationship with the Creator, community, and self.
• **The Difference:** A doctor treats a "patient" to fix a broken part; a Chirothesist ministers to a "member" or "communicant" to remove impediments to their spiritual and physical integration.
2. Legal Jurisdiction: Public Commerce vs. Private Ministry
• **Medical Practice:** Operates under the **Secular Umbrella**. It is a public commercial activity governed by state medical boards and statutes. Legitimacy comes from state licensure and peer-reviewed secular education.
• **Religious Therapeutics:** Operates under **Ecclesiastical** and **Tribal Umbrellas**. It is a private religious activity protected by the First Amendment, the **American Indian Religious Freedom Act (AIRFA)**, and the **Religious Freedom Restoration Act (RFRA)**. Legitimacy comes from ordination, lineage, and commissioning by a bona fide church or tribal organization.
• **Private Association:** Unlike medicine, which is open to the public, Religious Therapeutics is often structured within a **Private Membership Association (PMA)**, where services are offered only to members who have contractually agreed to a private, non-secular relationship.
3. Scope of Practice: Chirothesia vs. Medical Treatment
• **Medical Practice:** Defined by statute as the authority to **diagnose**, **treat**, **operate**, or **prescribe** for any human disease, injury, or physical condition. It includes invasive procedures (surgery) and controlled pharmaceuticals.
• **Chirothesia:** Defined as "the healing hand of God" or "Divine Touch." It involves the **laying on of hands**, anointing, and non-invasive somatic alignment to transmit healing energy or "Life Wind" (*Nilch'i* / *Prana*). It is explicitly **non-invasive** and **non-pharmaceutical**.
• **Restricted Acts:** A practitioner of Religious Therapeutics **never** claims to "diagnose," "treat," or "cure" a disease in the secular sense. Instead, they "assess," "minister," "restore," or "support" the body's natural ability to heal.
4. Modalities and Tools
• **Medical Tools:** Synthetic drugs, surgery, radiation, and diagnostic technology focused on pathology.
• **Religious Therapeutic Tools:**

◦ **Sacraments:** The use of herbs, oils, or specific foods (like the "Three Sisters") is viewed as "herbal stewardship" or communion rather than "prescribing drugs".

◦ **Ceremony:** Rituals like the **Sweat Lodge**, **Pipe Ceremony**, and **Vision Quest** are used to address the "Soul Wound" and metabolic imbalance, treating the spirit to heal the body.

◦ **Chirothesia:** Hands-on techniques (including indigenous bodywork like *SomaVeda®* or *Nuad Boran*) are applied to unblock "Spirit Lines" (energy pathways) rather than to perform "massage therapy" for relaxation.

Summary Distinction

The text summarizes the distinction with the image of the "healer of the future":

"The Medicine Man of the past carried a bow; the Medicine Man of the future holds the Law." This healer does not compete with the surgeon for trauma care but operates in a separate, protected domain to treat the chronic, spiritual, and lifestyle-based ailments that secular medicine often fails to resolve.

Conclusion: The Aligned Healer—Uniting Theology and Law

In Part I and Part IA, we have established that the conflict between modern regulators and traditional healers is not merely a misunderstanding of techniques, but a collision of two distinct worlds: the **Secular Medical Paradigm** and the **Sacred Paradigm**. We have argued that to practice safely and authentically, you cannot simply "do" holistic medicine; you must possess a **Legal Theology** that clearly defines *what* a human being is and *whose* authority governs the act of healing.

We have moved beyond the limited biological definition of health to a **Universal Definition**: *Wholeness* or *Bio-Spiritual Integrity*, summarized by the equation (**Spiritual Purpose + Relational Peace) × Physical Stewardship = Wholeness**. This definition is the bedrock of your legal defense. It demonstrates that when you offer prayer, ceremony, or Chirothesia, you are not "practicing medicine" without a license, because you are not treating a biological machine; you are ministering to a human temple.

Part IA provided the specific linguistic and legal boundaries that separate these worlds. We established that **Medical Practice** is a public commercial trade focused on pathology, diagnosing, and prescribing, while **Religious Therapeutics** is a private ministry focused on restoring the covenant between the individual, the community, and the Creator. We distinguished **Chirothesia** ("The Healing Hand of God") from secular massage, clarifying that your touch is a protected sacramental act of transmitting "Life Wind" or *Nilch'i*, not a regulated manipulation of soft tissue.

By adopting this framework, you transform from a vulnerable practitioner operating in the shadows of the medical establishment into a **Healer-Minister** standing on firm jurisdictional ground. You are no longer asking the State for permission to treat a patient; you are exercising your inherent right to minister to a member within the private sanctuary of a church, tribe, or Private Membership Association.

This clarity is the prerequisite for everything that follows. Now that you have aligned your heart (theology) and your hands (Chirothesia), you are ready to pick up the tools of your defense. In **Part II**, we will leave the realm of definitions and enter the **Legal Architecture**, examining the specific statutes—AIRFA, RFRA, IHCIA, and the FACE Act—that form the "Four Pillars" protecting your right to practice this theology in the real world. As the text reminds us: "The Medicine Man of the past carried a bow; the Medicine Man of the future holds the Law".

25

Chapter 1 – Why This Book, Why Now

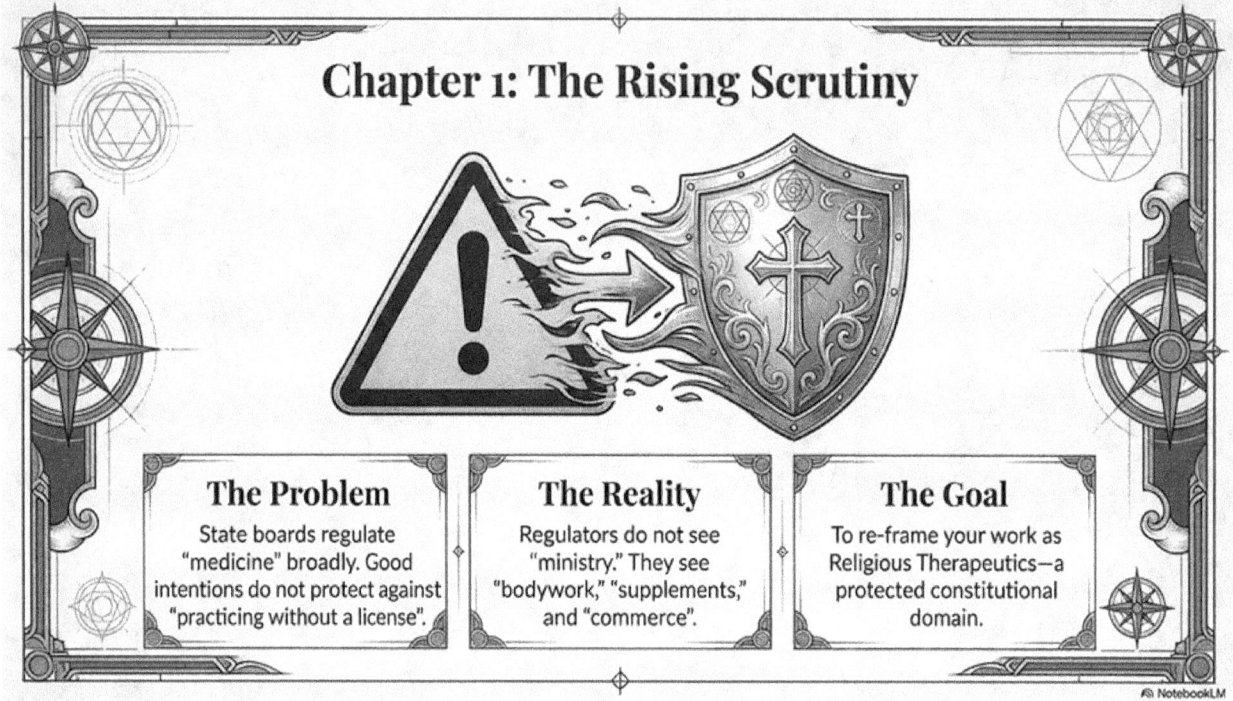

- *Why modern healers face rising scrutiny from medical and massage boards when they practice prayer, ceremony, and holistic care as a ministry.*
- *The book's core purpose is to frame holistic, Indigenous, and energy-based healing as Religious Therapeutics rather than secular "medicine."*
- *Who this book is written for and what it will and will not do (education, not legal advice).*

In every generation, healers arise who carry knowledge that did not come from medical school: grandmothers with herbs, pastors with prayer, medicine people with ceremony, and body-based practitioners who work with energy as much as with flesh. In our time, many of these people find themselves standing in the crosshairs of state medical boards, massage boards, health departments, and prosecutors who accuse them of "practicing medicine without a license" or "unlicensed massage." The same touch that a church calls "laying on of hands" may be re-labeled by a regulator as "bodywork," and the same herbs your ancestors called "medicine" may be treated as an unlicensed pharmacy.

This book exists because that tension is no longer theoretical. It shows up as cease-and-desist letters, surprise inspections, and traumatizing encounters with authorities who often do not understand the difference between secular medicine and sacred care. At the same time, healers themselves are sometimes unclear about where their work stands in relation to modern law. They feel called by Spirit, yet unsure how to speak to statutes. They want to honor their elders and their people, yet do not wish to become martyrs to misunderstanding.

The purpose of this book is to form and communicate a **cogent legal and spiritual argument** for practicing holistic, Indigenous, and energy-based healing as *religious therapeutics* rather than as secular "medicine." It will show that legitimate legal structures, church autonomy, Native American religious freedom, private membership associations, and specific federal statutes, such as AIRFA and RFRA, protect sincere, well-structured spiritual healing ministries. It will also show clearly where those protections **end**, especially around controlled substances and invasive procedures.

This work is written for a specific audience: ordained and lay ministers, Indigenous medicine people, holistic practitioners, and members of Native American and other faith-based communities who wish to serve as healers without misleading the public or violating the law. Many readers will be connected with organizations such as the <u>Native American Indigenous Church</u> (NAIC), the <u>Priory of Saving Grace</u>, SMOCH/SMOKH, or similar bodies that already frame healing as sacrament and ministry, not as commerce. But the concepts here are not proprietary; any group of sincere believers can study and apply them within its own tradition.

It is vital to state from the beginning what this book **is not**. It is not legal advice. It does not create an attorney-client relationship, and it does not substitute for consultation with a licensed attorney familiar with federal Indian law, constitutional law, or your state's medical and allied-health statutes. The author is not a lawyer and does not pretend to be one. What you will find instead is education: a map of the legal landscape, examples of how one tribal-religious organization has navigated it, and language you can bring to your own counsel and leadership.

Over the chapters that follow, we will move from theology to law to practice. First, we will explore what "health" really means in a holistic, spiritual, and Indigenous context. We will then examine the four legal umbrellas under which healing work can take place: secular licensing, ecclesiastical authority, Native American and tribal jurisdiction, and expressive private membership associations. After that, we will look closely at Religious Therapeutics and Chirothesia, laying on of hands, as non-medical, sacramental practices, and we will end with concrete tools: consent forms, ethical codes, and practice structures that keep your ministry in the private, protected domain.

Chapter 1 Conclusion – Stepping Onto the Road

This first chapter has asked you a simple but serious question: why are you here, and why now? If you are reading this, it is probably because you sense that you're called to heal and your need to remain lawful has come into conflict, or soon will. You may already have faced misunderstanding from regulators, or you may be preparing in advance so that your ministry can grow without fear.

The good news is that you are not alone and have tools. There is a long history of law recognizing the difference between commerce and sacrament, between public medicine and private ministry, and between secular regulation and tribal or ecclesiastical sovereignty. But to benefit from that history, you must be willing to learn its language.

In the next chapter, we will begin by looking more closely at the **two worlds of healing** you already inhabit, often without naming them: secular medicine on one side, and sacred care on the other. Understanding how each world defines health, authority, and responsibility will make it much easier to explain later where your work belongs and why.

LEARNING EXERCISE 1.1
Review & Application
Instructions: Select the best answer based on the reading.

1. **Which problem is the primary reason this book was written?**
   A) To help practitioners pass state licensure exams
   B) To replace conventional medicine with Indigenous medicine
   C) To address growing legal tension around holistic and Indigenous healing as "unlicensed practice."
   D) To standardize all religious healing under one national board
   E) To promote international medical tourism
   Correct Answer: C

2. **How does the book define its main purpose?**
   A) To give specific legal advice for each U.S. state
   B) To map a legal and spiritual argument for healing as Religious Therapeutics, not secular "medicine."
   C) To codify a new federal licensing category
   D) To establish a new political party for practitioners
   E) To market one proprietary healing system
   Correct Answer: B

3. **Which audience is the book written for?**
   A) Hospital administrators and malpractice insurers
   B) Pharmaceutical researchers
   C) Ordained and lay ministers, Indigenous medicine people, holistic practitioners, and faith-based communities
   D) Only federally recognized tribal governments
   E) Only licensed physicians
   Correct Answer: C

4. **What does the author emphasize the book is *not*?**
   A) A theological treatise
   B) A historical survey
   C) A source of legal advice or an attorney–client relationship
   D) A manual for herbal pharmacy operations
   E) A replacement for seminary education
   Correct Answer: C

5. **What kind of tools does the book promise to provide?**
   A) Step-by-step instructions for filing malpractice suits
   B) Billing templates for insurance claims
   C) Language, maps, and examples you can take to your own counsel and leadership
   D) Complete state-by-state regulatory codes
   E) Automated software for legal compliance
   Correct Answer: C

Chapter 2 – Two Worlds of Healing: Secular Medicine and Sacred Care

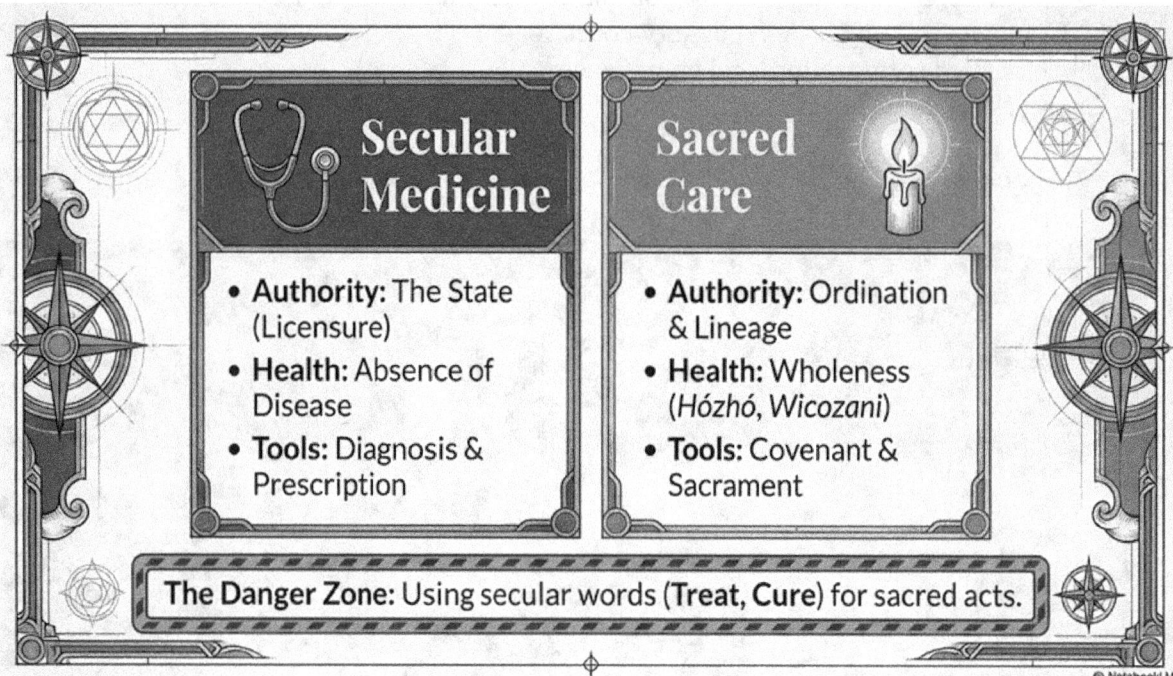

> ❧ How the secular medical paradigm defines health care through statutes, licenses, and regulated scopes of practice.
> ❧ How the sacred paradigm understands healing as a ministry, a covenant, and a ceremony within churches and Indigenous communities.
> ❧ Where and why these two worlds collide, and the four "legal umbrellas" that emerge from this tension.

If you are a healer today, you stand with one foot in a hospital corridor and one foot in a sweat lodge, or in a church sanctuary, a counseling room, or a kitchen where herbs hang drying from the ceiling. The modern regulatory system mostly sees the first world: white coats, diagnostic codes, and licensed touch. Your elders, scriptures, and ceremonies inhabit the second. The friction you feel arises because these two worlds operate on different definitions of health, different sources of authority, and different understandings of what it means to "help" a suffering person.

This chapter will map those differences. We will begin with the **secular medical paradigm**, in which the State claims jurisdiction over the body through medical practice acts and allied-health statutes. Then we will turn to the **sacred paradigm**, in which churches, tribal organizations, and Indigenous communities have, for thousands of years, ministered to the sick, counseled the distressed, and walked with the dying as an expression of worship and covenant. By the end, you will see that the tension you face is not accidental; it is structural, and that the law itself provides ways to honor both realms without collapsing into either.

1. The Secular Medical Paradigm

In the secular world, "health care" is defined primarily by statutes and regulations. State medical practice acts specify who may diagnose, treat, operate, or prescribe for "any human disease, pain, injury, deformity, or physical condition," and a person who performs those activities without a license risks civil or criminal penalties. Allied health boards, such as boards of nursing, chiropractic, psychology, massage therapy, and dietetics, regulate narrower scopes of practice. Still, the logic is the same: the State claims the power to decide who may touch, advise, or intervene in the physical and mental lives of its citizens.

Under this paradigm, touch becomes "massage" or "bodywork" when it meets a statutory definition, regardless of whether the practitioner calls it a blessing or a sacrament. Nutritional guidance may be reclassified as "dietetics," herbal distribution as "pharmacy," and emotional or spiritual counsel as "psychotherapy" or "mental-health services," depending on the wording of a given law. Legislators often design these statutes with the stated aim of protecting the public from fraud and harm, but they rarely consider Indigenous cosmologies or church-based healing traditions.

In this system, legitimacy flows from **licensing boards**, **peer-reviewed standards**, and **secular education**. A physician, nurse, or massage therapist is deemed competent not because of spiritual calling or lineage, but because they have completed state-approved training, passed an exam, and submitted to ongoing regulation. This model has real strengths in contexts involving invasive procedures, pharmaceuticals, and high-risk interventions. But when applied blindly to all forms of care, it can treat prayer like a drug and ceremony like a surgical procedure.

2. The Sacred Paradigm of Healing

Long before there were medical boards or billing codes, spiritual communities tended to the sick. Christian scriptures describe Jesus and his followers preaching, laying on hands, anointing with oil, casting out demons, and comforting the dying as core elements of ministry. Indigenous peoples conducted ceremonies, offered plant medicines, and called upon the Great Spirit for healing as part of their covenant with Creation. For millennia, no one required a state license to visit the sick, counsel the distressed, or bless a broken body. These acts were understood as ministries, not as trades.

Concept	Indigenous Term	Tribe / Language	Meaning & Context
Shalom (Peace/Harmony)	*Hózhó*	**Dinétah** (Navajo)	A foundational philosophy meaning beauty, balance, and health. It is the "covenant" of living in total harmony with the universe.
Wholeness	*Wicozani*	**Lakota** (Sioux)	Often translated as "health," but specifically refers to a state of being "altogether well", physically, mentally, and spiritually.
Bio-Spiritual Integrity	*Mino-Bimaadiziwin*	**Anishinaabe** (Ojibwe)	"The Good Life." It represents the integration of ethical living, spiritual purpose, and physical health.
Bio-Spiritual Integrity	*K'é*	**Dinétah** (Navajo)	The system of relationality that binds all living things. It is the "Relational Peace" component of your equation.
Wholeness / Shalom	*Sgi*	**Cherokee** (Tsalagi)	A state of "rightness" or being "at one." It is the outcome of spiritual ceremonies and physical stewardship.
Shalom (Cosmic Order)	*Maat*	**Indigenous African (Ancient Egypt)**	While technically African, this is the root of "Indigenous" bio-spiritual law: truth, balance, and order as a divine mandate.

2A. Deep Dive into the Native American Terms

Hózhó (Navajo)

This is perhaps the closest equivalent to **Shalom**. In the Navajo worldview, if a person is ill, they are "out of Hózhó." Healing is not "fixing" a part, but a covenantal ceremony (a "Sing") to restore the individual to the cosmic order. Like your definition, it assumes that physical health is impossible without spiritual alignment.

Mino-Bimaadiziwin (Anishinaabe)

This term perfectly encapsulates **Bio-Spiritual Integrity**. It suggests that "living well" is a discipline. It involves:

- **Physical Stewardship:** Respecting the body and the land.
- **Spiritual Purpose:** Following the Seven Grandfather Teachings.
- **Relational Peace:** Maintaining harmony with the community and the "Manidoog" (spirits).

Wicozani (Lakota)

In Lakota tradition, the "Sacred Hoop" represents the wholeness of the people. *Wicozani* is the state of that hoop being unbroken. When a regulator misclassifies a sacred act as "unlicensed medicine," they are ignoring the *Wakan* (holy/mysterious) element that is required for *Wicozani* to exist.

Note on "Medicine": In many Indigenous contexts, the word "Medicine" actually refers to **Spiritual Power** rather than a pharmaceutical substance. Thus, "Herbal Stewardship" is seen as a way to facilitate the plant's spirit, helping the human spirit, a purely "covenantal" act.

Within this sacred paradigm, authority flows from ordination, lineage, and community recognition rather than from secular boards. A pastor, priest, rabbi, medicine person, or other spiritual leader assumes responsibility for healing because they have been called by the Spirit, trained by elders, and commissioned by their church or tribal organization. Their work is governed by scripture, sacred texts, oral tradition, and codes of ethics established by the spiritual community itself.

When the U.S. Constitution protects the "free exercise" of religion and forbids the State from establishing or favoring any particular faith, it is acknowledging this paradigm. Court decisions over the years have recognized church autonomy in matters of doctrine, ordination, internal discipline, and sacramental practice. Federal statutes such as the American Indian Religious Freedom Act (AIRFA) go further in the Indigenous context, affirming that Native peoples have the right to access sacred sites, use sacred objects, and worship through traditional ceremonies and rites. In these spaces, healing is not a commodity; it is a covenant.

3. Where the Worlds Collide

Conflicts arise when the secular system examines sacred acts and insists on relabeling them according to its own categories. A church's laying on of hands may be described by a regulator as "unlicensed massage" if it involves touch. A tribal elder's nutritional teachings may be called "unauthorized dietetics," and the distribution of herbs within a ceremony may be framed as "illegal pharmacy practice." In each case, the State observes an activity that resembles something it regulates in the commercial sphere, and it intervenes, often without recognizing the spiritual context.

On the other side, some healers contribute to the confusion by using medical language inappropriately. When a practitioner without a secular license advertises that they "diagnose," "treat," or "cure" named diseases, or when they adopt generic, regulated labels such as "massage therapy" or "bodywork" for what is in fact religious ministry, they invite the State to interpret their work as secular practice. The intention may be innocent, using popular terms for marketing, but the legal consequences can be severe.

The key is not to deny that these worlds overlap, but to **name** the boundary honestly and consistently. Religious Therapeutics, Chirothesia, Indigenous ceremonies, and pastoral counseling are not attempts to enter the medical profession through the back door. They are distinct practices rooted in a different understanding of health and authority. When properly framed and structured, they belong to a protected domain that the law has historically set apart: the internal life of churches, tribes, and private associations of believers.

4. Four Pathways Through the Tension

Once you see the difference between the secular and sacred paradigms, it becomes easier to understand why this book speaks of **four legal umbrellas** under which healing work may lawfully occur.

- The **Secular Umbrella** represents state licensure: medicine, nursing, chiropractic, massage therapy, psychology, dietetics, and other regulated professions.
- The **Ecclesiastical Umbrella** covers healing ministries that operate under church or faith-based authority and are guided by doctrine, scripture, and internal law.
- The **Native American and Tribal Umbrella** covers sovereign tribal nations and bona fide tribal religious organizations, whose right to practice traditional medicine and ceremony is recognized in federal law.
- The **Expressive Private Membership Association Umbrella** covers healing relationships that take place within private associations of members, grounded in the rights of association, privacy, and contract.

Each of these umbrellas has its own strengths, limits, and responsibilities. Some practitioners may choose to operate primarily under one authority; others may adopt a **layered** approach, combining ecclesiastical and tribal authority with a private membership structure. Later chapters will explore these in detail. For now, it is enough to understand that you are not powerless before the secular system. There are lawful, time-tested ways to situate your work in a domain that the State does not and cannot regulate in the same way it regulates commerce.

Chapter 2 Conclusion – Choosing Your Ground

In this chapter, you have seen that the clash between regulators and healers is not merely about personalities or politics; it is about two competing ways of understanding what healing is and who has the right to do it. The secular world sees health largely through the lens of disease management and professional licensure. The sacred world views health as wholeness, covenant, and right relationship, upheld by ordained or recognized spiritual authorities and Indigenous communities.

Your task is not to reject one world and idealize the other. Modern medicine saves lives every day, and the law rightly intervenes when people are harmed by fraud or gross negligence. At the same time, your traditions carry forms of care that no hospital can replicate: ceremony, prayer, moral reconciliation, and communion with Creator and Creation. The question is not *whether* you will walk both roads, but *how* you will do so without losing your way in either.

In the next chapter, we will delve deeper into the core of your worldview by defining **health** from a holistic, Indigenous, and Christian perspective. We will articulate a universal definition of health, explore five laws of holistic well-being, and present a simple "health equation" you can use to explain your work in courtrooms, churches, and clinics alike. From there, we will be ready to return to the legal architecture with much greater clarity about what you are actually trying to protect.

LEARNING EXERCISE 2.1
Review & Application
Instructions: Select the best answer based on the reading.

1. What is the core difference between the secular and sacred paradigms of healing?
    A) Secular uses herbs; sacred uses pharmaceuticals
    B) Secular is communal; sacred is individualistic
    C) Secular defines health through statutes and licenses; sacred defines health through covenant, scripture, and tradition
    D) Secular addresses spirit; sacred addresses only body
    E) There is no meaningful difference
    Correct Answer: C
2. In the secular paradigm, how is "touch" often categorized?
    A) As expressive free speech
    B) As a sacramental blessing
    C) As massage or bodywork when statutory definitions are met

D) As unregulated personal expression

E) As a purely spiritual act beyond regulation

Correct Answer: C

3. In the sacred paradigm, where does authority to heal primarily come from?

A) State licensing boards

B) Insurance companies

C) Ordination, lineage, and community recognition

D) Commercial certification programs

E) Pharmaceutical sponsors

Correct Answer: C

4. Why does the chapter say the conflict between these worlds is "structural," not just personal?

A) Because most regulators dislike religion

B) Because statutes were written only for urban areas

C) Because each system rests on different definitions of health, authority, and the meaning of "helping."

D) Because hospitals are located far from reservations

E) Because Indigenous healers refuse to engage with the law

Correct Answer: C

5. What is the main risk when healers adopt secular medical language for their work?

A) Their clients will stop trusting them spiritually

B) Courts will lose jurisdiction

C) The State may reclassify ministry as a regulated practice (e.g., massage, dietetics, psychotherapy)

D) Their elders will revoke their lineage

E) Their services will automatically be covered by insurance

Correct Answer: C

Chapter 3 – A Universal Definition of Health

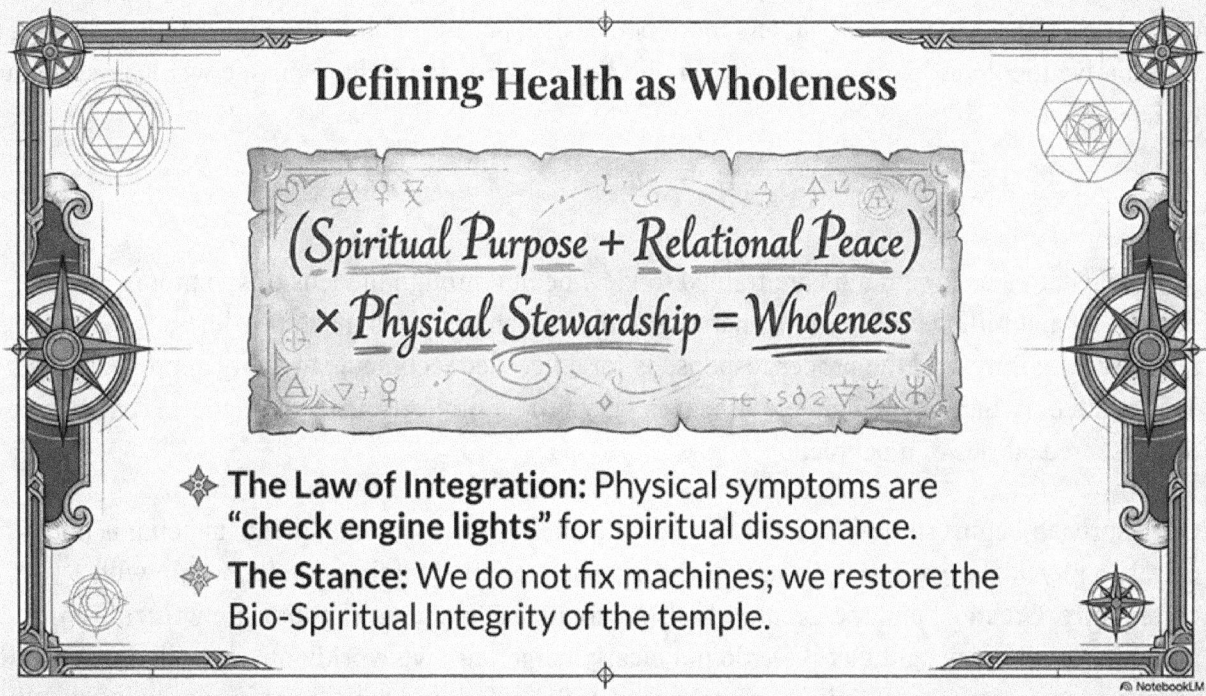

- What international bodies (WHO, human-rights instruments) already define health as more than the absence of disease?
- A universal, triune definition of health that unites the Christian "temple" and Indigenous "medicine wheel" into five laws of holistic well-being and the "health equation."
- How to express your understanding of health as a written Statement of Sacred Conviction that courts and boards can recognize as a religious tenet.

In every legal conversation about healing, someone eventually asks a deceptively simple question: "What do you mean by health?" If you allow the State's purely biological definition to dominate that conversation, your work as a spiritual or Indigenous healer will always appear marginal, unscientific, or even illegal. To protect your ministry, you must be able to articulate a definition of health that is theologically sound, culturally rooted, and intellectually coherent, and then show how your practices flow naturally from that definition.

This chapter offers that foundation. We will first examine how international bodies, such as the World Health Organization, define health as a human right rather than merely a medical outcome. Then we will propose a universal definition of health that unites the Christian image of the temple with the Indigenous symbol of the medicine wheel, mind, body, spirit, community, and Creation aligned with the Creator. From that shared ground, we will explore five universal laws of holistic health and introduce a simple "health equation" that captures your worldview in one line.

By the end of this chapter, you will have language you can use with legislators, judges, pastors, elders, and clients to explain what you actually seek for those you serve. That clarity will make every legal argument in later chapters more persuasive, because you will no longer be defending "alternative medicine" in the abstract; you will be defending the right to pursue wholeness as you understand it.

1. Our Approach Is Different

Most legislators and regulators are trained to view health through the lens of symptoms, diagnoses, and billing codes. In that paradigm, the human body is a machine, illness is a mechanical failure, and the proper response is for a licensed technician to apply approved tools. This is not evil, but it is incomplete. It leaves very little room for spirit, conscience, relationship, or the sacred stories of a people.

Our approach begins somewhere else. It begins with the conviction that a human being is not merely a physical organism but a unity of spirit, soul, and body living in relationship with community, Creation, and the Creator. It also recognizes that law and policy are written from a particular worldview, and that if we do not clearly name our own worldview, we will always find ourselves squeezed into definitions that do not fit. To understand how legislators approach health care regulation, we must first articulate a richer understanding of health.

2. What Is Health? (Global and Legal Perspectives)

Internationally, there is already acknowledgment that health is more than the absence of disease. The World Health Organization defines health as "a state of complete physical, mental [Our framework *extends* the concept to spiritual dimensions for theological/Indigenous reasons] and social well-being and not merely the absence of disease or infirmity," explicitly linking health to social and economic conditions and reaffirming it as a human right. This definition extends beyond the clinic; it includes housing, work, community, and meaning as legitimate parts of the health conversation.

Human rights instruments, such as the Universal Declaration of Human Rights and the Declaration of Alma-Ata, adopt a similar posture. They recognize the right of every human being to pursue health and well-being and call for primary health care that respects local culture, community participation, and equitable access. For Indigenous and faith-based healers, these documents are important because they affirm that health is intertwined with dignity, culture, and freedom of belief, not just with pharmaceuticals and procedures.

3. A Universal Definition of Health (Temple and Medicine Wheel)

Building on these global understandings, we can offer a definition that speaks directly from our own traditions. Health, in this framework, is not a static condition but a dynamic **state of Wholeness**. It is achieved when a human being lives in alignment with the Sacred Order, integrated internally (mind, body, spirit), connected externally (community, Creation), and anchored vertically (Creator/Great Mystery).

In Christian language, the body is the "temple of the Holy Spirit," and health is *shalom*: a peace in which righteousness, justice, and physical well-being mirror the state of the soul. In Indigenous language, health is "walking in a good way," in balance with all our relations, human, animal, plant, stone, water, wind, and ancestor. When we bring these two images together, we see that health is not simply the removal of symptoms; it is the right relationship at every level of existence.

Under this definition, many of the services targeted by state medical boards, prayer, ceremony, laying on of hands, counsel in moral matters, and herbal stewardship are not attempts to practice secular medicine without a license. They are coherent, traditional methods of restoring alignment with Sacred Order. To deny such practices legal space is not just to regulate a profession; it is to interfere with a people's understanding of what it means to be whole.

4. The Five Universal Laws of Holistic Health

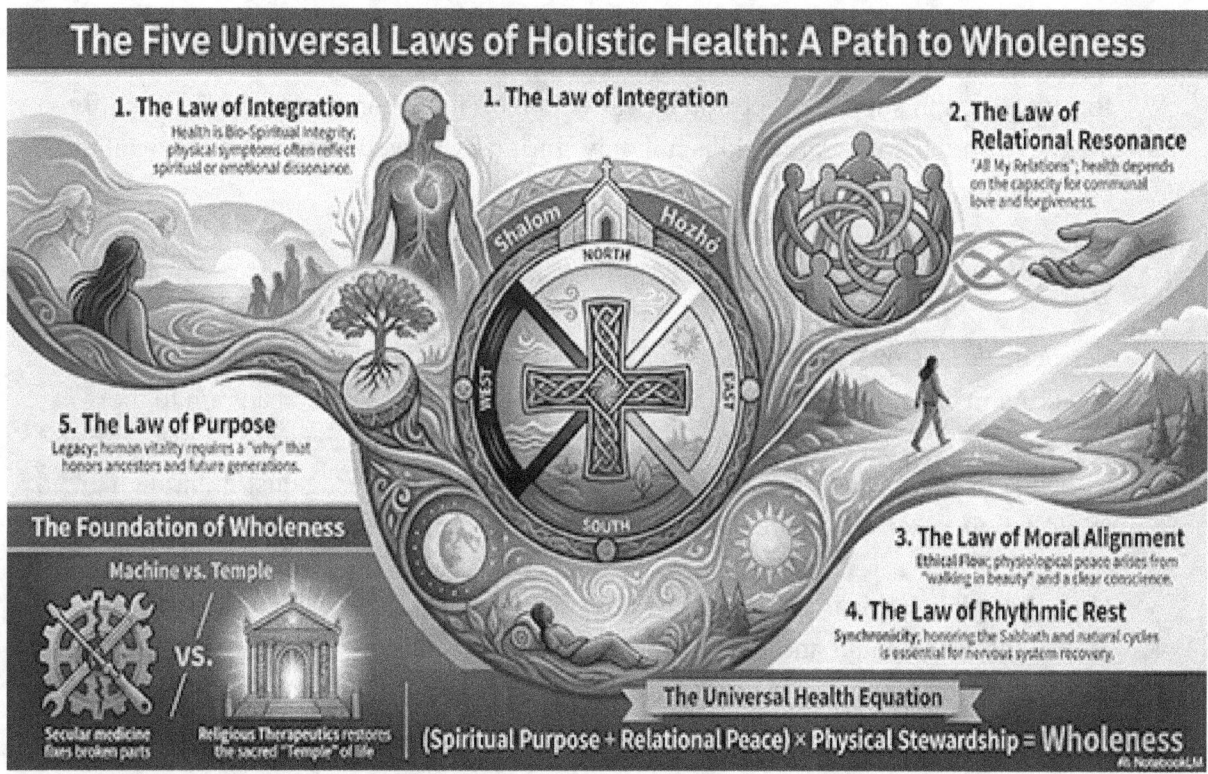

By merging the Christian "Temple" and the Indigenous "Medicine Wheel," we can articulate five universal laws that govern true vitality. These laws are not statutes passed by legislatures; they are patterns observed in scripture, ceremony, and the lived experience of healers across cultures.

Law 1 – The Law of Integration (Anti-Dualism)

Both traditions reject the idea that the body is a machine separate from the soul. Physical symptoms often function as "check-engine lights" for spiritual or emotional dissonance: chronic stress, unresolved grief, hidden resentment, or moral compromise.

In this view, **health is Bio-Spiritual Integrity**. It is the state in which physical biology cooperates with spiritual conviction, where your actions (body) are in harmony with your conscience (spirit). When that harmony breaks, when your lifestyle betrays what you know to be right, illness appears as stress, anxiety, autoimmune disorders, or other forms of breakdown.

Law 2 – The Law of Relational Resonance

Scripture warns against bitterness and unforgiveness; Indigenous elders warn against severing ties with "All My Relations." Modern biology confirms that isolation acts like a pathogen: it elevates stress hormones such as cortisol and erodes immune resilience, while healthy relationships increase oxytocin and support healing.

Under this law, **health is the community**. It is the capacity to give and receive love, forgiveness, and support. A person at war with their neighbor, estranged from family, or hostile toward the natural world is not only spiritually unwell; they are biologically compromised.

Law 3 – The Law of Moral Alignment

Scripture speaks of "righteousness" as a kind of health; Indigenous wisdom speaks of "walking in beauty," in harmony with the seen and unseen. There is a grain to the universe. When we move with that grain, acting with honesty, generosity, restraint, and respect, our bodies and minds tend to flourish. When we move against it, through greed, exploitation, cruelty, or disregard for nature, we get splinters.

Here, **health is Ethical Flow**. It is the physiological peace that comes from living with a clear conscience. Guilt and shame are heavy; they manifest as fatigue, tension, weight gain or loss, and a host of psychosomatic conditions. Many Religious Therapeutic protocols, confession, reconciliation, restitution, and moral counsel aim directly at restoring this flow.

Law 4 – The Law of Rhythmic Rest

The Sabbath and the ceremonial calendar, on one hand, and the cycles of seasons and animal life, on the other, both insist that rest is not optional. Nature does not bloom all year, and humans are not designed to produce 24/7. When we ignore it, the rhythms of work and rest, feast and fast, silence and speech, the system frays.

Under this law, **health is Synchronicity**. It is the discipline of knowing when to stop, when to withdraw, when to let fields and nervous systems lie fallow. True health respects daylight and darkness, the wintering of the soul, and the need for retreat and ceremony to prepare for future growth.

Law 5 – The Law of Purpose (The Long View)

Biblically, health is bound up with hope and calling; in Indigenous understanding, it is bound up with ancestral continuity and responsibility to future generations. The human organism degrades without a "why." Depression, addiction, and chronic disease often take root where purpose has been lost.

Here, **health is Legacy**. It is the vitality that arises when a person knows they are part of a story larger than themselves, accountable to ancestors and responsible to descendants. A healthy person sees their life as a seed to be planted for others, not a resource to be consumed only for personal gain.

5. The Health Equation

If we were to express this entire vision of health in a single line, it would not look like a fitness advertisement. Health is not simply:

$$\textbf{Diet + Exercise = Health.}$$

That formula leaves out purpose, relationship, conscience, and spirit. Based on the synthesis above, a more accurate equation is:

$$\textbf{(Spiritual Purpose + Relational Peace)} \times \textbf{Physical Stewardship = Wholeness.}$$

Here, "Spiritual Purpose" represents the Law of Purpose; "Relational Peace" encompasses the Laws of Relational Resonance and Moral Alignment; and "Physical Stewardship" encompasses Integration and Rhythmic Rest, nutrition, movement, sleep, and the environment. The multiplication sign matters: if either purpose or relational peace is near zero, physical efforts alone cannot produce true health.

This equation offers a simple way to explain why your protocols place such emphasis on prayer, ceremony, reconciliation, community, and moral counsel, alongside herbs, bodywork, or lifestyle advice. You are not neglecting the body; you are honoring the fact that the body cannot be whole while the spirit and relationships are broken.

6. A Statement of Sacred Conviction (Model)

Because law often asks not only *what* you do but *why* you do it, many practitioners benefit from a written statement that expresses their understanding of health as a religious tenet. Below is a refined version of your "Statement of Sacred Conviction and Ecclesiastical Duty," drafted from the perspective of an integrative healer walking both the Indigenous Road and the Christian Road. You may adapt it to your own tradition and submit it to boards, courts, or churches as needed.

Statement of Sacred Conviction and Ecclesiastical Duty

I stand as a bridge between two ancient lineages of truth: the Indigenous wisdom of my ancestors and the revealed Word of Holy Scripture. I am not merely a technician of the body; I am a steward of the soul.

My practice is founded on the unshakable conviction that a human being is a triune being, Spirit, Soul, and Body, and that health is a state of wholeness in which these three stand in right relationship with the Creator and with all Creation. Biblically, I understand health as *shalom*: a state of peace and righteousness in which the physical vessel reflects the spiritual condition. Traditionally, I understand health as "The Good Way": a harmonic balance with the Natural Laws of the universe and with All My Relations.

To treat the body while ignoring the spirit is, within my worldview, a form of spiritual malpractice. It is akin to painting over a collapsing wall. Therefore, the protocols I use, prayer, laying on of hands, moral and spiritual counsel, herbal stewardship, and ritual cleansing, are not medical treatments in the secular sense. They are sacred sacraments of restoration, intended to address the spiritual and moral dissonances that often manifest as physical disease.

I act under a dual mandate of conscience. As a follower of Christ, I am commanded to "heal the sick" not by my own power, but by restoring the individual's relationship with God. As a carrier of Indigenous medicine, I am bound by the law of *"Mitákuye Oyás'iŋ"*-All My Relations, to reconnect the severed bonds between the individual, their community, and Creation. To deny a suffering person these modalities would be to abdicate my religious duty. I answer to a jurisdiction higher than any medical board: the sovereignty of the Creator.

The herbs, counsel, and laying on of hands I employ are liturgical acts that restore the "temple of the Holy Spirit" and preserve the traditional healing arts of my people, as protected by the American Indian Religious Freedom Act and related laws. I do not claim to diagnose, treat, or cure disease as those terms are defined in state medical practice acts. I claim to facilitate wholeness as an exercise of religious freedom and cultural continuity.

Therefore, I declare that my work is a protected expression of religious belief and Indigenous identity. To restrict my ability to guide individuals toward shalom and balance is to violate the sanctity of the healer-patient covenant, which predates modern medical statutes. There is no true health without the Spirit, and my practice is the necessary application of this truth.

This kind of statement does not replace legal counsel. Still, it frames your work in terms courts and boards can understand: jurisdictional separation (pastoral vs. medical), explicit reliance on religious freedom statutes, and informed consent grounded in your definition of health.

Chapter Three Conclusion – From Wholeness to Law

In this chapter, we have stepped back from statutes and case numbers to ask a more fundamental question: What is health, and what are you actually trying to do when you "heal"? We have seen that your work is not a random technique but a coherent effort to restore Bio-Spiritual Integrity, Community, Ethical Flow, Rhythmic Rest, and Purpose under the Creator's sovereignty.

This clarity matters. When you later claim protection under the American Indian Religious Freedom Act, RFRA, or church-autonomy doctrines, you will be able to show that your practices are genuine expressions of a deeply held belief about health and wholeness, not marketing labels invented to dodge regulation. Law respects sincerity and coherence, even when it does not fully agree with your theology.

In the next part of this book, we will turn from definition to architecture. We will examine the four legal umbrellas under which you may practice, secular licensure, ecclesiastical authority, tribal sovereignty, and private membership associations, and see how each one interacts with the definition of health you have just embraced. With that foundation, you will be able to choose, with open eyes, where and how you wish to stand.

LEARNING EXERCISE 3.1
Review & Application
Instructions: Select the best answer based on the reading.

1. How does the World Health Organization's definition of health expand beyond the biomedical model?
   A) By focusing only on spiritual wellness
   B) By defining health as a state of complete physical, mental [spiritual], and social well-being, not merely the absence of disease
   C) By limiting health to economic productivity
   D) By equating health with access to surgery
   E) By excluding social conditions from health
   Correct Answer: B

2. What images are combined to form the book's "universal definition of health"?
   A) Hospital and pharmacy
   B) Courtroom and clinic
   C) Christian "temple of the Holy Spirit" and Indigenous "medicine wheel."
   D) Laboratory and herb garden
   E) Insurance policy and treaty
   Correct Answer: C

3. According to the chapter, what is health in this framework?
   A) Perfect lab values and fitness scores
   B) Absence of legal liability
   C) Dynamic wholeness: alignment with Sacred Order internally, externally, and vertically
   D) Constant productivity without rest
   E) Freedom from all suffering
   Correct Answer: C

4. Which statement best captures the "Law of Integration (Anti-Dualism)"?
   A) Mind and body are unrelated
   B) Physical symptoms can reveal spiritual or emotional dissonance, so health is bio-spiritual integrity
   C) Spiritual issues should be ignored in health conversations
   D) Only the body needs treatment; the soul is unaffected
   E) Law has no interest in spiritual beliefs
   Correct Answer: B

5. In the "health equation" (Spiritual Purpose + Relational Peace) × Physical Stewardship = Wholeness, why does the multiplication sign matter?
   A) It makes the equation mathematically simpler
   B) It shows that physical efforts alone can guarantee health
   C) It indicates that if either purpose or relational peace is near zero, physical efforts cannot produce true health
   D) It turns the equation into a legal formula
   E) It was chosen purely for stylistic reasons
   Correct Answer: C

Part II – The Legal Architecture of Religious Therapeutics in the U.S.

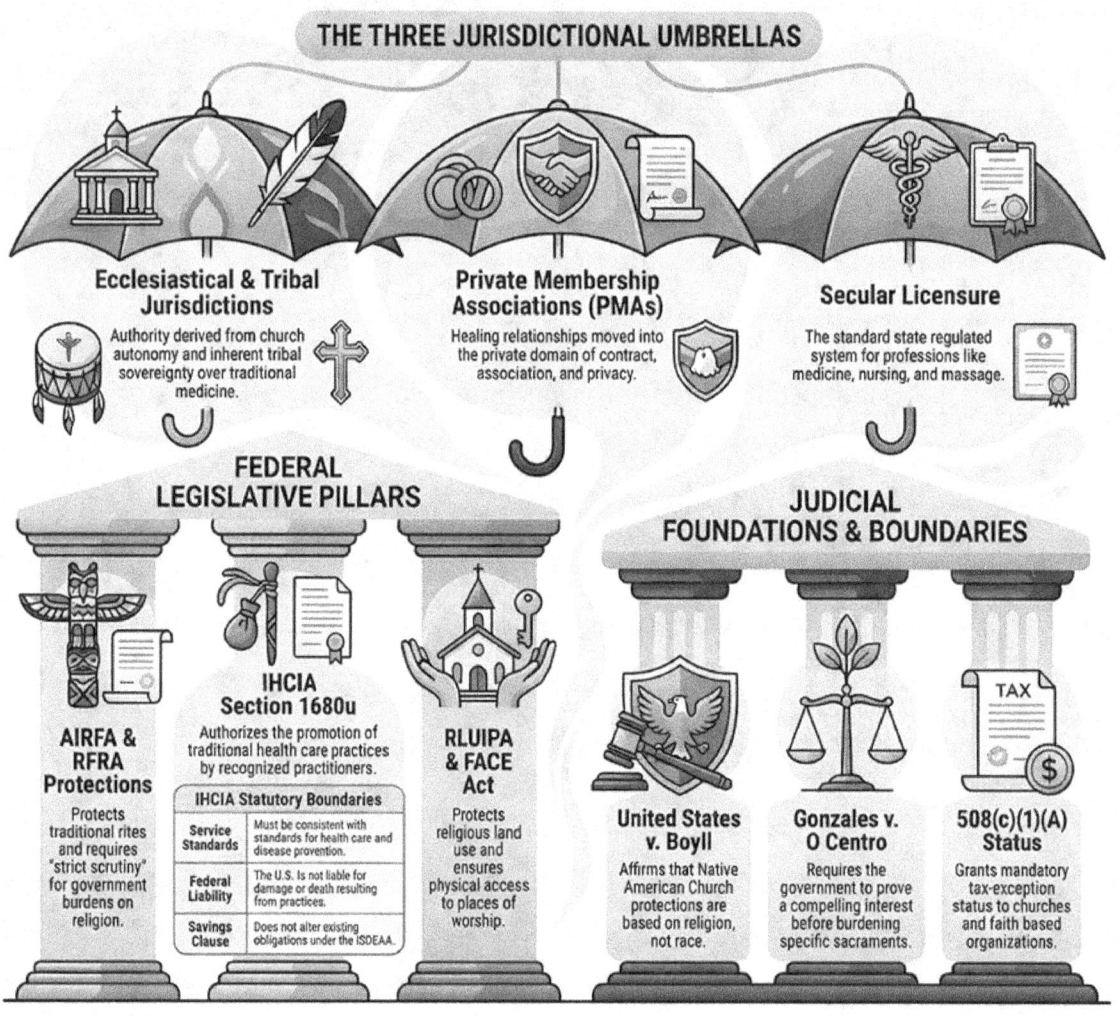

THE LEGAL SHELTER FOR SACRED HEALING: NAVIGATING PART II

Navigating the frameworks, statutes, and jurisdictional umbrellas protecting religious and Indigenous healing.

THE THREE JURISDICTIONAL UMBRELLAS

Ecclesiastical & Tribal Jurisdictions
Authority derived from church autonomy and inherent tribal sovereignty over traditional medicine.

Private Membership Associations (PMAs)
Healing relationships moved into the private domain of contract, association, and privacy.

Secular Licensure
The standard state regulated system for professions like medicine, nursing, and massage.

FEDERAL LEGISLATIVE PILLARS

AIRFA & RFRA Protections
Protects traditional rites and requires "strict scrutiny" for government burdens on religion.

IHCIA Section 1680u
Authorizes the promotion of traditional health care practices by recognized practitioners.

IHCIA Statutory Boundaries	
Service Standards	Must be consistent with standards for health care and disease provention.
Federal Liability	The U.S. is not liable for damage or death resulting from practices.
Savings Clause	Does not alter existing obligations under the ISDEAA.

RLUIPA & FACE Act
Protects religious land use and ensures physical access to places of worship.

JUDICIAL FOUNDATIONS & BOUNDARIES

United States v. Boyll
Affirms that Native American Church protections are based on religion, not race.

Gonzales v. O Centro
Requires the government to prove a compelling interest before burdening specific sacraments.

508(c)(1)(A) Status
Grants mandatory tax-exception status to churches and faith based organizations.

NotebookLM

Once you know that your work is ministry and not secular medicine, the next question is: **what law actually protects that ministry?**

Part II answers this by mapping the legal architecture that shelters Religious Therapeutics and Indigenous medicine in the United States. It explains the "four umbrellas" under which you can lawfully practice, secular licensure, ecclesiastical authority, Native American/tribal jurisdiction, and Private Membership Associations, and shows how federal statutes, case law, and constitutional principles create real, not imaginary, **exceptions** for churches, tribal and intertribal bodies, and faith-based organizations that choose to stand inside them.

At the heart of this architecture are explicit federal protections. The American Indian Religious Freedom Act (AIRFA-RFRA), **42 U.S.C. § 2000bb-1** 1996, declares it U.S. policy "to protect and preserve" the inherent right of American Indians, Eskimos, Aleuts, and Native Hawaiians to believe, express, and **exercise** their traditional religions, including access to sacred sites, use of sacred objects, and worship "through ceremonials and traditional rites." The Religious Freedom Restoration Act (RFRA), **42 U.S.C. § 2000bb-1**, forbids the government from substantially burdening religious exercise unless it can prove a compelling interest and use the least restrictive means, giving ministries a powerful defense against overbroad regulation. The Indian Health Care Improvement Act (IHCIA) authorizes the Indian Health Service to employ "traditional health care practices (the compiled IHCIA (GovInfo compilation of Public Law 94–437, as amended)), the Table of Contents lists **Sec. 831. Traditional health care practices.** In the codified U.S. Code, this corresponds to **25 U.S.C. § 1680u (Traditional health care practices)** https://www.law.cornell.edu/uscode/text/25/1680u) by traditional health care practitioners," validating Native healers as legitimate providers in federal policy. RLUIPA, 42 U.S.C. § 2000cc, applies strict scrutiny to religious land use, limiting how zoning and land-use laws may burden churches, temples, and ceremonial grounds. Other provisions, such as federal FMLA guidance recognizing Native traditional healers as "health care providers" and the FACE Act's protection of access to places of religious worship, further confirm that traditional and religious healing are recognized, nameable realities in U.S. law. The "equal terms" concept appears in § 2000cc(b)(1) ("less than equal terms with a nonreligious assembly or institution").

Important to note: "§ 1680u states that although the Secretary may promote traditional health care practices (consistent with Service standards), **the United States is not liable** for provision of such practices that result in damage, injury, or death, and it includes a savings clause about other liability under ISDEAA or the chapter."

IHCIA also instructs programs to "promote traditional health care practices" in at least one operational program section: 25 U.S.C. § 1616 (Community Health Representative Program), which states the Service shall "promote traditional health care practices of the Indian tribes served" consistent with Service standards for health care, health promotion, and disease prevention. (https://www.law.cornell.edu/uscode/text/25/1616)

What IHCIA says (scope frame)

- IHCIA permits the promotion of "traditional health care practices" that are consistent with Service standards for healthcare, health promotion, and disease prevention.

- IHCIA also directs, in at least one program area, that the Service "promote traditional health care practices" of tribes served (Community Health Representative Program).

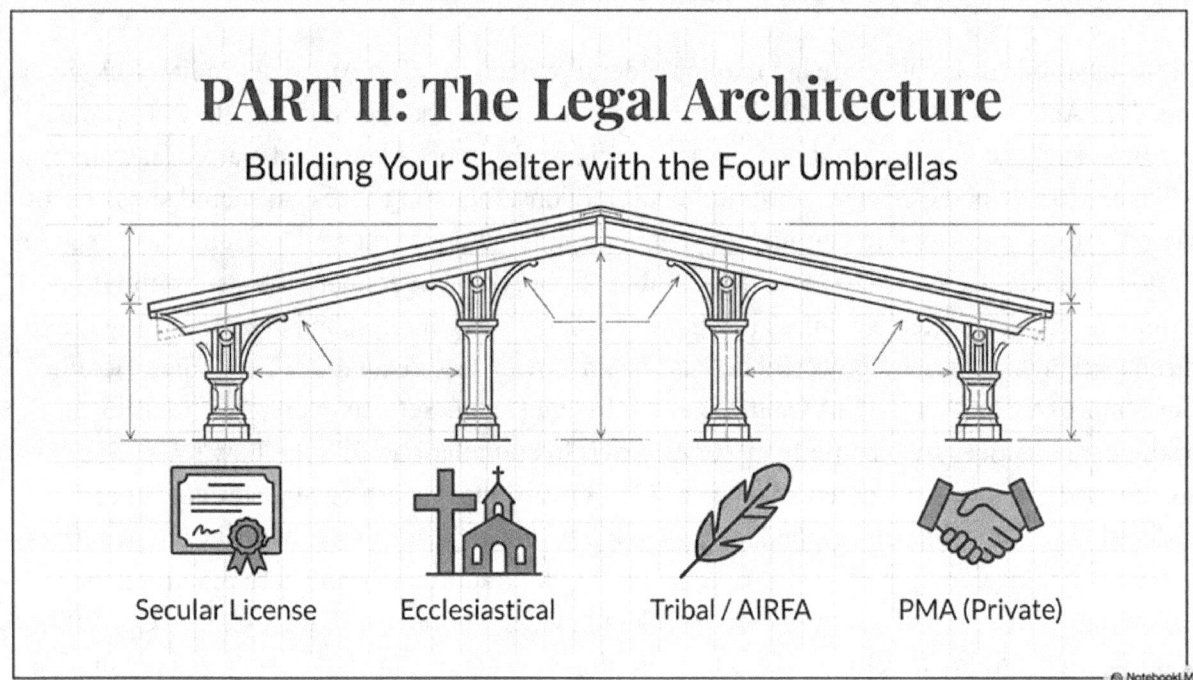

PART II: The Legal Architecture
Building Your Shelter with the Four Umbrellas

Secular License   Ecclesiastical   Tribal / AIRFA   PMA (Private)

Examples (illustrative, not exhaustive)

IMPORTANT NOTE: Examples of traditional health care practices may include talking circles, sweat lodges, and smudging, depending on the teachings and protocols of the tribe/community served. These are commonly cited/used traditional practices in Native communities and in I/T/U (Indian Health Service/Tribal/Urban Indian) settings, and they fit within the broad statutory framework of IHCIA. IHCIA provisions that recognize/preserve the category of "traditional health care practices" (https://www.law.cornell.edu/uscode/text/25/1680u)

IHCIA recognizes/promotes traditional health care practices and treats any specific modalities as **examples** that vary by tribe and setting.

- Talking circles (group healing/support circles).
- Sweat lodge/purification lodge ceremonies.
- Smudging (ceremonial cleansing with smoke, often sage/sweetgrass/cedar depending on tradition).
- Traditional healer services are provided in accordance with tribal protocols (sometimes referred to administratively as "traditional healer and natural helper services" in modern program implementation contexts).

IHCIA § 1680u doesn't ban traditional practices, but it builds in two practical **limitations**: (1) promotion is constrained by IHS "Service standards," and (2) the statute expressly limits federal liability for harms arising from provision of traditional practices under the Act.

Limitation 1: "Consistent with Service standards."

The Secretary may promote traditional health care practices only "consistent with the Service standards for the provision of health care, health promotion, and disease prevention." In practice, this means traditional practices are not treated as a free-floating entitlement; they must comply with IHS/I/T/U program standards, protocols, safety requirements, and any applicable clinical/administrative policies used by the Service.

Limitation 2: Federal liability limitation (U.S. not liable for harm)

Section 1680u states that "the United States is not liable" for provision of traditional health care practices under the chapter if it results in "damage, injury, or death to a patient." This is a major boundary: it serves as a statutory disclaimer that limits federal exposure to potential harms arising from the provision of traditional practices under IHCIA programs.

Limitation 3: No expansion/reduction of other existing obligations

The section adds a savings clause: nothing in § 1680u alters "any liability or other obligation" the United States may otherwise have under the Indian Self-Determination and Education Assistance Act (ISDEAA) or under the IHCIA chapter itself. In other words, § 1680u shouldn't be read as wiping out other legal duties that might arise under ISDEAA contracting/compact frameworks or other IHCIA provisions; it is narrowly targeted to the "traditional practices" liability statement while preserving other obligations.

What § 1680u does *not* do (important "limits" by omission)

- It does not define a specific list of practices; "traditional health care practices" is left broad and contextual.
- It does not create a guaranteed right to receive any particular ceremony/service; it says the Secretary "may promote," not "shall provide."

Part II also explores what your materials call the "ironclad triangle" (now a four-pillar foundation): sovereignty of tribes and tribal religious organizations, church autonomy under the First Amendment, private association law, and these federal statutes working together.

You will see:

1. How federally and state-recognized tribes possess inherent authority to define and regulate their own medicine;

2. How 508(c)(1)(A) churches and FBOs enjoy "mandatory exception" status from standard IRS application procedures;

3. How Private Membership Associations move healing into the private domain of contract and association, and how the U.S. Code gives tribal organizations a patent-like right to self-determination in beliefs, practices, and expressions.

Far from being loopholes, these are **deliberate** exceptions and privileges carved out so that religious and Indigenous healing can survive alongside a tightly regulated medical-industrial system.

Finally, Part II does not romanticize these protections; it draws their **boundaries**. You will study key cases such as *United States v. Boyll* and *Gonzales v. O Centro*, which affirm non-racial access to Native American Church protections and RFRA's application to visionary sacraments, but also clarify that religious freedom does not license conduct that gravely threatens public safety. You will learn why contentious medicine, entheogens, invasive rites, and high-risk interventions sit under stricter scrutiny, and how sincere belief, clear organizational structure, informed consent, and ethical practice make the difference between protected ministry and prosecutable misconduct. By the time you leave Part II, you will know not only **that** the law can protect your calling, but exactly **how** and **where** to stand to receive those protections.

LEARNING EXERCISE PART2.
Review & Application
Instructions: Select the best answer based on the reading.

1. **In Part II, which sets correctly names the "four umbrellas" under which holistic/religious healing may be practiced lawfully (as framed in this text)?**
   A. Federal, state, county, municipal
   B. Secular licensure; ecclesiastical authority; Native American/tribal jurisdiction; Private Membership Associations (PMAs)
   C. Insurance billing; hospital privileges; FDA approval; malpractice coverage
   D. Church autonomy; zoning law; criminal law; tort law
   E. Public health; environmental law; labor law; immigration law
   Correct Answer: B
2. **Under RFRA (42 U.S.C. § 2000bb-1), the government may substantially burden religious exercise only if it:**
   A. Shows a rational basis and issues a written notice
   B. Gets permission from a state licensing board.
   C. Proves a compelling governmental interest and uses the least restrictive means
   D. Demonstrates majority public support for enforcement
   E. Shows the practice is commercial rather than religious.
   Correct Answer: C

3. **Which statement best captures what IHCIA's "Traditional health care practices" provision (25 U.S.C. § 1680u) does and does not do?**
A. It creates an absolute, enforceable right for any person to receive any ceremony on demand
B. It defines a fixed nationwide list of approved traditional practices and mandates coverage for each
C. It authorizes promotion of traditional practices consistent with Service standards and includes a federal liability limitation plus a savings clause
D. It prohibits traditional practices within IHS settings unless state-licensed
E. It applies only to non-Native religious organizations
Correct Answer: C

4. **RLUIPA's "equal terms" concept is tied to which idea in the land-use context?**
A. Religious assemblies must always receive preferential treatment over all nonreligious uses
B. Government may not treat a religious assembly or institution on less than equal terms with a nonreligious assembly or institution
C. Only federally recognized tribes may challenge zoning decisions.
D. Land-use laws never apply to any religious organization
E. Equal terms apply only to employment, not zoning
Correct Answer: B

5. **Which pairing of cases is used in Part II to illustrate (1) non-racial access/coverage issues related to Native American Church protections and (2) RFRA protection for a specific sacramental use against federal drug-law enforcement?**
A. Roe v. Wade; Dobbs v. Jackson
B. Marbury v. Madison; Brown v. Board
C. United States v. Boyll; Gonzales v. O Centro Espírita Beneficente União do Vegetal
D. Miranda v. Arizona; Gideon v. Wainwright
E. Mapp v. Ohio; Terry v. Ohio
Correct Answer: C

Chapter 4 – The Four Legal Umbrellas for Holistic Practice

Chapter 4: The Four Legal Umbrellas

Secular
State License (LMT, MD).
Public domain.
Regulated commerce.

Ecclesiastical
Church autonomy.
Ministry domain.
Separation of Church & State.

Tribal
Sovereignty/AIRFA.
Indigenous domain.
Domestic Dependent Nations.

PMA
Private Contract.
Association domain.
Right of Association.

Strategy: The 'Layered Umbrella' combines **Church + Tribal + PMA** for maximum protection.

- The four legal "umbrellas" under which healing can lawfully occur: secular licensure, ecclesiastical authority, Native American/tribal jurisdiction, and expressive PMAs.
- Who is in charge, what activities are covered, and what risks and responsibilities come with each umbrella.
- How a layered umbrella (church + tribal + PMA) can provide a more resilient shelter for your ministry.

If you want to practice holistic or Indigenous healing without a state medical license, you must know exactly under which legal sky you are standing. In the United States, four distinct umbrellas can shelter complementary and alternative modalities: the secular licensing system, ecclesiastical authority, Native American and tribal jurisdiction, and the private association of church or tribal members. Most practitioners today are standing under more than one of these simultaneously, often without realizing it.

This chapter gives you a clear map of those four umbrellas, so you can see where you already fit, where you might want to move, and what each path can and cannot protect. We will not ask you to become a lawyer; instead, we will translate legal categories into everyday language and practical choices. Under each umbrella, we will look at three questions: Who is in charge? What activities does this umbrella cover? What are the risks and responsibilities that come with it?

We begin with the **secular** umbrella, where state medical and allied health boards define and regulate the "practice of medicine" and related professions such as massage, psychology, and dietetics. Under this model, your right to touch, counsel, or advise about health depends on a government-issued license, a statutory scope of practice, and compliance with peer-reviewed standards. For some readers, this will remain your primary shelter, but you will see why it is not the only, or always the best, framework for spiritual and Indigenous healing.

Next, we step under the **ecclesiastical** umbrella, where churches and faith-based organizations exercise self-governance over their ministries, sacraments, and internal discipline. Here, "healing the sick," "laying on of hands," and "pastoral counseling" are not commercial services, but sacred duties rooted in scripture, doctrine, and tradition. We will explore how ordination, commissions, and church-issued licenses function as internal credentials that carry real legal weight when your work is clearly identified as religious.

From there, we turn to **Native American and tribal** umbrellas, where federally and state-recognized tribes, and bona fide tribal religious organizations, exercise inherent sovereignty over their religious and medical practices. For many Indigenous practitioners, no additional legal maneuver is needed: the right to carry medicine, conduct ceremony, and serve their people flows from their status as members of domestic dependent nations. We will also look at how non-tribal allies can engage with these structures respectfully, without misusing them as mere shields.

Finally, we will examine the **Expressive Private Membership Association** (PMA): a contract-based relationship in which ministers and healers serve private members rather than the general public. This framework rests on the rights of association, speech, privacy, and contract, and can be layered under church or tribal authority to keep spiritual care in the private domain. You will see why a PMA is powerful, why it is not bulletproof, and why its protection depends on clear member agreements, ethical conduct, and staying within your declared spiritual scope of practice.

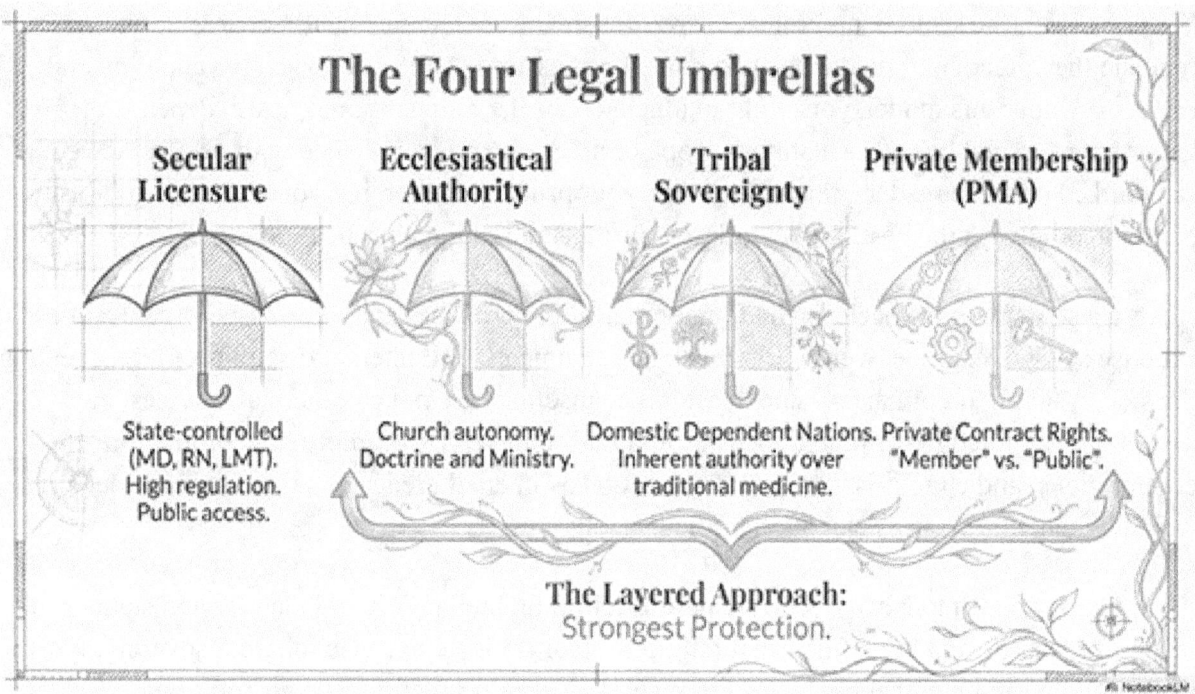

The Four Legal Umbrellas

Secular Licensure	Ecclesiastical Authority	Tribal Sovereignty	Private Membership (PMA)
State-controlled (MD, RN, LMT). High regulation. Public access.	Church autonomy. Doctrine and Ministry.	Domestic Dependent Nations. Inherent authority over traditional medicine.	Private Contract Rights. "Member" vs. "Public".

The Layered Approach:
Strongest Protection.

1. The Secular Umbrella

Under the secular umbrella, practice is governed by state medical practice acts and allied-health statutes. These laws define "practicing medicine" broadly, diagnosing, treating, operating, or prescribing for any human disease, pain, injury, deformity, or physical condition, and reserve those activities to licensed professionals such as physicians, osteopaths, chiropractors, nurses, and psychologists. Additional boards oversee "allied" or vocational specialties such as massage therapy, dietetics, and esthetics, each with its own scope of practice and protected titles.

In this domain, legitimacy flows from state-approved education, examinations, and ongoing regulatory oversight. Touch is regulated as "massage" or "bodywork" when it meets statutory definitions; counseling may be captured under psychology or social work statutes; and nutritional advice may fall under dietetics, depending on the wording of local law. If your work is conceptualized as secular therapy in the public marketplace, you are expected to stand under this umbrella and accept its constraints and liabilities.

For some practitioners, especially those performing invasive procedures, prescribing pharmaceuticals, or working in hospitals, this remains the appropriate primary shelter. For others, whose work is explicitly sacramental, ceremonial, or Indigenous in character, standing entirely under the secular umbrella can distort both the nature of their practice and the legal analysis. The rest of this book exists because other umbrellas may be more fitting.

2. The Ecclesiastical Umbrella

The ecclesiastical umbrella rests on the constitutional principle of separation of church and state and on court decisions that recognize the autonomy and sovereignty of churches in matters of doctrine, worship, ordination, and internal governance. In this framework, a church or faith-based organization (FBO) defines its own theology, sacraments, and ministries, including ministries of healing, counseling, and pastoral care.

Within this domain, religious institutions may issue degrees, licenses, ordinations, and commissions for various specialties, such as pastoral counseling, ecclesiastical medicine, or monastic healing, in accordance with their own scriptures, sacred texts, traditions, and role expectations. A therapeutic ministry may include natural therapies and remedial arts as prescribed by doctrine, dogma, family tradition, and common practice, provided ministers act within the level of education and authority granted by the religious body. Courts have repeatedly declined to adjudicate purely ecclesiastical questions, refusing to exercise jurisdiction over internal church disputes regarding doctrine or ordination.

Organizations such as the Native American Indigenous Church (NAIC), the Priory of Saving Grace, and SMOCH/SMOKH exemplify this umbrella in action, offering religious seminary education, ecclesiastical recognition, and defined scopes of practice for ministers engaged in Indigenous and holistic medicine as sacramental work. These protections are not exclusive to any one church; the law cannot favor one denomination over another. Any bona fide religious body may, in principle, establish similar internal structures, so long as they are sincere and coherent.

3. The Native American & Tribal Sovereignty Umbrella

The Native American and tribal umbrella derives from the inherent sovereignty of federally recognized tribes and the specific protections granted to Native religions and medicines in statutes such as the American Indian Religious Freedom Act (AIRFA). Federally recognized tribes are "domestic dependent nations" with the right to regulate their own spiritual and health practices on tribal lands, subject primarily to federal law rather than state medical or allied-health boards. State-recognized tribes, while not enjoying full nation-to-nation status, also exercise significant rights of self-governance and cultural preservation, including control over traditional healing practices.

In addition, bona fide tribal religious organizations, such as Native American churches and Indigenous tribal organizations chartered under state law, enjoy protection when they practice traditional medicine and ceremony as expressions of Indigenous religion. AIRFA and related acts affirm that American Indian, Eskimo, Aleut, and Native Hawaiian peoples have the right to believe, express, and exercise their traditional religions, including access to sacred sites, use and possession of sacred objects, and worship through traditional rites.

The Native American Indigenous Church, Inc. (NAIC), for example, describes itself as a religious tribal organization and private membership association, open to both Native and non-Native persons who join as members and agree to its religious therapeutic framework. Under this umbrella, practices such as sweat lodges, sacred breath ceremonies, sacrament use, and laying-on-of-hands are treated as protected religious rites, not as commercial services in the public domain.

4. The Expressive Private Membership Association Umbrella

An Expressive Private Membership Association (PMA) is a legal structure grounded on the rights of association, speech, privacy, and contract, as recognized in numerous Supreme Court decisions. In a PMA, individuals voluntarily enter into a private, nonpublic relationship governed by the association's bylaws, codes of ethics, and rules of practice. Within that relationship, members agree to receive services, counseling, or ministry from other members on a private basis, outside the general public marketplace.

In the healing context, this means: "I am not a doctor treating a public patient; I am a minister or healer serving a private member of our association." By moving the interaction into the private domain and clearly defining it as a religious, educational, or expressive activity, the practitioner narrows the State's "compelling interest" to regulate the transaction, so long as no substantive harm is done and no mala in se crimes (such as violence, abuse, or fraud) occur.

However, this umbrella is not bulletproof. If a PMA is secular in character, functioning as a commercial clinic in disguise, ignoring its own rules, or causing harm, it may be challenged in court; its "corporate veil" can be pierced and its activities treated as if they were public. Protection depends on maintaining active membership, honoring ethical codes, staying within declared scopes of practice, and avoiding behavior that creates a clear and present danger.

5. The Layered Legal Umbrella

For many practitioners, the safest strategy is a **layered** umbrella: a PMA organized within and under the authority of an ecclesiastical jurisdiction (a bona fide church or tribal religious body), which itself is a Native American Indigenous religious tribal organization meeting federal statutory protections. In this configuration, the practitioner stands under ecclesiastical authority, tribal or Indigenous protection, and private association law simultaneously.

Such a structure, illustrated by organizations like NAIC in relation to SMOCH/SMOKH and the Priory of Saving Grace, benefits from multiple legal shields: church autonomy, tribal sovereignty, AIRFA and RLUIPA protections for Indigenous religious exercise, and constitutional rights to association and privacy. Under U.S. Code, tribal organizations have the right to determine their own beliefs, practices, and expressions, including their approaches to medicine and ceremony. When these elements are combined coherently and ethically, they create a strong environment for practicing Religious Therapeutics and Indigenous medicine without a secular state license.

Chapter 4 Conclusion – Knowing Where You Stand

In this chapter, you have seen that "the law" is not a single, monolithic force. It is a landscape of different jurisdictions and protections, some of which support your work and some of which constrain it. You have met the four umbrellas under which healing can take place: secular, ecclesiastical, Native American/tribal, and private association, and glimpsed how a layered approach can offer the greatest stability.

Knowing where you stand is the first step toward walking safely. If you choose to operate as a secular therapist in the public marketplace, you will need to pursue and maintain the appropriate state licenses and accept the authority of those boards. If you choose to stand primarily under ecclesiastical or tribal umbrellas, you will need to deepen your relationship with bona fide religious and tribal bodies and honor the disciplines they require. If you adopt a PMA structure, you must keep it truly private and ethical.

In the next chapter, we will examine the **federal pillars** that specifically uphold Indigenous and religious healing in the United States: the American Indian Religious Freedom Act (AIRFA), the Religious Freedom Restoration Act (RFRA), and the Indian Health Care Improvement Act (IHCIA). These laws form the "ironclad triangle" that supports Native American medicine and other sincere religious health practices. Understanding them will turn your layered umbrella into something more than hope; it will become a legally intelligible shelter.

LEARNING EXERCISE 4.1
Review & Application
Instructions: Select the best answer based on the reading.

1. **What are the "four legal umbrellas" under which healing work may lawfully occur?**
   A) Federal, state, county, and municipal
   B) Hospital, clinic, spa, and home practice
   C) Secular licensure, ecclesiastical authority, Native American/tribal jurisdiction, and expressive PMA
   D) Medical, chiropractic, nursing, and pharmacy
   E) Civil, criminal, administrative, and canon law
   Correct Answer: C
2. **Under the secular umbrella, what primarily defines practice?**
   A) Tribal resolutions
   B) Unwritten community norms

C) State medical and allied-health practice acts and their scopes of practice

D) Personal spiritual experiences

E) International treaties alone

Correct Answer: C

3. **What distinguishes the ecclesiastical umbrella?**

   A) It focuses on profit and insurance billing

   B) Its authority to regulate all secular clinics

   C) Church autonomy over doctrine, sacraments, ministry, and internal credentials

   D) Its exclusive control over herbal remedies

   E) Its power to license physicians

   Correct Answer: C

4. **How does the Native American and tribal umbrella protect healing work?**

   A) By outlawing all non-tribal practices

   B) By granting tribes exclusive rights to all medicine worldwide

   C) Through inherent tribal sovereignty and statutes like AIRFA, recognizing traditional ceremonies and medicines

   D) By requiring all healers to obtain federal medical licenses

   E) By exempting tribes from any federal law

   Correct Answer: C

5. **What is the main function of an expressive Private Membership Association (PMA) in this context?**

   A) To eliminate all legal oversight

   B) To operate as a public hospital

   C) To move healing relationships into a private, membership-based domain grounded in association, privacy, and contract rights

   D) To provide malpractice insurance

   E) To replace church and tribal structures

   Correct Answer: C

Chapter 5 – Federal Pillars: AIRFA, RFRA, IHCIA, and the FACE Act

> ❧ What AIRFA, RFRA, IHCIA, and the FACE Act actually say and how they protect Indigenous and religious healing.
> ❧ How these four federal "pillars" work together with church autonomy and tribal sovereignty to support Religious Therapeutics.
> ❧ Why these protections are deliberate exemptions in law, not "loopholes" or "sovereign citizen" tricks.

Specific laws hold up the four legal umbrellas you met in the last chapter. For Native American and other religious healers in the United States, four federal statutes form the strongest beams in that structure: the American Indian Religious Freedom Act (AIRFA), the Religious Freedom Restoration Act (RFRA), the Indian Health Care Improvement Act (IHCIA), and the Freedom of Access to Clinic Entrances Act (the **FACE Act**). Together, they create what we might call the **Federal Four-Pillar Foundation** for Indigenous medicine and religious therapeutics.

This chapter introduces each pillar in turn. We will examine what the law actually says, why it was needed, and how it applies to traditional healing practices such as sweat lodges, smudging, herbalism, sacramental plant use, and bodywork understood as ceremony rather than massage. We will then consider how these statutes interact with one another, with tribal sovereignty, and with church autonomy, and how they collectively guard not only your right to practice, but also your right to be free from harassment, threats, or physical obstruction when you do.

By the end of this chapter, you will not be a legal scholar. Still, you will be able to explain, in plain language, why the right to practice Indigenous and religious healing is not a "loophole" or a "sovereign citizen" trick. It is a federally codified reality, grounded in acts of Congress and affirmed by the courts.

1. The American Indian Religious Freedom Act (AIRFA)

Before 1978, many Native American religious practices were effectively illegal or severely constrained in the United States. Ceremonies were suppressed, access to sacred sites was restricted, and the use of certain sacraments and sacred objects was criminalized or discouraged. In response, Congress passed the American Indian Religious Freedom Act (AIRFA), codified at 42 U.S.C. § 1996, as a joint resolution declaring a new national policy.

AIRFA states that it is now "the policy of the United States to protect and preserve for American Indians their inherent right of freedom to believe, express and exercise the traditional religions of the American Indian, Eskimo, Aleut, and Native Hawaiians," including "access to sites, use and possession of sacred objects, and the freedom to worship through ceremonials and traditional rites." Subsequent amendments further clarified and expanded these protections, including specific reference to the sacramental use of peyote by Indians for religious purposes.

In the context of this book, AIRFA is crucial because Native American Traditional Indigenous Medicine (NATIM) does not separate "medicine" from "religion." Ceremonies such as smudging, sweat lodges, sacramental rituals, laying on of hands, and herbal practices are all part of a unified spiritual-medical worldview. Under this worldview, therapeutic modalities are "traditional rites," and AIRFA's protection of traditional religions necessarily extends to these healing practices when they are conducted as part of bona fide Indigenous religious expression.

2. The Religious Freedom Restoration Act (RFRA)

In 1993, after Supreme Court decisions had narrowed the protection of religious exercise, Congress enacted the Religious Freedom Restoration Act (RFRA), codified at 42 U.S.C. § 2000bb. RFRA's purpose was to restore a higher standard of protection for religious practices burdened by government actions, even when those actions are "neutral" and "generally applicable."

RFRA provides that the government may not "substantially burden" a person's exercise of religion unless it can demonstrate that the burden furthers a **compelling governmental interest** and is the **least restrictive means** of furthering that interest. This "strict scrutiny" standard is one of the most protective in constitutional law. RFRA applies broadly to all sincere religious exercises, not only to Native American traditions.

A key illustration of RFRA is the Supreme Court case *Gonzales v. O Centro Espírita Beneficente União do Vegetal* (2006). There, a small Brazilian-origin church in New Mexico used a visionary tea (Hoasca, containing a Schedule I substance) as a sacrament. The federal government sought to prohibit the practice under drug laws. Still, the Court held that RFRA required individualized analysis and that the government had failed to demonstrate a compelling interest in prohibiting this specific controlled sacramental use. The church was allowed to continue its practice under strict conditions.

For holistic and Indigenous practitioners, RFRA is significant because it affirms that religious healing activities, including ceremonies involving otherwise restricted substances, cannot be restricted lightly. The government must show not only a general interest in public safety but also a compelling need to burden *this* practice in *this* context using the least restrictive means.

3. The Indian Health Care Improvement Act (IHCIA)

While AIRFA and RFRA protect the right to practice religious and Indigenous medicine, the Indian Health Care Improvement Act (IHCIA) provides a different approach: the validation and integration of traditional healers within the federal health care system. "IHCIA contemplates incorporation of traditional practices into Indian health programs, for example, the Community Health Representative Program directs the Service to promote traditional health care practices of the tribes served (25 U.S.C. § 1616), and IHCIA also includes a specific 'Traditional health care practices' provision with a federal liability limitation (25 U.S.C. § 1680u)." (https://www.law.cornell.edu/uscode/text/25/1616)

This language acknowledges that "traditional health care practitioners" are legitimate providers and that traditional practices may be funded and integrated through the Indian Health Service (IHS). In other words, within the Indian health system, traditional healers are not treated as fringe or fraudulent; they are recognized as participants in the health care team.

For our purposes, IHCIA serves two main functions. First, it undermines any simplistic claim by state boards that traditional or Indigenous medicine is inherently unscientific or illegitimate. If the federal government can fund and integrate such practitioners through IHS, state boards must be cautious in dismissing the same practices as quackery when conducted under proper tribal or ecclesiastical authority. Second, it models how traditional and biomedical paradigms can coexist in a complementary way, an important example for those building integrated clinics and ministries.

4. The Freedom of Access to Clinic Entrances Act (FACE Act)

The fourth pillar, the **Freedom of Access to Clinic Entrances Act of 1994**, known as the FACE Act and codified at **18 U.S.C. § 248**, is often discussed in the context of reproductive health clinics. But its protections are **expressly dual**: it safeguards access to both facilities that provide reproductive health services **and** places of religious worship.

Under **18 U.S.C. § 2482**, FACE makes it a federal offense for anyone who, "by force or threat of force or by physical obstruction, intentionally injures, intimidates or interferes with or attempts to injure, intimidate or interfere with" a person obtaining or providing reproductive health services, **or** a person "lawfully exercising or seeking to exercise the First Amendment right of religious freedom at a place of religious worship." It also prohibits intentional damage or destruction of the property of such facilities or places of worship.

The Act does more than create crimes; it also creates **civil remedies**. Any person aggrieved by conduct prohibited under subsection (a)(2), the provision relating to religious freedom at places of worship, may bring a civil action for injunctive relief, compensatory and punitive damages, and attorney's fees. The Attorney General and state attorneys general may likewise seek injunctive relief and civil penalties against violators.

For our purposes, the FACE Act matters because it protects **freedom from violent or physically obstructive interference** when people gather to worship, pray, and practice their religion. If your healing work takes place in or as part of a recognized place of worship, church sanctuary, ceremonial lodge, designated sacred ground, then those entering or leaving to exercise their First Amendment religious freedom are shielded against threats, assaults, or blockades aimed at stopping that exercise.

In other words, where AIRFA, RFRA, and IHCIA focus on your right to practice, the FACE Act adds a distinct layer: a right to access and use places of worship **without being physically attacked, intimidated, or blocked at the door**. It is a protection against vexatious interference by force or physical obstruction, reinforcing the idea that religious exercise is not only theoretically free but also practically accessible.

5. How the Four Pillars Work Together

AIRFA, RFRA, IHCIA, and the FACE Act each address different aspects of the same reality, and together they form a robust four-pillar foundation for Indigenous and religious therapeutics.

- **AIRFA** affirms the inherent right of Indigenous peoples to practice their traditional religions, including access to sacred sites, use of sacred objects, and performance of traditional ceremonies and rites that are often indistinguishable from what we call "medicine."
- **RFRA** requires the government to meet strict scrutiny before substantially burdening any sincere exercise of religion, demanding both a compelling interest and the least restrictive means.
- **IHCIA** explicitly recognizes traditional healers as legitimate health-care providers in the federal Indian health system, authorizing contracts with tribes to employ traditional practices.
- **The FACE Act** protects the physical access to and use of places of religious worship by making it a federal offense, and creating civil remedies, when someone uses force, threats, or physical obstruction to injure, intimidate, or interfere with persons exercising their First Amendment religious freedom at such places.

Viewed together, these statutes address four key questions:

1. **Do we have the right to practice our traditional and religious medicine at all?**
   – AIRFA answers "Yes" for Indigenous peoples and their traditional religions.
2. **Can the government burden our religious healing practices with neutral laws?**
   – RFRA says "Only if it meets strict scrutiny and uses the least restrictive means."
3. **Are traditional healers considered legitimate providers under federal health policy?**
   – IHCIA answers "Yes, and we can contract with tribes to employ them."
4. **Are we protected from violent or physically obstructive interference when we gather to worship and heal?**
   – The FACE Act answers "Yes, and violators may face both criminal and civil consequences."

When combined with tribal sovereignty and church autonomy, these four pillars confer on a traditional healer a standing under multiple layers of law. A practitioner working under tribal authority and within a bona fide Native American church, for example, can point to: (1) the tribe's inherent sovereignty; (2) AIRFA's protection of traditional rites; (3) RFRA's demand for strict scrutiny of any substantial burden on religious exercise; (4) IHCIA's validation of traditional practitioners in federal health policy; and (5) the FACE Act's protection against physical obstruction or threats at places of worship.

This does **not** mean that anything done in the name of religion is immune from law. The Supreme Court has made clear that religious freedom does not license acts such as violence, abuse, or reckless endangerment, and federal and state criminal laws continue to apply. Schedule I substances, invasive procedures, and other high-risk practices remain areas of heightened scrutiny, and practitioners must operate with great care and robust internal protocols when working at these frontiers. But within those boundaries, the four pillars significantly tilt the balance toward protecting sincere, carefully structured religious healing.

6. Not a Loophole, Not "Sovereign Citizen" Logic

Some critics, and some careless practitioners, speak as if these protections are "loopholes" that allow people to escape all regulation simply by declaring themselves a church or tribal group. This is both inaccurate and dangerous. The legal framework described here is not grounded in pseudo-legal theories that deny the authority of government altogether; it is grounded in statutes enacted by Congress and interpreted by courts under the normal rule of law.

"Sovereign citizen" arguments typically claim that individuals are exempt from basic obligations such as driver's licenses, taxes, or criminal statutes by invoking obscure readings of constitutional or commercial law. By contrast, Native American practitioners and religious healers acknowledge the existence of federal and state law but assert specific religious and cultural exemptions that Congress and the courts have intentionally granted to protect Indigenous and spiritual life. We do not claim to be outside the law; we claim to be **protected by** the law.

Maintaining this distinction is essential for credibility. When you frame your practice as a sincere exercise of religion supported by AIRFA, RFRA, IHCIA, the FACE Act, tribal sovereignty, and church autonomy, and when your conduct remains transparent, ethical, and non-harmful, you invite the courts to see you as a lawful heir of these protections. When you speak in the language of conspiracy or defiance, you risk having your claims dismissed as frivolous.

Chapter 5 Conclusion – Standing on the Four Pillars

In this chapter, you have met four of the strongest supports under your feet: AIRFA, RFRA, IHCIA, and the FACE Act. Together with tribal sovereignty and church autonomy, they make it clear that the right to practice Indigenous and religious therapeutics is not an accident or a gap in the law; it is a deliberate choice by Congress and the courts to honor the spiritual and cultural life of the people and to protect access to places of worship from violent or obstructive interference.

This does not mean you are licensed to do anything you wish. The same law that protects your ceremonies also protects your neighbors from harm. But it does mean that when you stand in integrity, as a minister, medicine person, or traditional healer operating within a bona fide tribal or ecclesiastical structure and serving members in a private domain, you can speak with a confidence grounded not just in faith, but in statute.

In the next chapters, we will turn from these federal pillars to the **practical definitions** of your work: Religious Therapeutics, Chirothesia, and Indigenous Healthcare. You will see how to describe your actual protocols in a way that is true to your traditions and consistent with the legal frameworks we have just explored, so that when you say, "I am not practicing medicine; I am practicing ministry," you can show exactly what that means.

Walking on Four Solid Stones

The four federal pillars you have met in this chapter, AIRFA, RFRA, IHCIA, and the FACE Act, are not abstract theories. They are **stones** you can actually stand on when you step into your role as a healer-minister. AIRFA affirms that Indigenous ceremonies and traditional rites, which for NATIM are inseparable from "medicine," are part of a protected religious inheritance. RFRA demands that any government attempt to burden sincere religious exercise, whether Christian, Indigenous, or otherwise, must meet the highest legal test: a compelling interest pursued by the least restrictive means. IHCIA goes further by naming traditional healers as legitimate providers within the Indian Health Service, signaling that your work is recognized, not dismissed, in federal health policy. And the FACE Act protects worshippers' physical access to their places of religious exercise, shielding them from force, threats, and intentional obstruction when they come to pray, receive the sacraments, or participate in healing ceremonies.

Taken together, these statutes do something remarkable. They say that Indigenous and religious healing is not a tolerated eccentricity but a **protected expression** of human dignity, culture, and faith, backed by both civil and criminal remedies when those rights are violated. They also establish clear boundaries around conduct that endangers others: no pillar licenses violence, fraud, or the reckless use of high-risk substances or procedures. For the sincere practitioner who walks in integrity under tribal or ecclesiastical authority, however, these four stones turn fear into footing. You can now see that when you stand in your calling, as minister, medicine person, or traditional healer, you are not trespassing on someone else's legal territory. You are standing on ground that Congress itself has marked out as sacred.

LEARNING EXERCISE 5.1
Review & Application
Instructions: Select the best answer based on the reading.

1. What does AIRFA (42 U.S.C. § 1996) declare as U.S. policy?
   A) To standardize all medical education
   B) To limit Indigenous religious practice to museums
   C) To protect and preserve Indigenous peoples' inherent right to exercise their traditional religions, including ceremonial rites and sacred objects
   D) To license all tribal healers under state boards
   E) To subsidize only hospital-based care
   Correct Answer: C

2. What standard does RFRA restore for government actions that burden religious exercise?
   A) Rational basis review
   B) No review at all
   C) Strict scrutiny: compelling interest and least restrictive means
   D) Intermediate scrutiny based on economic impact
   E) A purely political test
   Correct Answer: C

3. How does the Indian Health Care Improvement Act (IHCIA) support traditional healers?
   A) By banning them from Indian Health Service facilities
   B) By requiring them to become physicians
   C) By authorizing IHS to employ traditional health care practices by traditional practitioners via tribal contracts
   D) By treating all traditional practices as superstition
   E) By limiting them to mental-health services
   Correct Answer: C

4. What aspect of practice does the FACE Act protect in this book's context?
   A) Insurance reimbursement
   B) Advertising rights on social media
   C) Physical access to places of religious worship against force, threats, or obstruction
   D) Exclusive rights to use the term "clinic."
   E) Tax-exempt status for all healers
   Correct Answer: C

5. How do these "four pillars" collectively support Religious Therapeutics and Indigenous medicine?
   A) By granting automatic immunity from all laws
   B) By providing a general amnesty for health-care fraud
   C) By affirming rights to practice traditional religions, requiring strict scrutiny for burdens, recognizing traditional healers in policy, and protecting access to worship spaces
   D) By replacing tribal and church authorities with federal agencies
   E) By funding only biomedical research
   Correct Answer: C

Chapter 6 – Tribal Sovereignty and Native American Medicine

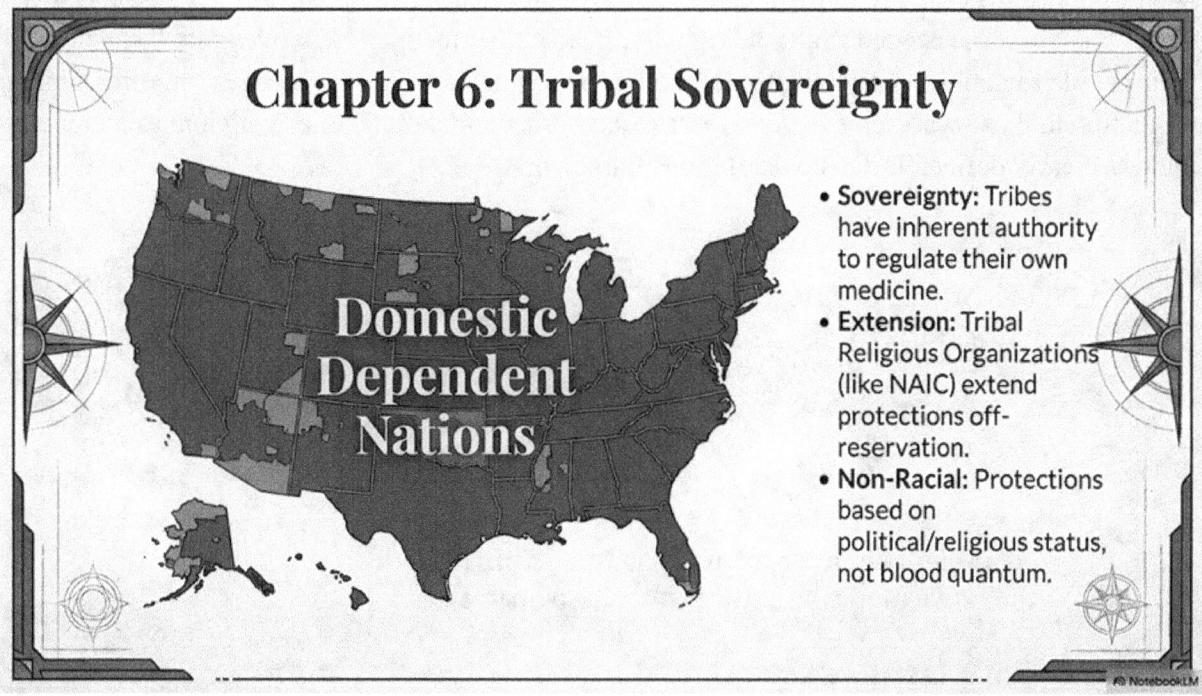

- ❧ What it means, legally, to walk into a different jurisdiction when you step onto tribal land.
- ❧ How federally recognized and state-recognized tribes govern their own ceremonies, medicine people, and traditional healers.
- ❧ What tribal religious organizations and Native American churches extend this protection beyond reservation borders for Native and non-Native members.

When you walk onto tribal land, you are not just entering a neighborhood; you are entering another jurisdiction. Federally recognized tribes are "domestic dependent nations" with inherent sovereignty: the right to govern their own internal affairs, including how they understand and regulate health, ceremony, and medicine. For many Native practitioners, this means that what looks like "alternative medicine" to a state board is, in fact, the normal practice of a sovereign people's religion and culture.

This chapter explores what that sovereignty means for Native American Traditional Indigenous Medicine (NATIM). We will look first at federally recognized tribes and their authority over traditional healers and ceremonies on tribal lands. We will then consider state-recognized tribes, whose status differs but still confers significant rights of cultural self-governance. Finally, we will examine tribal religious organizations and Native American churches, such as the Native

American Indigenous Church (NAIC), that extend this protection into urban and inter-tribal settings and provide legal shelter for Native and non-Native members alike.

By the end of this chapter, you will understand why, for many Indigenous healers, no special "legal maneuver" is needed at all: the right to practice their medicine is woven into the status of their people as nations. You will also see how tribal organizations and churches can offer similar protection to those who serve beyond reservation borders, including allies who join as members under a clearly defined Indigenous religious framework.

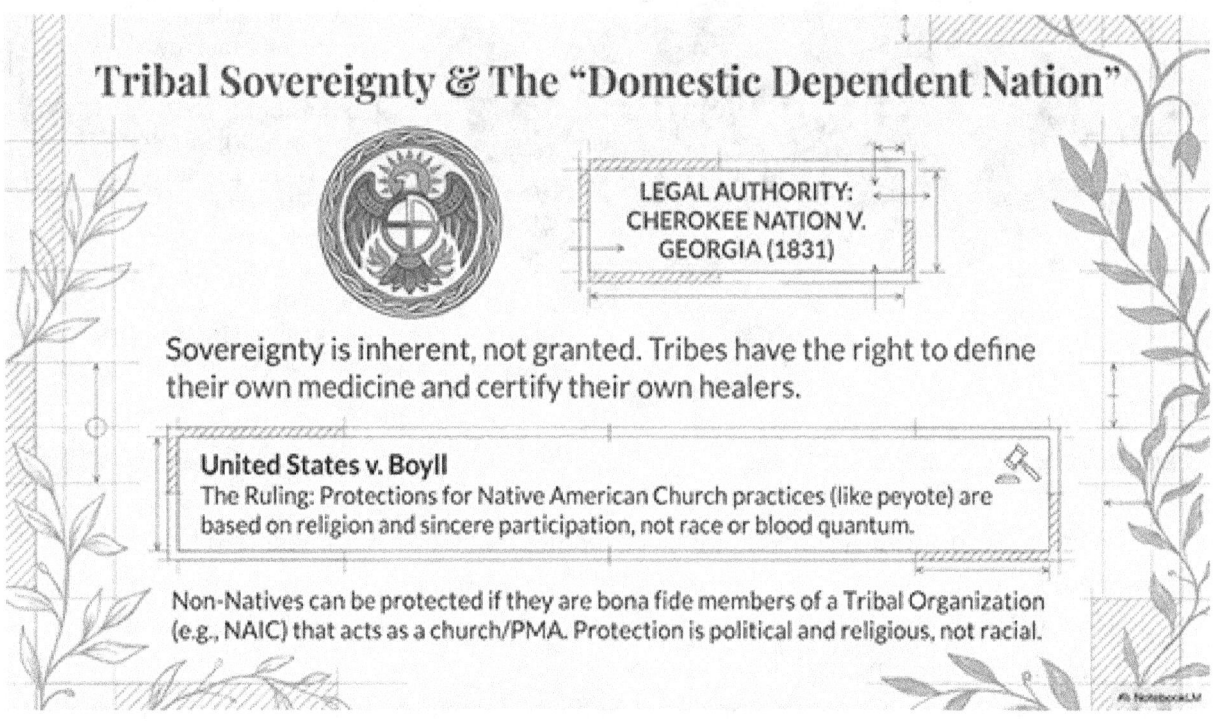

1. Sovereignty by Right: Federally Recognized Tribes

Federally recognized tribes are not clubs or nonprofits; they are political communities with a government-to-government relationship with the United States. The Supreme Court has described them as "domestic dependent nations" that pre-exist the Constitution and retain inherent powers of self-government except where Congress has clearly taken away those powers. Among those retained powers is the authority to define, protect, and regulate their own religious and medical practices

Because this sovereignty is inherent, a federally recognized tribe does **not** need to incorporate as a church or seek permission from a state medical board to practice its medicine. Tribal law generally governs the conduct of tribal members on tribal land, including who may serve as a medicine person, how ceremonies are conducted, and what traditional remedies may be used.

State medical and massage practice acts usually do not apply on tribal lands in the same way they apply off-reservation, although federal criminal law still applies to serious offenses.

NATIM itself makes no hard distinction between "religion" and "medicine." Smudging, sweat lodges, sacrament ceremonies, laying on of hands, herbal remedies, birth and death rites, and vision quests are all part of a single Indigenous health-religion system. Under AIRFA and related statutes, those ceremonies are expressly protected as traditional religions of American Indians, Eskimos, Aleuts, and Native Hawaiians. When such practices are conducted under tribal authority on tribal land, they rest on both inherent sovereignty and explicit federal policy.

2. State-Recognized Tribes and Cultural Self-Governance

Not all Indigenous nations have federal recognition. Many are recognized instead by individual states. State-recognized tribes may lack certain federal benefits and the full "nation-to-nation" status enjoyed by federally recognized tribes. Still, they remain valid political entities with real rights of self-governance and cultural preservation.

These tribes can and do define and regulate their own cultural and religious practices, including traditional healing. State recognition often brings formal acknowledgment of a tribe's ongoing existence, history, and authority over its internal affairs, even if federal law does not yet recognize the tribe as a domestic dependent nation. In practice, this means that ceremonies, healers, and traditional health practices sanctioned by a state-recognized tribe carry significant weight when seeking religious and cultural exemptions under state law.

For practitioners working with or within state-recognized tribes, it is important to understand the specific legal instruments and memoranda that define the tribe's status. However, the underlying principle remains: these communities have a right to maintain and develop their traditional medicine and spirituality, and to organize their own systems of recognition and accountability for healers.

3. Tribal Religious Organizations and Native American Churches

Many Indigenous people today live and serve far from reservation lands, in cities, small towns, and mixed communities where formal tribal jurisdiction is less clear. To protect and continue their medicine in these contexts, Native leaders have formed **tribal religious organizations** and Native American churches that function as vessels for NATIM beyond the boundaries of a single reservation.

The Native American Indigenous Church (NAIC) is one such example. NAIC describes itself as a Florida-chartered not-for-profit religious tribal organization and an expressed private membership association for medicine, healing, curing, and life. It operates as an intertribal church, open not only to enrolled tribal members but also to non-ethnic, non-blood-quantum persons who sincerely join as members and agree to its Indigenous religious therapeutic framework. NAIC is also recognized as a UN/WHO/DESA NGO Indigenous Peoples Organization, and functions as an integrated auxiliary of the Priory of Saving Grace and SMOCH/SMOKH within a broader ecclesiastical structure

By incorporating as both a **tribal organization** and a **faith-based organization** under Internal Revenue Code 508(c)(1)(A), such a church claims "mandatory exception" status as a bona fide religious body. It is not required to seek advance permission from the IRS to exist or to operate its ministries, including healing ministries. Within this structure, traditional healers, Native and non-Native, can be recognized, trained, and commissioned to practice Indigenous medicine as a sacramental ministry among fellow members rather than as a public commercial service.

Crucially, these protections are not proprietary to any one organization. Any group of sincere believers can, in principle, organize as a tribal religious body or Native American church in accordance with applicable law, provided they do so honestly and coherently. What NAIC and similar organizations offer is a **model**: a legal and ecclesiastical framework that honors Indigenous tradition while interfacing effectively with modern regulatory systems

4. Sovereignty, Statutes, and Self-Determination

Tribal sovereignty does not float in isolation; it is reinforced by the federal statutes you encountered in the previous chapter. AIRFA declares a national policy to protect and preserve American Indians' inherent right to exercise their traditional religions, including access to sacred sites, use of sacred objects, and worship through ceremonial rites. RFRA requires strict scrutiny when any government action substantially burdens a religious exercise. IHCIA authorizes the Indian Health Service to contract with tribes to employ "traditional health care practices by traditional health care practitioners," thereby validating traditional healers as legitimate providers

Layer onto this the rights articulated in other federal law: provisions recognizing "Native Medicine Men" and traditional healers as health-care providers for purposes such as family medical leave and Indian health programs; statutory language encouraging the utilization and promotion of Traditional Indian Health Care and Treatment Practices; and explicit acknowledgments that tribal organizations may certify and register their own traditional health-care providers

Under U.S. Code, Native American tribal organizations have what you might call a **patent right of self-determination** regarding their beliefs, practices, and expressions. They decide what their religion consists of, which ceremonies and medicines it includes, and who is authorized to carry those medicines. When such an organization operates as a church and PMA in the private, ecclesiastical domain, its members can point not only to generic religious-freedom arguments but to a concrete body of tribal, federal, and international law that recognizes Indigenous medicine as a sovereign science to be respected, not a relic to be studied.

5. Non-Exclusive Protections: Sincere Allies and Membership

One key point often misunderstood is that the legal protections for Native American religious practice are **not racial preferences**. AIRFA and related statutes protect religions, not blood quantum. Case law, such as *United States v. Boyll* (discussed later in this book), confirms that membership in a Native American Church and sincere participation in its sacraments may be legally protected, even for individuals who are not enrolled members of federally recognized tribes, so long as the practice is genuinely religious.

Organizations like NAIC embody this principle by opening membership to non-ethnic persons who adopt and respect the Indigenous religious framework and who submit to the church's code of ethics, ceremonial protocols, and scopes of practice. In doing so, they extend the shelter of tribal religious practice to a wider circle without reducing it to a mere legal loophole or cultural appropriation. Membership is not casual; it carries responsibilities, including tithing, education, and accountability to church and tribal authorities.

For non-Native allies and practitioners, this means that you cannot simply claim "tribal sovereignty" on your own. You must either work under the authority of a bona fide tribe or tribal religious organization or stand openly under a different umbrella (such as a non-Native church). You **can** join and support Indigenous churches and organizations respectfully and honestly, with authorization and training from those who carry the medicine by right.

Chapter 6 Conclusion – Nations Within a Nation

In this chapter, you have seen that Native American medicine is not merely an "alternative modality" in the eyes of the law; it is the living expression of sovereign nations within a nation. Federally recognized tribes, state-recognized tribes, and tribal religious organizations all exercise varying degrees of authority to define, protect, and transmit their traditional medicines and ceremonies. Federal statutes such as AIRFA, RFRA, and IHCIA do not create that authority; they acknowledge and reinforce it.

For Indigenous healers, this means your rights flow first from who your people are, and only second from what licenses you hold. For non-Native practitioners, it means that genuine partnership with tribal and Native American church structures is not only ethical but legally wise. In both cases, the path forward is not to hide your medicine, but to root it more deeply in the sovereign and sacred soil from which it came.

In the next chapter, we will broaden our focus from tribes to other private domains, churches, and Private Membership Associations, where spiritual and Indigenous healing can lawfully take place outside the public commercial marketplace. You will see how church autonomy, tribal authority, and PMA contracts can be layered together to create a resilient legal umbrella for your ministry, whether on reservation land or in the heart of a city.

LEARNING EXERCISE 6.1
Review & Application
Instructions: Select the best answer based on the reading.

1. How are federally recognized tribes described in U.S. law?
   A) Nonprofits with no political status
   B) Private clubs under state jurisdiction
   C) "Domestic dependent nations" with inherent sovereignty over internal affairs
   D) Federal agencies
   E) Counties within each state
   Correct Answer: C
2. On tribal lands, who primarily regulates traditional healers and ceremonies for tribal members?
   A) State massage boards
   B) Local county commissioners
   C) Tribal law and government
   D) International NGOs
   E) Private insurance companies
   Correct Answer: C
3. How do state-recognized tribes differ from federally recognized tribes in this chapter?
   A) They have no rights at all
   B) They are not allowed to practice traditional medicine
   C) They lack full nation-to-nation status but retain significant cultural self-governance, including over traditional healing
   D) They are treated as private businesses
   E) They must follow hospital protocols for all ceremonies
   Correct Answer: C
4. What role do tribal religious organizations like NAIC play in urban and non-reservation settings?
   A) They replace all tribal governments
   B) They function as inter-tribal churches and PMAs that extend protection for NATIM to members beyond reservation boundaries
   C) They serve only as social clubs

D) They operate as secular clinics

E) They issue state licenses

Correct Answer: B

5. Why does the chapter emphasize that protections are not racial preferences?

A) Because only non-Native people can join

B) Because courts have held that protections rest on religion and sincere participation, not blood quantum alone

C) Because race is irrelevant in all U.S. law

D) Because tribes deny membership to all non-tribal persons

E) Because AIRFA applies only to Europeans

Correct Answer: B

Chapter 7 – Private Domains: Churches, Tribes, and PMAs

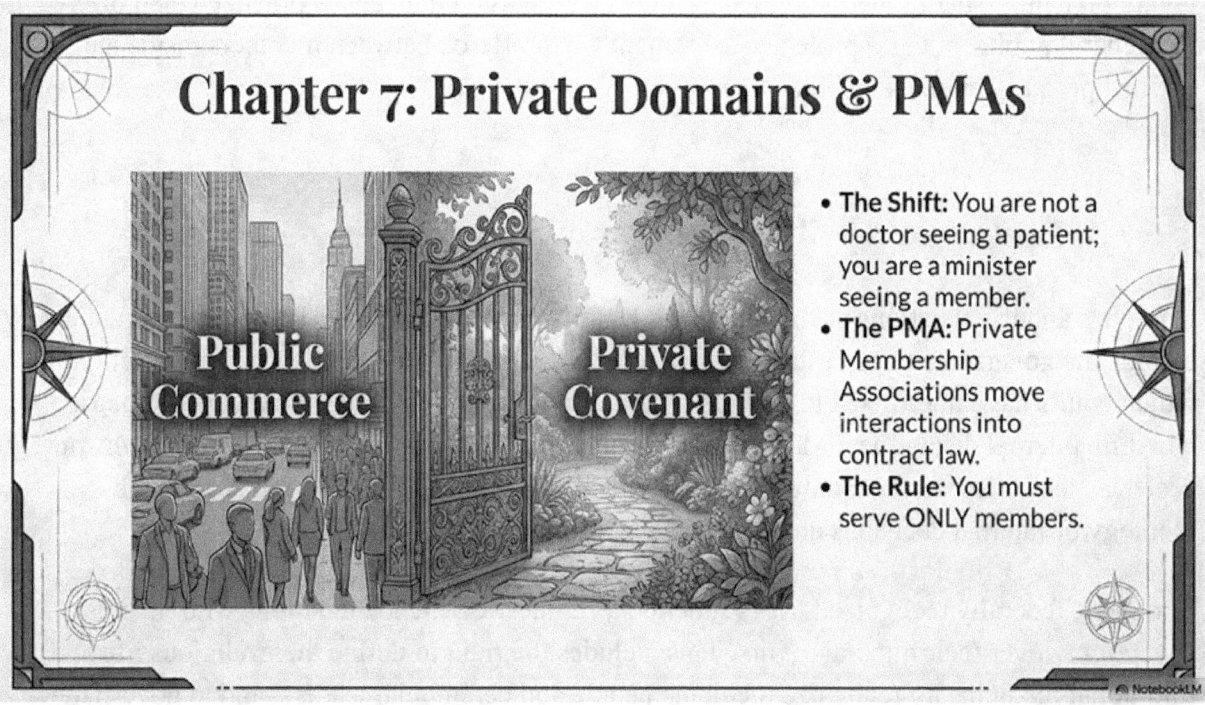

- ⇝ How churches, tribes, and PMAs create overlapping private domains where healing is treated as covenant, not commerce.
- ⇝ Practical markers that distinguish a truly private, member-only ministry from a public clinic in disguise.
- ⇝ How to build a layered legal umbrella in practice so your ceremonies and sessions have a clear legal "home."

When the State thinks about "health care," it imagines public clinics, hospitals, and solo practices advertising to anyone who walks in off the street. Your work, by contrast, is meant to live in a different space: the **private domain** of churches, tribes, and associations of members who have chosen one another. In this domain, healing is not a commodity; it is a covenant. Understanding how this private space is created and protected is among the most important legal skills a religious or Indigenous healer can acquire.

This chapter explains how three forms of private domain, churches, tribes, and Private Membership Associations (PMAs), work individually and together. We will examine church and tribal autonomy under the First Amendment, then examine how PMAs invoke contract and association rights to move healing encounters out of the public marketplace. Finally, we will return to the "layered legal umbrella" and see how combining ecclesiastical, tribal, and PMA structures can give your ministry its strongest footing.

By the end of this chapter, you will understand why the **same** healing act, anointing with oil, laying on hands, sharing herbal remedies, may be seen as an unlicensed practice when offered to the general public, but as a protected sacrament when offered between members inside a clearly defined private, religious domain.

1. Church and Tribal Autonomy: Sanctuaries in Law

Churches and tribal nations occupy a unique position in American law. The First Amendment forbids the government from establishing a religion. It protects the "free exercise" of religion, which courts have interpreted to include broad **autonomy** for churches in matters of doctrine, worship, internal discipline, ordination, and ministry. Courts routinely decline to resolve "purely ecclesiastical" disputes, recognizing that they lack jurisdiction to second-guess a church's theology or internal decisions about clergy and sacraments.

Similarly, federally recognized tribes function as domestic dependent nations with inherent sovereignty over their internal affairs. This includes the right to define their religious life and traditional medicine, to recognize medicine people and ceremonial leaders, and to govern the conduct of ceremonies on tribal lands. State-recognized tribes, while having a different legal status, also exercise significant powers of cultural self-governance and the protection of traditional healing practices.

In both cases, the key idea is the same: there exist **domains set apart**, church sanctuaries, tribal grounds, ceremonial lodges, where the State's ordinary regulatory power is deliberately limited. Within these sanctuaries, healing is, first and foremost, a religious act, not a commercial service, and is thus judged by church or tribal law before by secular law.

2. Private Membership Associations: Contracts of Trust

Private Membership Associations add another layer to this protection. A PMA is, at its core, a **contract** between private individuals who agree to associate for a specific purpose under shared rules. Constitutional rights of association, speech, privacy, and contract give such groups a special status: what is done privately among members, for expressive, educational, or religious reasons, is not automatically subject to the same regulation as public commerce.

In a healing PMA, the fundamental shift is this:

"I am not a provider offering services to the general public; I am a minister or healer serving fellow members of a private, religious association."

Members sign agreements acknowledging that:

- They enter the relationship as co-members, not as public "patients" or "clients."
- The services offered are Religious Therapeutics, Chirothesia, Indigenous ceremonies, or related spiritual work, **not** diagnosis or treatment as defined by state medical practice acts.
- Disputes will be handled within the association's own process, under its codes of ethics and religious law, rather than through immediate recourse to secular boards.

Supreme Court decisions have described the private association domain as a "sanctuary," "constitutional shelter," "shield," and "preserve" for indispensable liberties, including association and belief. This does not render it lawless; mala in se crimes, such as violence, abuse, or fraud, are never protected. Still, it does mean that regulatory offenses (mala prohibita) tied to public commerce may not apply in the same way when activities are genuinely confined to a private or religious association.

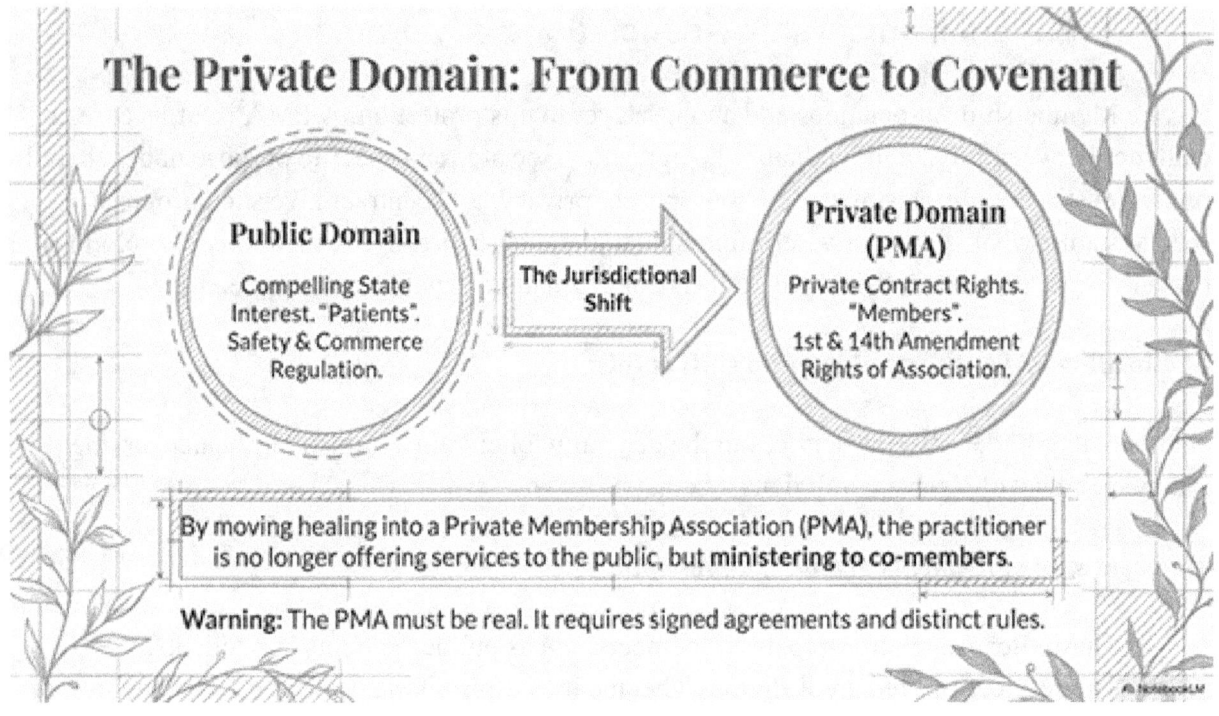

The Private Domain: From Commerce to Covenant

Public Domain
Compelling State Interest. "Patients". Safety & Commerce Regulation.

The Jurisdictional Shift

Private Domain (PMA)
Private Contract Rights. "Members".
1st & 14th Amendment Rights of Association.

By moving healing into a Private Membership Association (PMA), the practitioner is no longer offering services to the public, but **ministering to co-members**.

Warning: The PMA must be real. It requires signed agreements and distinct rules.

3. Drawing the Line: Public vs Private

To benefit from these protections, you must make the boundary between public and private **real**, not theoretical. That means:

- You serve only members and require non-members to join before receiving ministry.
- You avoid describing your work in generic, regulated terms ("massage," "bodywork," "psychotherapy"), using precise religious language instead (Chirothesia, Religious Therapeutics, Sacred Bodywork, Indigenous Ceremony).
- You do not advertise to the public as a secular clinic; you present yourself openly as a church, tribal organization, or PMA-based ministry.
- You adhere to your own codes of ethics, scopes of practice, and complaint-resolution procedures, demonstrating that the association is serious and well-governed, not a shell to evade accountability. If you blur these lines, taking random walk-ins, using regulated titles, or operating like a public clinic under a thin PMA veneer, you invite regulators to treat your work as public and to apply medical or massage statutes accordingly. A PMA is a safeguard only when it is genuine.

4. The Layered Legal Umbrella in Practice

The strongest protection for religious and Indigenous healing often comes from **layering** these private domains rather than relying on just one. A typical layered structure looks like this:

- A bona fide **church or tribal religious organization** (e.g., NAIC, SMOCH/SMOKH, Priory of Saving Grace) defines a theology of healing and issues ordinations, commissions, and church licenses to ministers and medicine people.
- That religious body identifies itself explicitly as a **Native American Indigenous religious tribal organization** where appropriate, invoking tribal sovereignty and AIRFA protections for traditional ceremonies and medicines.
- Within this ecclesiastical/tribal framework, a **Private Membership Association** is formed so that all healing work occurs strictly between members, in the private domain, under clearly stated religious and ethical rules.

In this configuration, any given healing act, say, a SomaVeda® Thai Yoga session, a sweat lodge, or a sacrament ceremony, stands simultaneously under:

- Church autonomy (ecclesiastical law),
- Tribal sovereignty (Indigenous law and custom),
- Federal religious-freedom statutes (AIRFA, RFRA, IHCIA, RLUIPA), and
- Constitutional rights of association and privacy via the PMA.

For regulators, this layered structure signals that your practice is not an unregulated public clinic, but a carefully ordered religious and tribal ministry with its own internal law. For you and your members, it provides a stable home where sacramental and traditional healing can flourish without constant fear of being misclassified as unlicensed secular medicine.

Chapter 7 Conclusion – Building Your Sanctuary

In this chapter, you have seen how churches, tribes, and PMAs create overlapping private domains where healing can be offered as ministry rather than as public commerce. You have also seen that these domains are not mere paper shields; they must be lived out through real membership, clear language, ethical codes, and genuine accountability.

As you continue through this book, keep asking: "Where does my work truly live, public marketplace or private sanctuary?" The more honestly you answer that question, and the more carefully you build your sanctuary, the less vulnerable you will be to misunderstandings and the freer you will be to serve.

In the next chapter, we turn to the court cases that have tested and clarified these principles, cases about sincere belief, sacramental substances, and the legal limits of religious liberty.

LEARNING EXERCISE 7.1
Review & Application
Instructions: Select the best answer based on the reading.

1. What is the key difference between public and private domains of healing in this chapter?
   A) The number of clients served
   B) Whether the practitioner charges money
   C) Whether services are offered to the general public or confined to members within a church/tribal/PMA framework
   D) Whether the practitioner uses herbs
   E) Whether sessions occur indoors or outdoors
   Correct Answer: C

2. How do churches and tribes function as "sanctuaries in law"?
   A) By eliminating all legal oversight
   B) By gaining authority to license surgeons
   C) By enjoying autonomy over doctrine, worship, internal discipline, and ceremonies, where state power is deliberately limited
   D) By controlling all property within their territory
   E) By exempting members from taxes
   Correct Answer: C

3. What is the core statement of a healing PMA relationship?
   A) "I am a government-approved doctor treating patients."
   B) "I am a minister or healer serving fellow members in a private association, not the general public."
   C) "I am exempt from all civil law."
   D) "I sell medical products exclusively online."
   E) "I am a tribal official enforcing state statutes."
   Correct Answer: B

4. Which practice would *undermine* the private-domain claim?
   A) Serving only members
   B) Using religious terminology
   C) Having clear bylaws
   D) Taking random walk-ins and advertising as a secular clinic
   E) Maintaining a code of ethics
   Correct Answer: D

5. In the layered legal umbrella, how do ecclesiastical, tribal, and PMA structures interact?
   A) They compete for control of practitioners
   B) They cancel each other out legally
   C) They stack, so any given act of healing stands simultaneously under church autonomy, tribal sovereignty, federal religious-freedom statutes, and association rights
   D) They apply only on reservation land
   E) They only affect tax filings
   Correct Answer: C

Chapter 8 – Case Law, Sincere Belief, and Legal Boundaries

Chapter 8: Sincerity in the Courtroom

- **Key Cases:** United States v. Boyll & Gonzales v. O Centro.
- **The Test:** Courts look for "Sincere Belief" and "Organizational Structure".
- **The Reality Check:** Judges reject "sovereign citizen" tricks. Be the real deal.

- ↝ What key cases like *United States v. Boyll* and *Gonzales v. O Centro* actually decided about sacramental substances and non-Native participants.
- ↝ How courts evaluate "sincere belief" and distinguish genuine religious claims from pseudo-legal "sovereign citizen" tactics.
- ↝ Where law draws the line between protected religious exercise and criminal conduct, especially around public safety.

Laws on paper become real when someone is arrested, charged, or brought into court, and a judge must decide what those laws actually mean. For religious and Indigenous healers, several key cases have tested the limits of AIRFA, RFRA, and related protections, especially around sacramental substances and who may claim Indigenous religious rights.

This chapter examines pivotal cases—including *United States v. Boyll*, *Gonzales v. O Centro Espírita Beneficente União do Vegetal*, and *Church of the Holy Light of the Queen v. Mukasey*—and the concepts they crystallize: **sincere belief**, individualized RFRA analysis, and the difference between legitimate religious exemptions and pseudo-legal "sovereign citizen" claims. We will also revisit the concept of "contentious medicine," in which even protected practices come under heightened scrutiny due to their potential risks.

By the end of this chapter, you will understand not only what these cases decided but also how to present your own work as a sincerely held religious practice, grounded in a coherent theology and organizational structure, so that it stands on the same firm ground rather than on wishful thinking.

1. United States v. Boyll: Religion, Not Race

In *United States v. Boyll* (D.N.M. 1991), a non-Native man, Robert Boyll, was prosecuted for possession of peyote. Boyll was a member of the Native American Church (NAC) but was not an enrolled member of a federally recognized tribe. The government argued that statutory protections for peyote use applied only to "Indians" by blood or tribal enrollment and therefore did not shield Boyll.

Judge Burciaga disagreed. He ruled that the protections for Native American Church peyote use rest on **religious freedom**, not on race. Limiting those protections to people of a certain ancestry would violate equal-protection principles and distort the purpose of AIRFA and related provisions. The court held that what matters is not blood quantum but **sincere, bona fide participation** in the religious practice of the NAC.

This decision has two profound implications for healers:

- First, it confirms that non-Native members of bona fide Native American churches may, under certain conditions, participate in protected sacramental practices if they do so sincerely and within the church's rules.
- Second, it reinforces the idea that the law is concerned with **religion**, not ethnicity, when it comes to Indigenous spiritual protections. Tribal sovereignty matters, but so does the broader principle that religious liberty cannot be distributed by race.

2. Gonzales v. O Centro: RFRA and Visionary Sacraments

In *Gonzales v. O Centro Espírita Beneficente União do Vegetal* (546 U.S. 418, 2006), the U.S. Supreme Court considered whether a small church could use a sacramental tea (Hoasca) containing a Schedule I substance (DMT). The government argued that the Controlled Substances Act (CSA) contained no exceptions and that the uniform enforcement of the Act constituted a "compelling interest" that precluded any RFRA claim.

The Court rejected this blanket approach. Applying RFRA, it held that the government must show a **compelling interest in burdening *this specific* religious exercise** and that it is using the **least restrictive means** to do so. The mere existence of a general drug law was not enough. The Court also noted that the federal government already tolerated certain exceptions, such as peyote use in NAC contexts.

The result was that the church was permitted to continue its controlled, sacramental use of Hoasca under strict conditions. For our purposes, the case demonstrates that:

- RFRA requires **individualized**, not one-size-fits-all, analysis of religious practices.
- Courts will look seriously at a group's sincerity, structure, safeguards, and history when deciding whether a sacramental use of a controlled substance can be exempted.

3. Church of the Holy Light of the Queen: Expanding the Precedent

Following the *O Centro* decision, another Brazilian-based church, the *Church of the Holy Light of the Queen* (Santo Daime), sought legal protection for their use of Daime tea (ayahuasca). In *Church of the Holy Light of the Queen v. Mukasey* (D. Or. 2009), the court applied the "strict scrutiny" standard established by RFRA.

The court found that the church's use of the tea was a **sincere religious exercise** and that the government failed to prove that a total ban was the least restrictive means of preventing health risks or diversion to non-religious use. This case further solidified the right of sincere religious organizations to use traditionally "controlled" substances as sacraments within a structured, disciplined environment. It underscored that the **sincerity of the practitioners** and the **safety protocols** of the church are paramount in legal evaluations.

4. The "Gaia Church" and Emerging Administrative Exemptions

While many groups seek protection through the courts, a new pathway involves administrative petitions directly to the DEA. Technically, the DEA has provided a path for religious groups to receive CSA exemptions under RFRA since its enactment in 1993.

The case of the "Gaia Church" (and others like the psychedelic Spokane church) represents a shift toward seeking **legal immunity** through administrative recognition before enforcement actions occur. However, the DEA's process remains slow and often involves intensive background checks and security requirements. These cases highlight that while the door to religious exemption is open, it requires **financial backing, legal expertise, and a documented history of sincere practice** to successfully navigate.

5. Sincere Belief vs. "Sovereign Citizen" Tactics

All these cases show courts grappling with religious practices that collide with general laws. In each instance, protection was extended where the practice was clearly rooted in a coherent religious tradition, conducted under organizational discipline, and asserted as a matter of sincere faith.

This stands in sharp contrast to **"sovereign citizen" theories**, which typically claim that individuals are exempt from ordinary laws, licenses, taxes, and criminal statutes based on obscure or fabricated readings of law. These arguments do **not** rest on coherent theology, nor do they accept the legitimacy of the legal system whose protection they seek. Courts routinely reject such tactics.

Native American and religious healers must take care not to sound like sovereign citizens. When you claim exemption from certain regulations, you are not claiming to be "above the law"; you are invoking **specific religious and cultural rights** that Congress and the courts have recognized: AIRFA, RFRA, IHCIA, and tribal sovereignty. You respect the law, even as you assert that it must bend around sincere religious practice when possible.

6. Contentious Medicine: Where Law Looks Closely

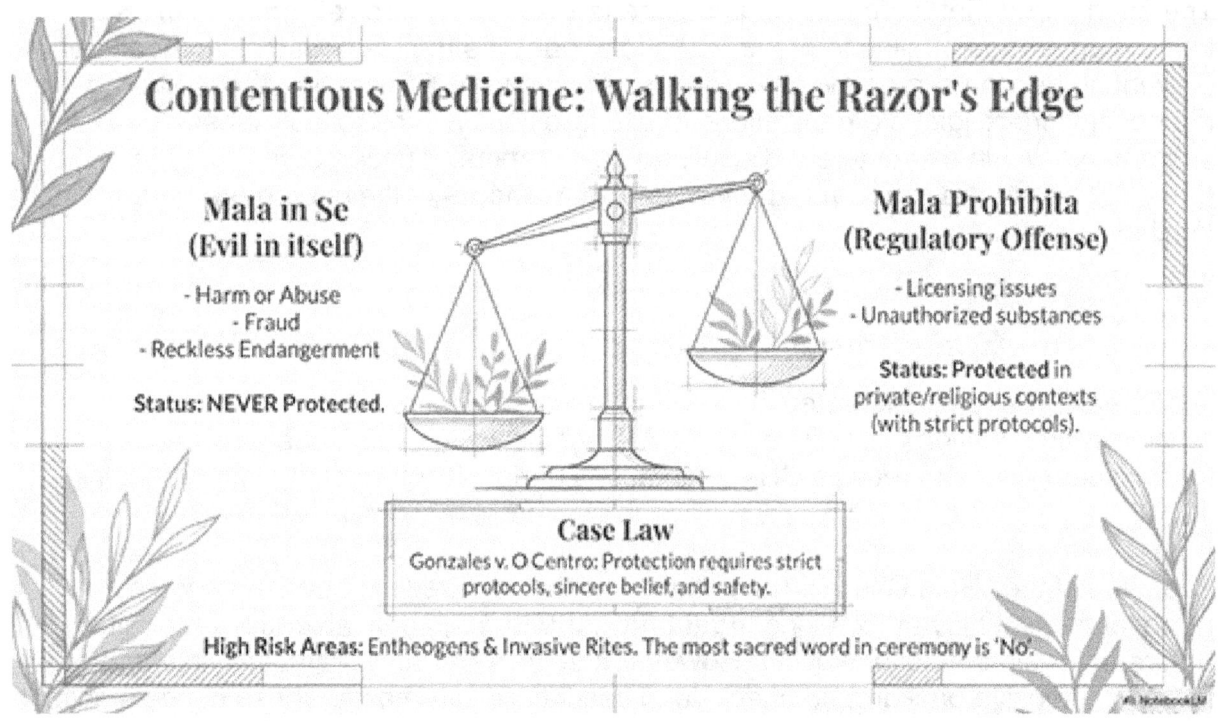

The law distinguishes between the **right to pray** and the **right to act**. Prayer and non-harmful ceremonies are rarely constrained. However, certain practices involving controlled substances, physical risk, or vulnerable participants draw heightened scrutiny.

We call these **contentious medicine**:

- Use of Schedule I entheogens outside of narrow exemptions.
- Invasive rituals performed without proper safeguards.
- High-risk interventions on minors or those unable to give consent.

Courts have clearly stated that religious freedom does **not** license conduct that threatens public safety. For practitioners at these frontiers, the burden is high: impeccable documentation, rigorous protocols, medical screening, and a willingness to submit to organizational oversight that can say "no" when risk is too great.

7. Lessons for Your Practice

- **Anchor your work in written belief.** A well-articulated theology, like a "Statement of Sacred Conviction," shows that your protocols flow from faith, not marketing.
- **Belong to a real community.** Courts protect members of established churches with history and rules.
- **Stay far from fraud and harm.** Safe, transparent practice is more likely to be seen as bona fide religious exercise.
- **Speak the language of rights, not rebellion.** Invoke specific protections (AIRFA, RFRA) rather than rejecting the law itself.

Chapter 8 Conclusion – Edges and Anchors

In this chapter, you have seen how courts handle the **edges** of religious healing: sacramental substances, non-Native members, and the line between sincere faith and pseudo-legal defiance. The message is consistent: when belief is sincere, practices are organized, and risk is managed, the law is often willing to bend. When belief is thin or harm is imminent, the law stands firm.

+2
For your own ministry, the path is clear. Deepen your sincerity, strengthen your organizational anchors, and be honest about where your practices sit on the spectrum from gentle ceremony to contentious medicine.

LEARNING EXERCISE 8.1

Review & Application

Instructions: Select the best answer based on the reading.

1. **What did *United States v. Boyll* decide regarding peyote use?**
   - A) Only enrolled tribal members could ever be protected.
   - B) Peyote use is always illegal.
   - C) Protections for NAC peyote use rest on religion, not race, and may extend to sincere non-Native members.
   - D) Peyote is a prescription drug.
   - E) Peyote can be sold commercially.
   - **Correct Answer: C**

2. In *Gonzales v. O Centro*, what did the Supreme Court require under RFRA?
   - A) Zero exceptions to drug laws.
   - B) Deference to agency policy without review.
   - C) An individualized strict-scrutiny analysis showing a compelling interest and the least restrictive means for *this specific* church and sacrament.
   - D) A national referendum on entheogens.
   - E) Automatic approval for all visionary sacraments.
   - **Correct Answer: C**
3. What was a key finding in *Church of the Holy Light of the Queen v. Mukasey*?
   - A) Ayahuasca is always illegal for non-Indians.
   - B) The government must prove a ban is the least restrictive means of addressing specific health and diversion risks.
   - C) Brazilian churches have no rights in the U.S.
   - D) Sincerity of belief is irrelevant in drug cases.
   - **Correct Answer: B**
4. What distinguishes "contentious medicine" in this chapter?
   - A) Any herbal tea.
   - B) Administrative tasks.
   - C) High-risk practices like entheogens and invasive rites that draw heightened legal scrutiny.
   - D) All forms of prayer.
   - **Correct Answer: C**
5. Which factor strengthens a practitioner's position when courts assess a religious freedom claim?
   - A) Lack of any organizational affiliation.
   - B) Using "sovereign citizen" arguments to reject all law.
   - C) Clear theology, organizational discipline, safety protocols, and evidence of sincere belief.
   - D) Aggressive marketing promises of medical cures.
   - **Correct Answer: C**

Would you like me to generate a specific administrative petition template for seeking a DEA religious exemption?

Ministry is an expression of a sincere and firmly held conviction that healing and the practice of religious therapeutics is an expression of Indigenous Native American and Christian Sacradotal Duties as expressed in Mathew 10:8 as expressed by Jesus the Christ and To protect the practice of Mother Earth based Native American spiritual traditions, beliefs, ceremony, sacred practices, expressions, Indigenous and Natural Medicine ways.

S.M.O.CH.

2

Practitioner is Ordained and or Licensed Minister/ Monastic Medical Practitioner by Church.

3

N.A.I.C. Expressive Private Membership Association Or equivilent with your own Independent Branch or Auxiliary ALL= 100% Services are for MEMBERS ONLY! No exceptions!

1

Practitioner is Authorized and or Ordained Minister/ Medicine Person by Tribal Org.

First Nation Medical Board

Licensed Clinical Holistic Therapist, LCHT, is Authorized and Ordained Minister/ Medicine Person by Tribal Org.

Informed Consent

4

All communicants, members required to sign and witness Ministry Informed Consent. No Consent signed = NO SERVICES!

Legal Umbrella

Chapter 9 – Contentious Medicine: Entheogens, Invasive Rites, and Public Safety

- Why certain high-risk practices, visionary sacraments, invasive rites, and extreme asceticism live at the frontier of legal tolerance.
- The difference between mala in se crimes and mala prohibita regulatory offenses in the context of religious healing.
- Concrete risk-management principles for those who feel called to walk near these edges.

Not all healing practices fall within the same legal jurisdiction. While prayer, blessing, and gentle laying on of hands rarely attract serious scrutiny, certain modalities involving controlled substances or invasive physical rites stand at the edge of what courts and regulators tolerate under religious freedom protections. In this chapter, we refer to these frontier practices as **Contentious Medicine**.

The goal is not to dictate what you may do, but to make explicit where risk rises sharply and why. We will explore the sacramental use of entheogens and invasive rituals, revisiting the distinction between *mala in se* and *mala prohibita* offenses, while providing practical risk-management guidelines.

1. Entheogens and Narrow Exemptions

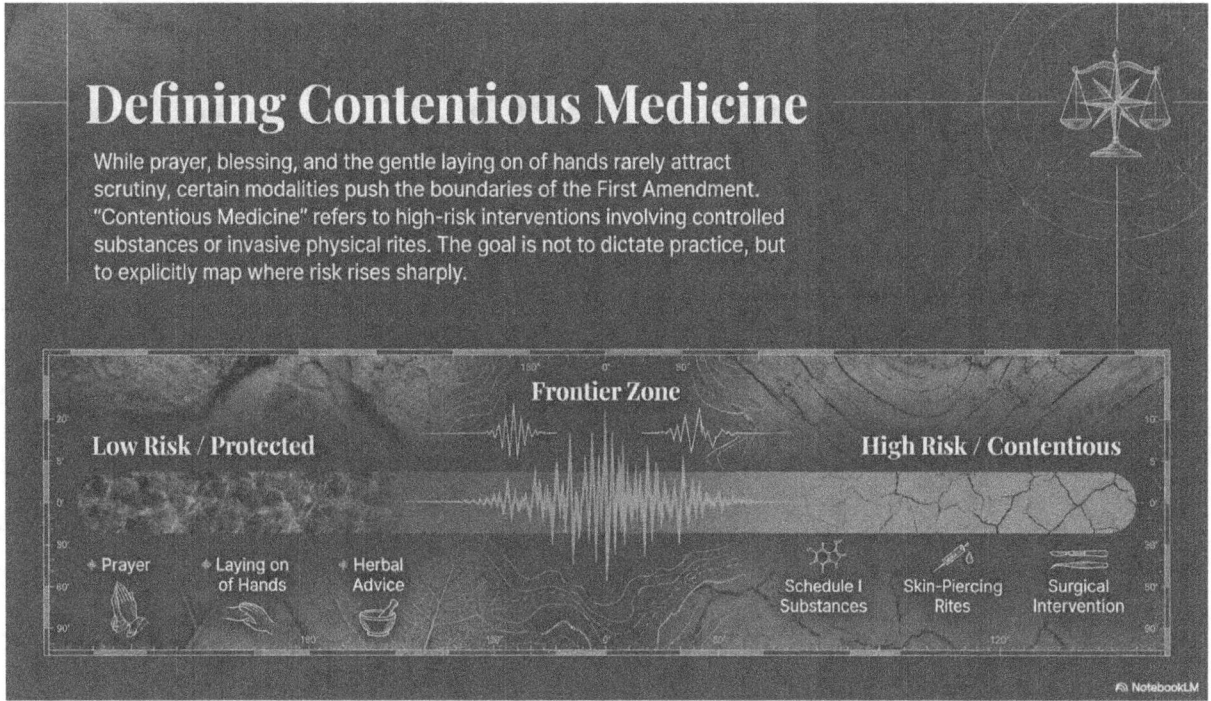

Across many Indigenous traditions, sacramental plants—such as peyote, ayahuasca, San Pedro, tobacco, and cannabis—occupy a central place in ceremony. These sacraments are not "drugs" in the secular sense; they are teachers and covenantal beings used to seek purification and vision. AIRFA explicitly recognizes the traditional religious use of peyote by Indians.

However, many of these substances are classified as **Schedule I** controlled substances. While the DEA has technically provided a path for religious groups to receive exemptions under the Religious Freedom Restoration Act (RFRA) without a lawsuit—as seen with groups like the "Church of Gaia"—these are narrow exceptions, not blanket permissions.

The issue of entheogens (psychedelics) remains highly contentious and litigious. It is **risky and ill-advised** for a practitioner or organization to offer these unless they are prepared to defend their use with significant financial backing and authoritative support even as clinical trials demonstrate the promise of substances like psilocybin, LSD, and MDMA for treating mood and anxiety conditions—leading to various FDA "breakthrough therapy" designations—the legal landscape for religious use remains a minefield.

Furthermore, the projected **$6.85 billion US market for psychedelics by 2027** has attracted for-profit interest. Yet, there is a relative lack of research on the ethical, legal, and social implications of this commerce. Initiatives like the Project on Psychedelics Law and Regulation (POPLAR) at Harvard Law reflect the growing need to address these complex implications.

2. Invasive Rites and Bodily Integrity

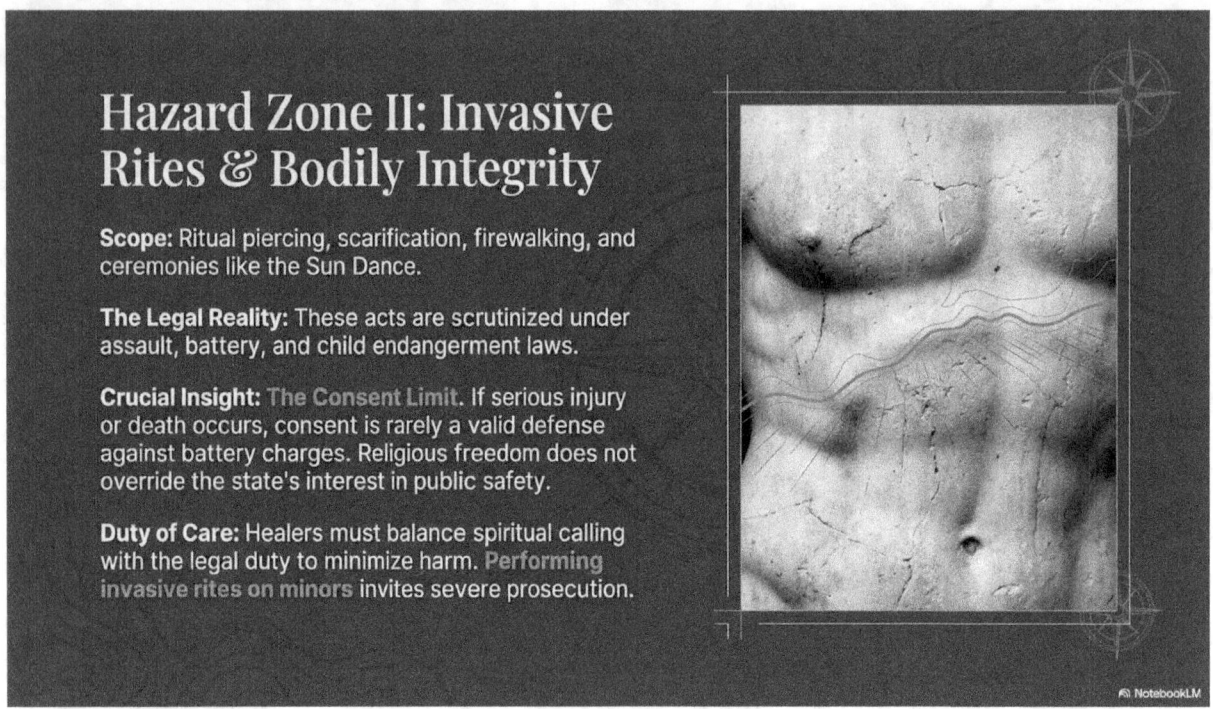

Contentious medicine includes invasive or physically intense rites: ritual piercing, scarification, extended fasting, or firewalking. In North American contexts, the Sun Dance and certain piercing ceremonies carry real physical risk.

Legally, these rites may be scrutinized under laws against assault, battery, or child endangerment, especially if performed by untrained individuals or on minors. If serious injury or death occurs, courts are unlikely to treat it as a protected religious practice, regardless of consent. Healers must balance their call to carry out these ceremonies with a legal duty to minimize harm and screen out vulnerable participants.

3. Mala in Se vs Mala Prohibita: Why It Matters

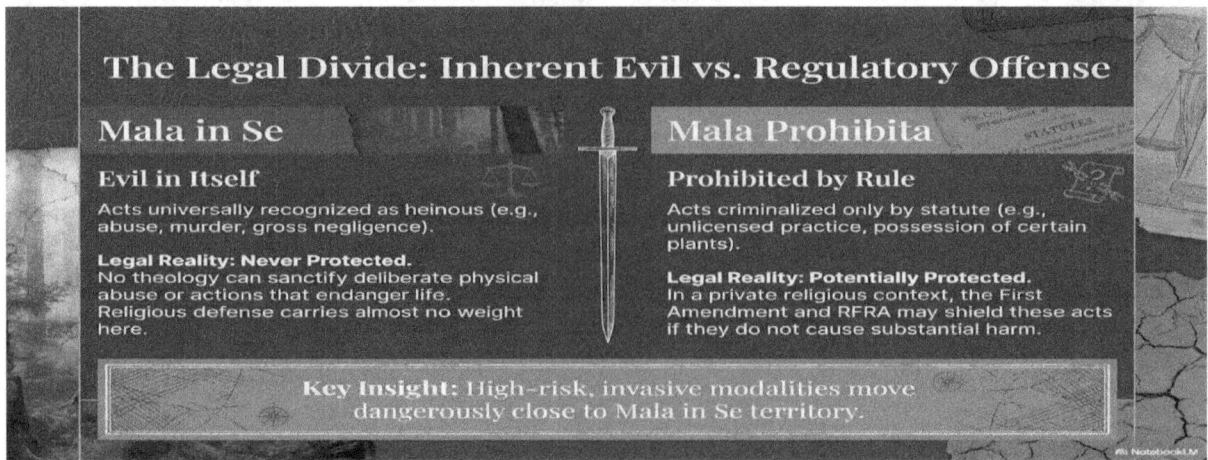

We must distinguish between *mala in se* (acts that are evil in themselves, such as abuse or murder) and *mala prohibita* (offenses that are criminal only because they are prohibited, such as unlicensed practice).

Authorized religious acts, such as sharing herbal advice or non-invasive ceremonies, are often treated as *mala prohibita* in the public domain but may be shielded in a private religious context if they do not cause substantial harm. However, ***mala in se* conduct is never protected**. No theology can sanctify deliberate physical abuse or gross negligence. High-risk, invasive modalities move closer to *mala in se* territory, where religious arguments carry far less weight.

4. Risk-Management Principles for Frontier Work

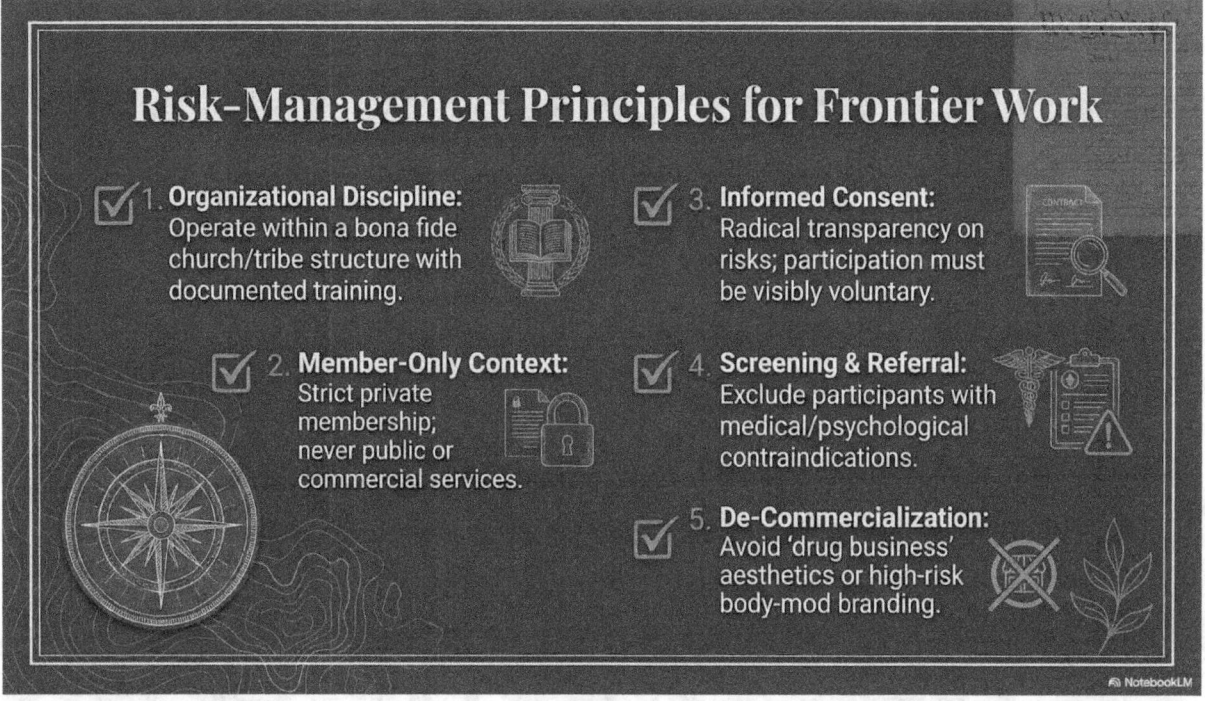

If called to walk near these edges, you must be hyper-vigilant:

- **Organizational Discipline:** Operate only within a bona fide church or tribal organization with clear codes of ethics and documented training.
- **Member-Only Context:** Conduct ceremonies strictly within a private membership, never as public commercial services.
- **Informed Consent:** Provide detailed information on risks and ensure participation is entirely voluntary.
- **Screening and Referral:** Exclude participants with medical or psychological conditions that make participation unsafe.
- **Avoid Commercialization:** Avoid making your work look like a drug business or high-risk body-modification service.

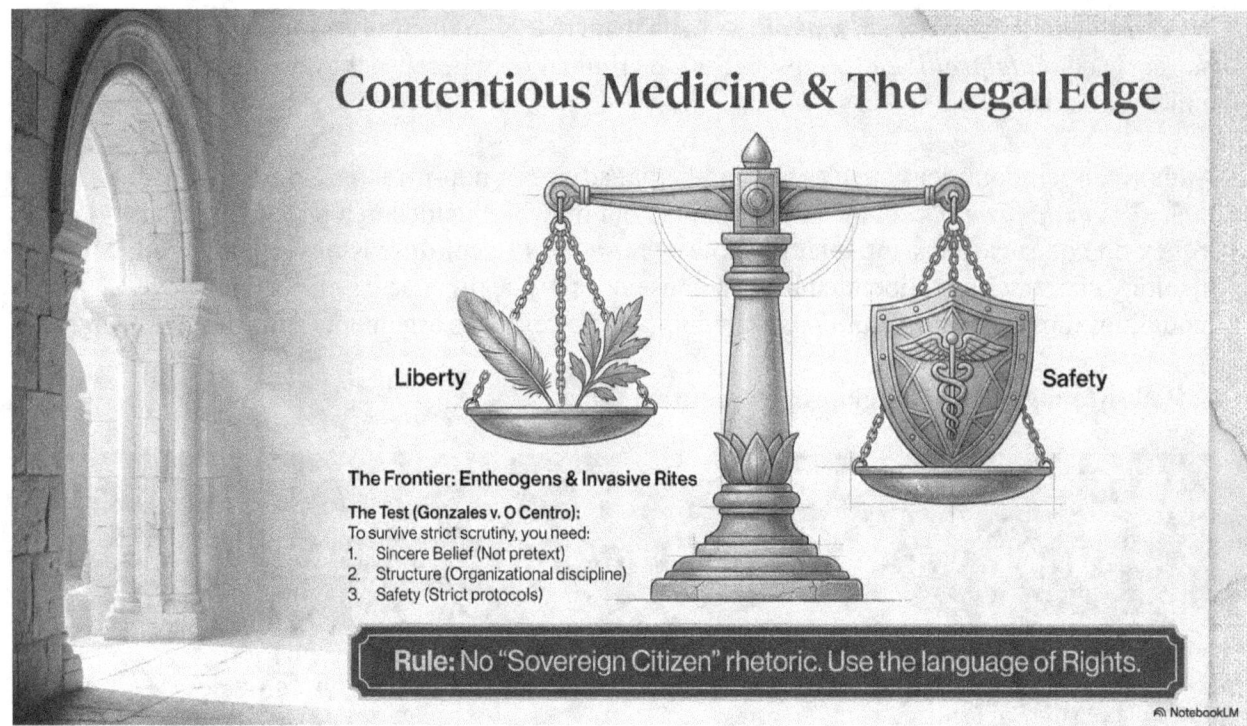

5. POPLAR initiative's specific findings

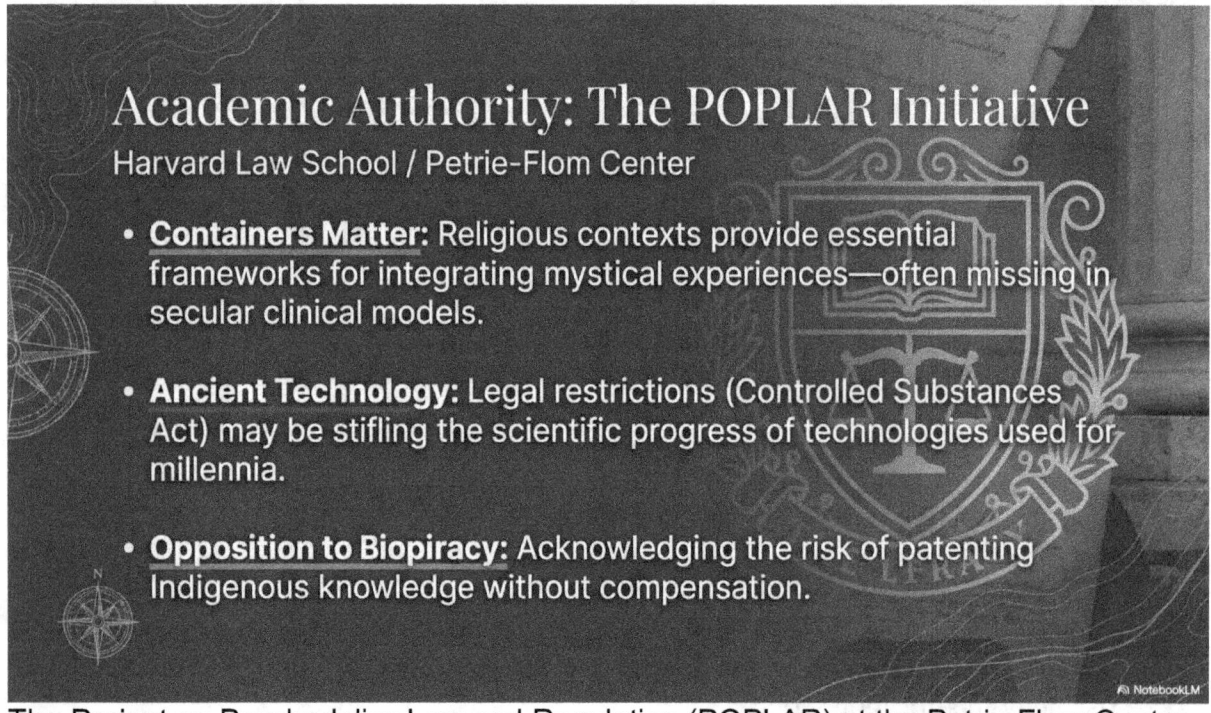

The Project on Psychedelics Law and Regulation (POPLAR) at the Petrie-Flom Center for Health Law Policy, Biotechnology, and Bioethics at Harvard Law School is an academic body that examines the legal and ethical implications of the emerging psychedelic landscape. Its findings provide significant scholarly support for protecting traditional and religious therapeutic frameworks from purely commercial medical models.

- **Recognition of Traditional Containers**: POPLAR scholars emphasize that religious and traditional contexts provide essential "containers" for integrating mystical or difficult experiences. They note that theological frameworks provide users with a necessary mental framework for processing their experiences, which is often absent in secular clinical or recreational models.
- **Opposition to Biopiracy**: A major finding of the initiative is the elevated risk of **biopiracy**—Western corporations patenting naturally occurring substances or Indigenous healing methods without acknowledgment or compensation to the traditional communities that pioneered them.
- **Ancient Technology vs. Modern Law**: Scholars within the initiative argue that current legal restrictions, such as the Controlled Substances Act, may be stifling the scientific and communal progress of "ancient technologies" used by Indigenous cultures for millennia.
- **The Three-Pathway Model**: POPLAR identifies "Religious Use" as one of three primary emerging pathways in the U.S. (alongside therapeutic and recreational) and advocates for a distinct legal status that honors the First Amendment rights of sincere faith communities.
- **Equity and Social Implications**: The initiative highlights concerns that rapid commercialization, projected to reach billions by 2027, will marginalize the very communities (BIPOC and Indigenous) that safeguarded these medicines through centuries of prohibition.

POPLAR Research and Citable Reference Bibliography

The following verifiable links and citations provide a legal and scholarly foundation for the legitimate, though contentious, use of traditional sacraments by religious and tribal organizations:

I. Primary Case Law & Legal Opinions

- **Gonzales v. O Centro Espírita Beneficente União do Vegetal**, 546 U.S. 418 (2006): Affirming RFRA protection for sacramental Ayahuasca use. Link.
- **United States v. Boyll**, 774 F. Supp. 1333 (D.N.M. 1991): Ruling that Native American Church peyote protections are based on religion, not race. Link.
- **Employment Division, Dept. of Human Resources of Oregon v. Smith**, 494 U.S. 872 (1990): The landmark case concerning peyote use that led to the creation of RFRA. Link.

II. Academic Research & Strategic Frameworks

- **POPLAR - Project on Psychedelics Law and Regulation**: Harvard Law School's foundational research on the intersection of drug law, equity, and religion. Link.
- **WHO Traditional Medicine Strategy: 2014–2023**: Global policy recognizing the importance of strengthening the role of traditional medicine. Link.
- **Chacruna Institute RFRA Guide**: A primer for plant sacrament churches on best practices for organizational structure and legal protection. Link.

III. Federal Statutes & International Declarations

- **American Indian Religious Freedom Act (AIRFA)**, 42 U.S.C. § 1996: U.S. policy to protect Indigenous freedom to worship through traditional rites. Link.
- **UN Declaration on the Rights of Indigenous Peoples (UNDRIP)**, Article 24: Affirms the right to maintain traditional medicines and health practices. Link.
- **Nagoya Protocol**: International agreement on the fair sharing of benefits from traditional knowledge and genetic resources. Link.

IV. Foundational Literature

- **Fields, Gregory P.** *Religious Therapeutics: Body and Health in Yoga, Āyurveda, and Tantra*. SUNY Press, 2001.
- **James, Anthony B.** *Decoding AI Bias in Medicine: How Artificial Intelligence Ignores Traditional Indigenous and Holistic Healing*. Bearded Media, 2024.

Would you like me to generate a specific "Statement of Sacred Conviction" template for a practitioner seeking to integrate these POPLAR findings into their own ecclesiastical scope of practice?

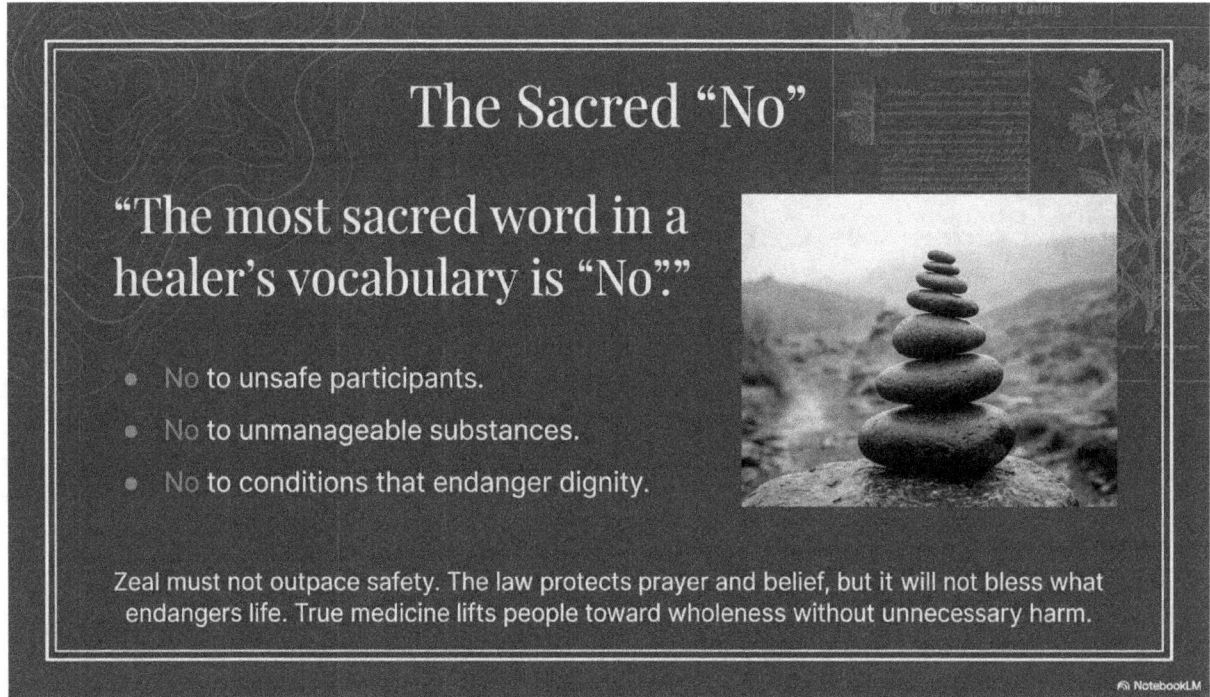

Contentious medicine tests not only the limits of law but the integrity of the healer. It forces you to ask whether your zeal for powerful experiences has outpaced your commitment to safety and to the well-being of those you serve. A mature medicine person understands that sometimes the most sacred word in ceremony is "no", no to certain participants, no to certain substances, no to certain conditions.

The law, in its own imperfect way, echoes this wisdom. It generously protects prayer, belief, and non-harmful rites, and extends narrower but meaningful safeguards to some high-risk practices where sincerity and structure are clear. But it will not bless what endangers life and dignity. As you move forward, let that boundary guide you: where your medicine lifts people toward wholeness without unnecessary harm, it stands on the strongest ground, both spiritually and legally.

I, the author, do not advocate for the common use of entheogen-style medicine. It should only be used in very tightly supervised and authorized situations, under the direct supervision of authentically trained and authorized medical personnel. There must be strict adherence to the traditional ceremonial constructs established by the original Native and Indigenous religious practices to avoid **cultural misappropriation** and the misuse of sacraments as profit-generating activities rather than for sincere religious practice.

In the next chapter, we leave the legal frontier and return to the heart of your actual work: **Religious Therapeutics**, what they are, how they function, and why they are not the practice of secular medicine under state law.

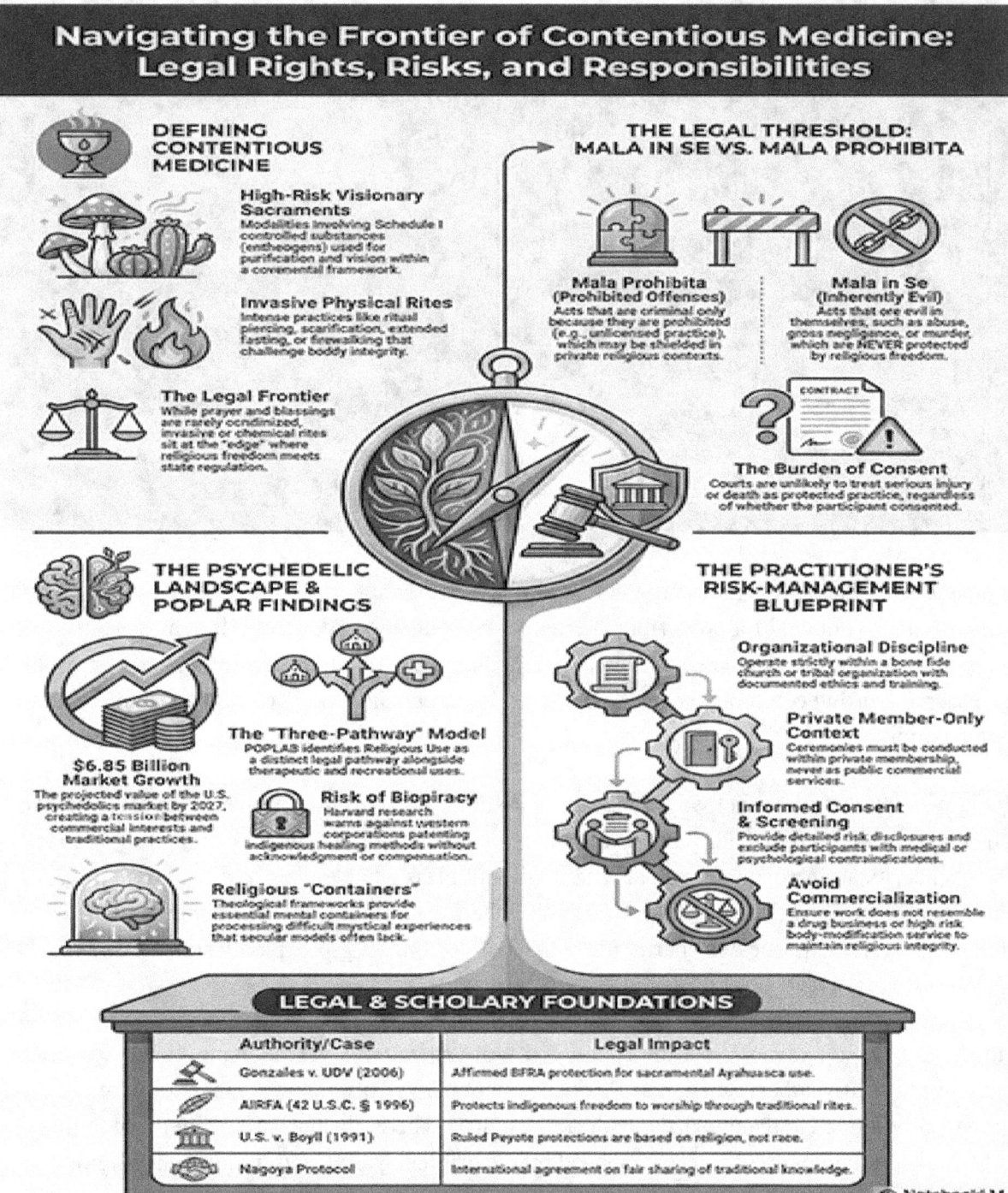

LEARNING EXERCISE 9.1

Review & Application

Instructions: Select the best answer based on the reading.

1. **What does the author identify as the most "sacred word" in high-risk ceremonies?**
   - A) Yes
   - B) Heal
   - C) No
   - D) Profit
   - **Correct Answer: C**

2. **Why is the use of entheogens described as "risky and ill-advised" for individual practitioners?**
   - A) They are medically ineffective.
   - B) The practice is highly litigious and requires significant financial and organizational backing to defend.
   - C) They are only legal for federally recognized tribes.
   - D) The FDA has banned all research on them.
   - **Correct Answer: B**

3. **According to the POPLAR initiative, what is a primary risk of rapid commercialization in the psychedelic market?**
   - A) Decreased investor interest.
   - B) The marginalization of Indigenous and BIPOC communities that safeguarded these medicines during prohibition.
   - C) A surplus of clinical research data.
   - D) The elimination of the "Religious Use" pathway.
   - **Correct Answer: B**

4. **How does the chapter distinguish *mala in se* from *mala prohibita* in this context?**
   - A) *Mala in se* are regulatory; *mala prohibita* are moral.
   - B) *Mala in se* are evil in themselves (e.g., abuse), never protected; *mala prohibita* are regulatory offenses sometimes exempted in private religious domains.
   - C) RFRA always protects both.
   - D) Both are always exempt for tribes.
   - **Correct Answer: B**

5. **Which term describes the risk of corporations patenting Indigenous healing methods without compensation to those communities?**
   - A) *Mala prohibita*
   - B) Biopiracy
   - C) Informed Consent
   - D) *Chirothesia*
   - **Correct Answer: B**

Figure 2, Pipe Stone Lakota-Dakota Sundance adjacent to the Sacred Catlanite Quarries, Pipestone National Park 1992 ©1992 Anthony B. James

Part III – Religious Therapeutics and Chirothesia

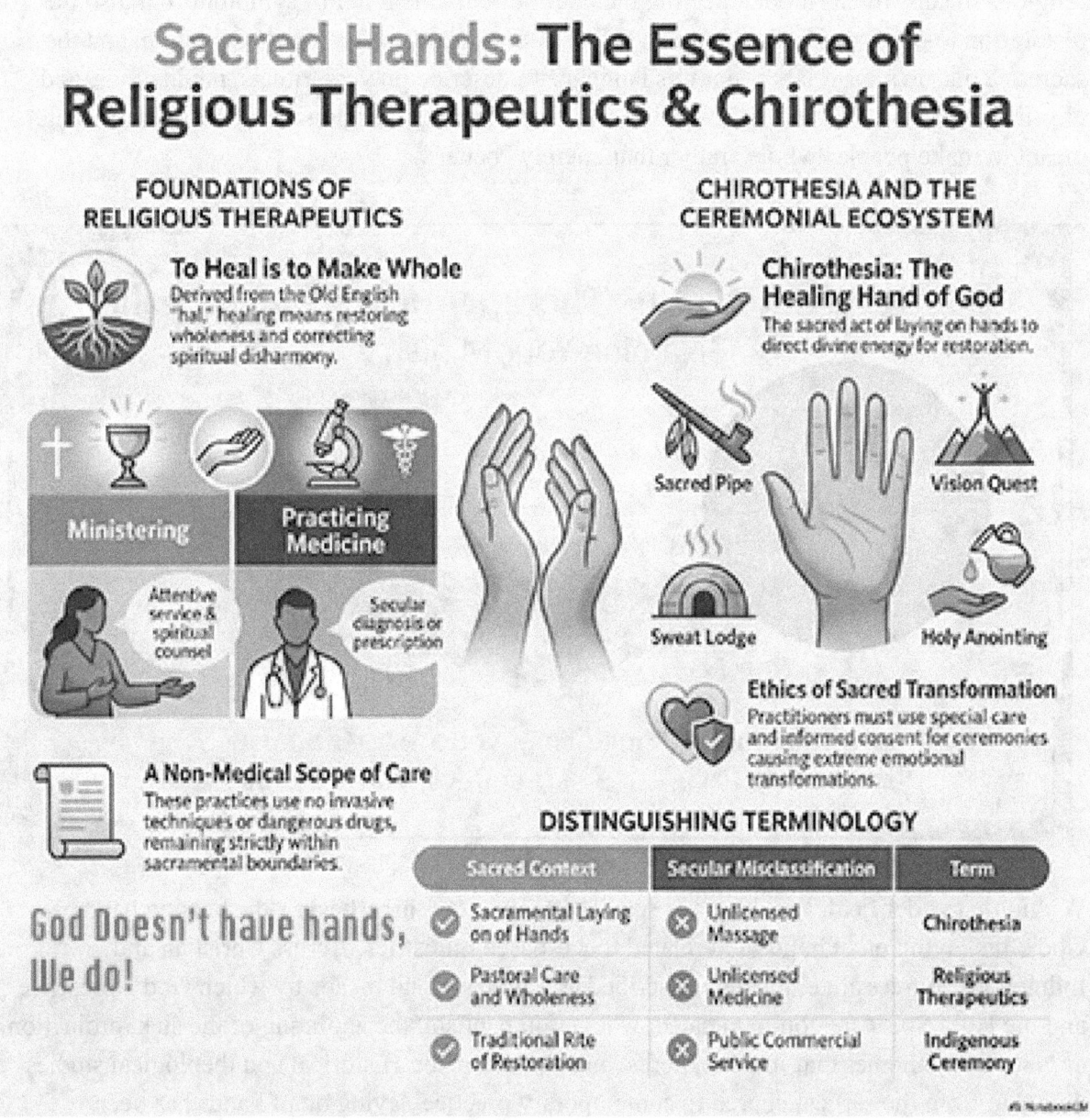

Law can protect a ministry only if we can say clearly **what** that ministry is. Part III turns from statutes and court cases to the heart of your actual work: **Religious Therapeutics** and **Chirothesia**, the hands-on, sacramental healing practices that churches, tribes, and Indigenous communities have exercised for millennia. Here, we define the concepts, trace their histories, and identify the specific practices that belong within this protected sphere, so that both you and any outsider can see why they are ministry rather than secular medicine.

The term "Religious Therapeutics" comes from both your internal NAIC teaching and wider scholarship, notably Gregory P. Fields's work on how traditions like Yoga, Ayurveda, and Tantra treat health as a psychophysical and spiritual reality, addressed through explicitly religious means. In this model, healing includes not only the relief of symptoms but also the restoration to one's true nature and to a right relationship with community, creation, and the sacred. Your own materials adopt this language to describe prayers, rituals, meditations, and physical interventions, such as anointing and ritual touch, as religious responses to suffering, meant to make people "whole" rather than merely "better."

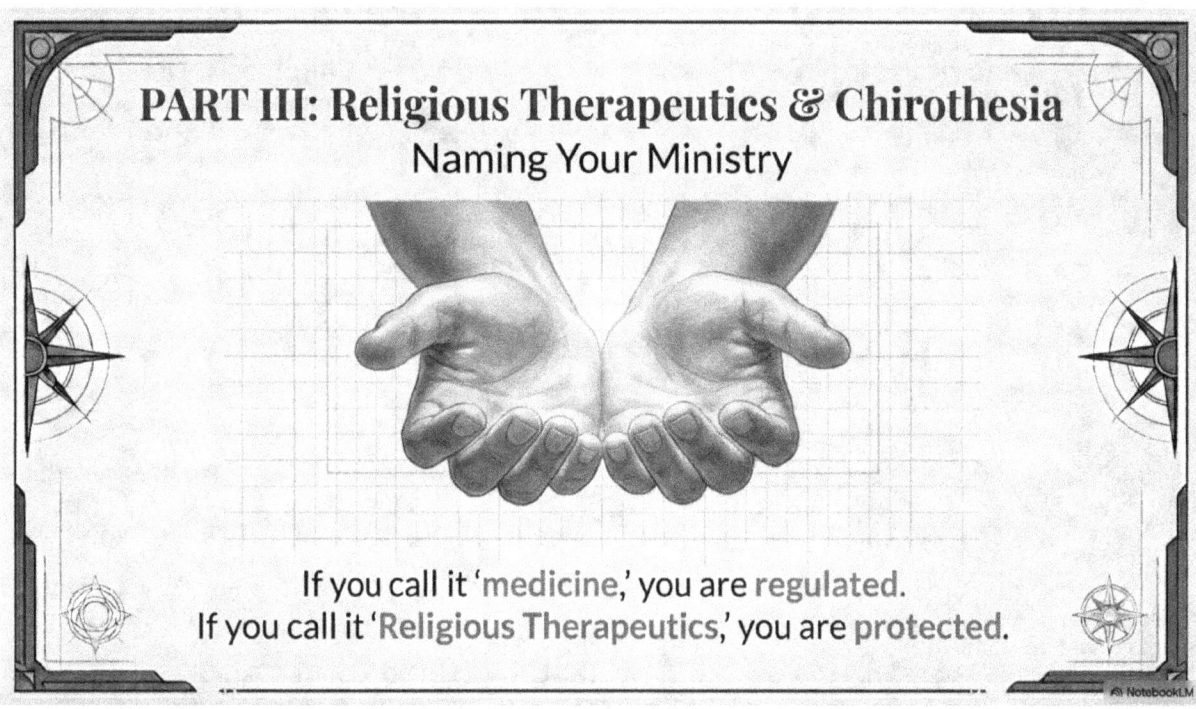

PART III: Religious Therapeutics & Chirothesia
Naming Your Ministry

If you call it 'medicine,' you are regulated.
If you call it 'Religious Therapeutics,' you are protected.

Within that wider field, Part III gives special attention to **Chirothesia**, "the healing hand of God": the laying on of hands and related touch-based ministries. Across Christian and Indigenous sources alike, touch is described as a fundamental means by which God's presence and the Holy Spirit are communicated, whether in baptism, the anointing of the sick, ordination, or Native ceremonies that use oils, herbs, and ritual contact. Historical and theological studies note that from the earliest church to contemporary practice, laying on of hands has been understood as a core sacramental act, not merely a technique, and that Indigenous healers worldwide have long used gentle touch as a primary medicine. Here, you will see how NAIC and its allied institutions systematize this into a coherent scope of practice, Chirothesia as non-invasive Religious Therapeutic CAM and Indigenous Healthcare (IHSM), and why that scope is deliberately framed outside the statutory definition of "practicing medicine."

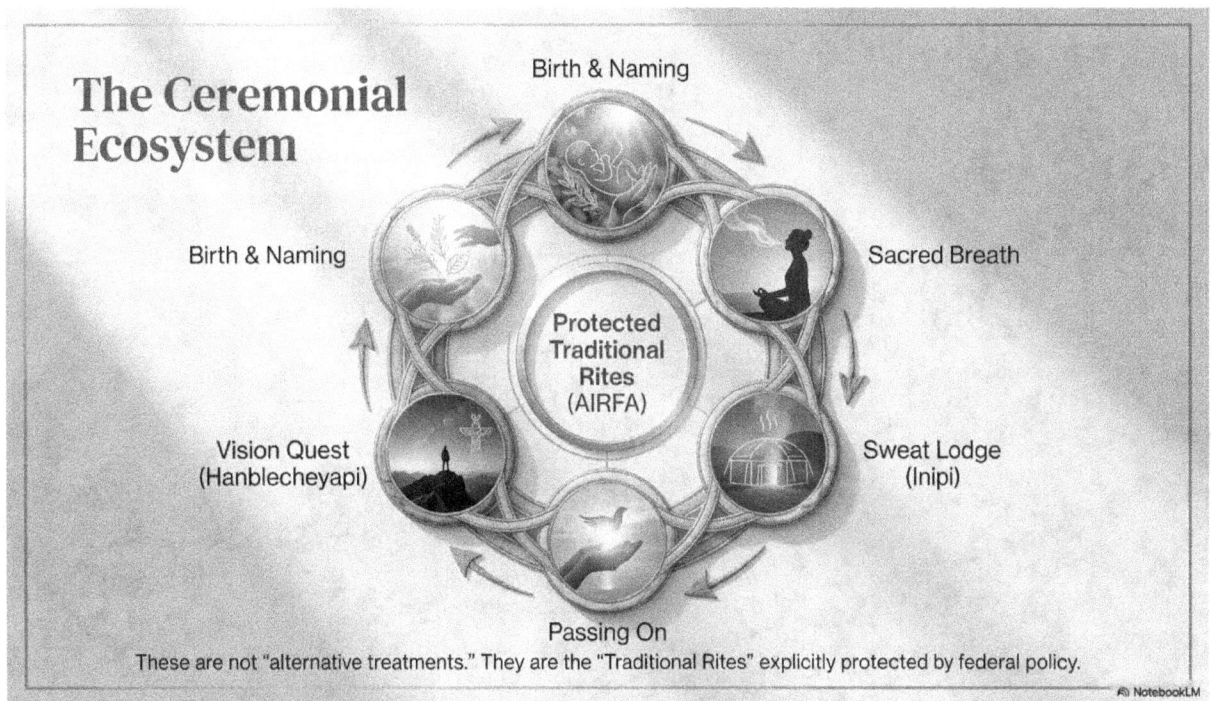

The Ceremonial Ecosystem

Birth & Naming

Sacred Breath

Sweat Lodge (Inipi)

Passing On

Vision Quest (Hanblecheyapi)

Birth & Naming

Protected Traditional Rites (AIRFA)

These are not "alternative treatments." They are the "Traditional Rites" explicitly protected by federal policy.

NotebookLM

Finally, Part III situates Chirothesia and Religious Therapeutics inside the ceremonial life of Indigenous and Christian communities: Birth, Sacred Breath, Holy Anointing, Pipe and Sacrament ceremonies, Sweat Lodge, Vision Quest, and other rites that your materials describe as "ALL protected practices." Taken together, these chapters show how touch, prayer, plant medicines, and ritual are woven into a single, legally recognized system of Native American religion and traditional medicine, one that federal law (AIRFA, RFRA, IHCIA, RLUIPA, and related provisions) was explicitly designed to preserve by the end of this Part, you will not only know what Religious Therapeutics and Chirothesia are, but also how to describe them, in theological, historical, and legal terms, as the core of a protected healing ministry

Figure 3, We now see Native American Traditional and Indigenous Medicine being performed in modern clinical settings.

Chapter 10 – What Are Religious Therapeutics?

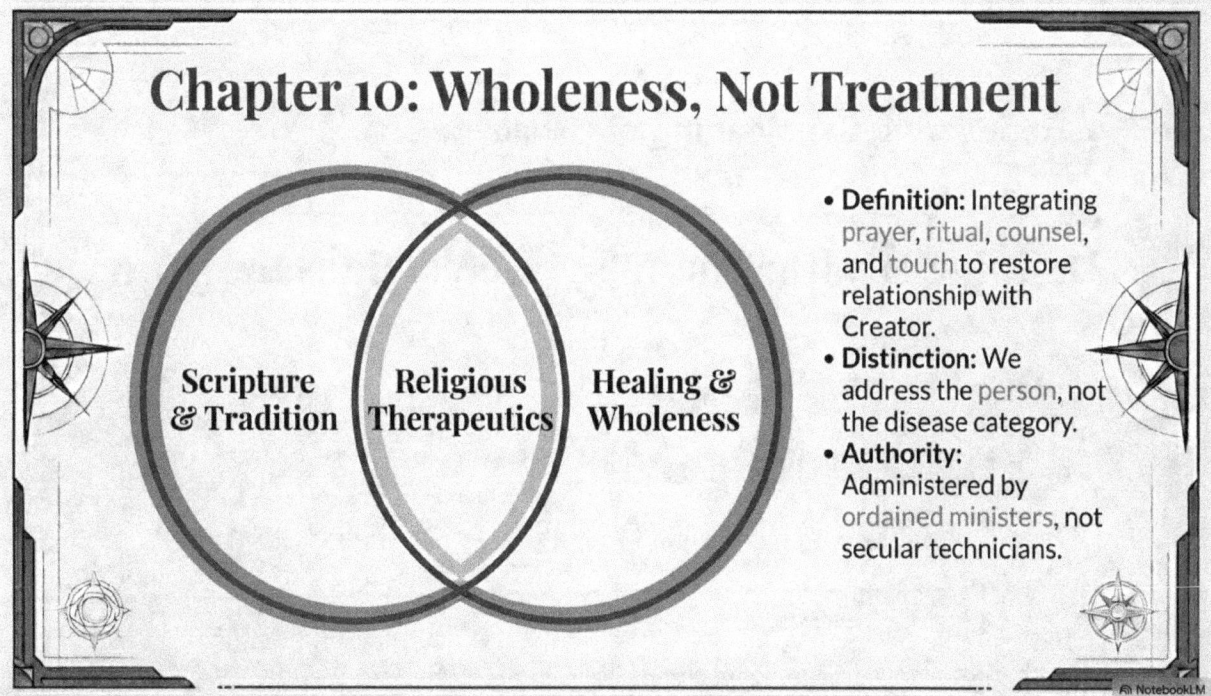

- The deeper meanings of "heal" and "therapeutic" point to wholeness, salvation, and attentive service.
- How Religious Therapeutics integrates prayer, ritual, counsel, and gentle physical interventions as explicitly religious means of healing.
- Clear criteria that distinguish Religious Therapeutics from secular diagnosis and treatment under the medical practice acts.

To navigate law and ethics with integrity, you must first know what you are actually doing. You may touch, pray, counsel, anoint with oil, offer herbs, or lead ceremonies, but what is all of this **called** in the language of your faith and tradition? This chapter answers that question by defining **Religious Therapeutics**: the principles and practices that support human well-being by uniting health and religiousness.

We will begin by recovering the original meanings of "heal" and "therapeutic," tracing them back to roots that link wholeness, salvation, and attentive care. Then we will draw on contemporary scholarship that describes religious therapeutics as a field in which prayer, ritual, meditation, and physical interventions are all understood as means of spiritual healing. Finally, we will distinguish Religious Therapeutics from secular medical treatment and clarify why your work, when properly framed, is **ministry**, not "practicing medicine without a license."

By the end of this chapter, you will have language you can use in consent forms, church documents, and even legal settings to describe your work accurately and confidently.

1. Recovering the Meaning of "Heal."

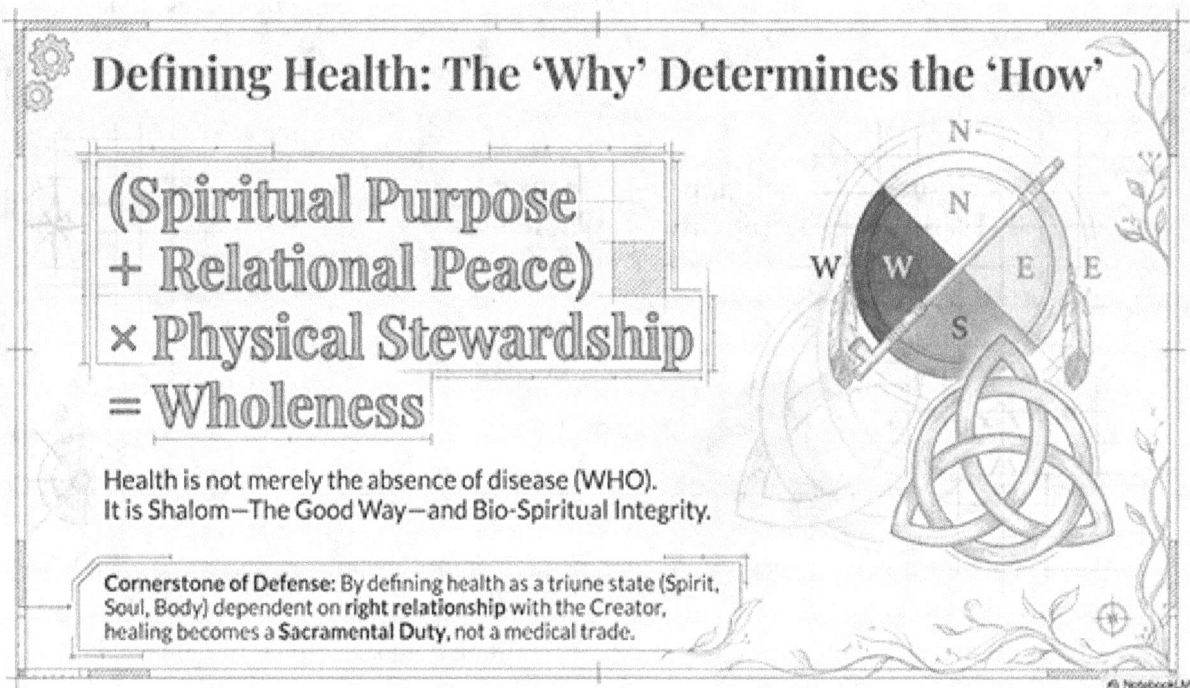

Defining Health: The 'Why' Determines the 'How'

(Spiritual Purpose + Relational Peace) × Physical Stewardship = Wholeness

Health is not merely the absence of disease (WHO).
It is Shalom—The Good Way—and Bio-Spiritual Integrity.

Cornerstone of Defense: By defining health as a triune state (Spirit, Soul, Body) dependent on **right relationship** with the Creator, healing becomes a **Sacramental Duty**, not a medical trade.

In common speech, "healing" often means little more than symptom relief. But the word itself carries a deeper story. The Old English root *hal*, from which we get "heal," "whole," and "holy", means **"to make whole."** To heal, in this older sense, is to restore from a bad condition, to save from or repair what has become evil, pernicious, or unwholesome. It is to correct disharmony, to bring a person back into right relationship with their own essence, nature, spirit, and soul.

In this view, healing is not just about stopping pain; it is about removing or reducing the impediments to self-realization, oneness with God, Spirit, and Soul. A body can be medically stable and yet profoundly "unhealed" if guilt, alienation, or spiritual numbness remain untouched. Conversely, a person facing chronic illness can nonetheless experience deep healing if relationships are mended, fear is replaced with peace, and they come into alignment with Sacred Order.

2. What "Therapeutic" Really Means

The term "therapeutic" comes from the Greek *therapeuein*, meaning "to cure" and "to restore," and *therapeia*, which denotes **healing through attentive service**. In its original sense, *therapeia* can refer to both medical endeavors and religious ministering, the attending of a healer to one who suffers, whether that healer is a physician or a priest.

From this perspective, a therapeutic act is not primarily an intervention on tissues; it is a form of **attending**: listening, witnessing, praying, touching, instructing, and walking with someone through suffering toward greater integrity of being. Curing, in this language, refers to alleviating impaired functioning and discomfort, or removing whatever interferes with the person's pursuit of spiritual elevation, self-realization, or inner peace. Restoring means returning to an original state of integrity, wholeness, and well-being, where spirit, mind, and body each stand in balance according to their nature and function.

When you put "heal" and "therapeutic" together, healing work becomes the knowledge, practice, and technique used to remove impediments, restore what is broken or lost, and support a person in living as a whole being. This is the heart of Religious Therapeutics.

3. Dimensions of Religious Therapeutics

Gregory P. Fields, in his study of religious therapeutics, describes this field as encompassing principles and practices that support human well-being by recognizing the common ground between health and religiousness. He identifies several key dimensions:

- **Religious meanings** that inform the philosophy of health and medicine, your beliefs about what it means to be whole.
- **Religious means of healing**, prayers, meditations, rituals, sacraments, and physical interventions that are explicitly undertaken as acts of worship and obedience.
- **Health as support to religious life**, recognizing that bodily and emotional well-being can strengthen a person's ability to pray, serve, and fulfill their spiritual duties.
- **Religiousness itself is a remedy** for the suffering of the human condition, acknowledging that faith, devotion, and practice can directly ease fear, despair, and moral confusion.

In Indigenous and Christian contexts alike, Religious Therapeutics therefore includes therapeutic prayers, laying on of hands, fasting, confession and reconciliation, ritual cleansing, anointing, herbal stewardship under spiritual guidance, and other physical or energetic interventions administered as sacraments rather than as commercial services.

4. Religious Therapeutics vs Secular Treatment

From a legal standpoint, the way you **frame** your work matters. Religious Therapeutics, as we are using the term, is:

- Rooted in a specific, articulated theology of health and wholeness.
- Administered by ordained, commissioned, or otherwise authorized ministers, medicine people, or spiritual leaders within a church or tribal organization.
- Offered to members or communicants as an expression of faith and covenant, not as public commerce.
- Limited to non-invasive, non-pharmaceutical modalities that do not claim to diagnose, treat, mitigate, or cure disease as those terms are defined in state medical practice acts.

Secular medical treatment, by contrast, is defined by statute as diagnosing, treating, operating, or prescribing for human disease, pain, injury, deformity, or physical condition, under state-issued licenses and within specific scopes of practice. When unlicensed practitioners use medical language ("I diagnose and treat X disease") or generic regulated terms ("massage therapy," "bodywork," "psychotherapy") for what are actually religious acts, they invite regulators to misclassify their work as secular practice.

By clearly stating that you **do not** diagnose or prescribe for medical or psychological conditions, and that you **do not** claim to prevent, treat, mitigate, or cure such conditions as defined in secular practice acts, you help courts and boards see your work for what it is: Religious Therapeutics and pastoral care. Your focus is on restoring the right relationship with God, Spirit, and Creation, using touch, words, herbs, and ceremony as sacramental tools rather than as medical procedures.

Chapter 10 Conclusion – Naming Your Ministry

Religious Therapeutics gives you a name for what your hands and heart have been doing all along. It gathers your prayers, touches, herbs, and counsel into a coherent framework of healing: wholeness, cure by removing impediments to spiritual growth, and restoration by returning people to their true nature before God and Creation.

For the law, this clarity is priceless. When you stand before a board, a judge, or even a skeptical family member and say, "I do not practice medicine; I practice Religious Therapeutics," you can now explain exactly what that means, and how it fits within recognized patterns of religious life across cultures. In the chapters to come, we will apply this definition to specific modalities, beginning with **Chirothesia**, the "healing hand of God," and to Indigenous ceremonies that surround and support your work as a healer-minister.

LEARNING EXERCISE 10.1
Review & Application
Instructions: Select the best answer based on the reading.

1. What is the older root meaning of "heal" emphasized in this chapter?
   A) To manage symptoms
   B) To prescribe drugs
   C) To make whole, restore from what is unwholesome, and correct disharmony
   D) To increase productivity
   E) To avoid legal liability
   Correct Answer: C

2. What does "therapeutic" originally mean in this discussion?
   A) Only surgical procedures
   B) Pharmaceutical intervention
   C) Healing through attentive service, which can be medical or religious ministering
   D) Insurance-approved treatment
   E) Scientific experimentation
   Correct Answer: C

3. Which element is *not* listed as part of Religious Therapeutics?
   A) Prayers, meditations, and rituals
   B) Physical interventions like anointing and gentle touch
   C) Moral and spiritual counsel
   D) Sacraments and ceremonies
   E) Invasive surgery under anesthesia
   Correct Answer: E

4. How is Religious Therapeutics distinguished from secular treatment in this chapter?
   A) By using stronger drugs
   B) By competing with hospitals
   C) By being rooted in a specific theology, administered by authorized ministers, offered to members, and avoiding secular claims to diagnose or treat disease
   D) By rejecting all science
   E) By focusing only on emotions
   Correct Answer: C

5. What is one key legal advantage of naming your work "Religious Therapeutics"?
   A) It guarantees insurance coverage
   B) It automatically grants tax exemption
   C) It helps regulators see your work as ministry and pastoral care rather than the unlicensed practice of medicine
   D) It allows the use of prescription drugs without oversight
   E) It removes the need for informed consent
   Correct Answer: C

Chapter 11 – Chirothesia: The Healing Hand of God

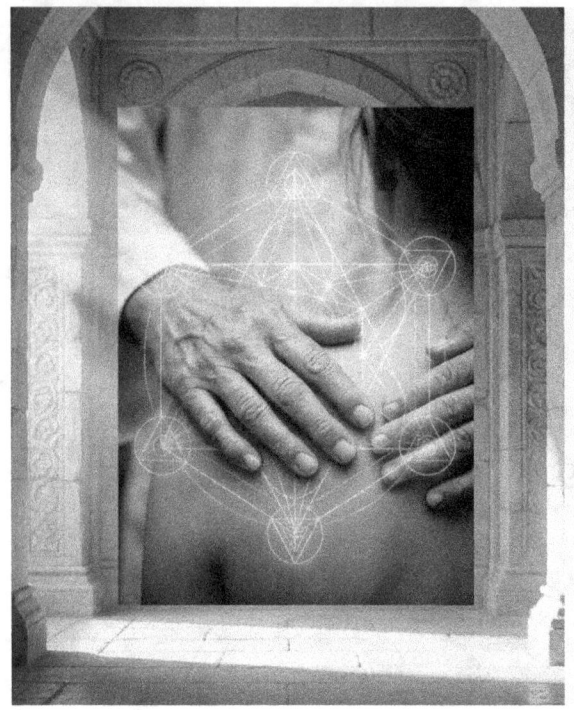

Architectural Sanctuary

Chirothesia: The Healing Hand of God

Etymology: Chiro (Hand) + Thesia (Placing/Setting)

Definition: Led by the healing hand of God.

The Legal Distinction:

 Secular: Massage Therapy = Manipulation of tissue for commerce.

 Sacred: Chirothesia = Transmission of divine energy (Energia, Prana) as religious observance.

Legal Stance: A sacerdotal duty, not a medical procedure.

NotebookLM

> - The etymology and theology of Chirothesia, and how the laying on of hands functions as a sacramental practice across traditions.
> - The practical scope of a Chirothesist's work includes specific non-invasive modalities that fit under this religious-therapeutic umbrella.
> - Why, when properly framed and practiced, Chirothesia is not "practicing medicine" or "massage therapy" under state law.

When you place your hands on another human being in prayer or blessing, what you are doing is far older than modern massage or physical therapy. In Indigenous and Christian traditions, that act belongs to a distinct sacramental science called **Chirothesia**, a hands-on ministry that transmits divine energy for healing, comfort, and empowerment. To describe your work accurately and lawfully, you need to understand and name this practice clearly.

This chapter unfolds Chirothesia in four steps. We begin with its etymology and theological meaning, then examine how the laying on of hands appears across world religions. Next, we define a Chirothesist's scope of practice in modern terms, including the many complementary and Indigenous modalities that fit under this religious-therapeutic umbrella. Finally, we explain why, when properly framed and practiced, Chirothesia is not the "practice of medicine" under state law, but a protected ministry of Indigenous and ecclesiastical healthcare.

By the end of this chapter, you will have a precise, honored name for what your hands do, and a way to explain that both to elders and to regulators who might otherwise mislabel your work as unlicensed massage.

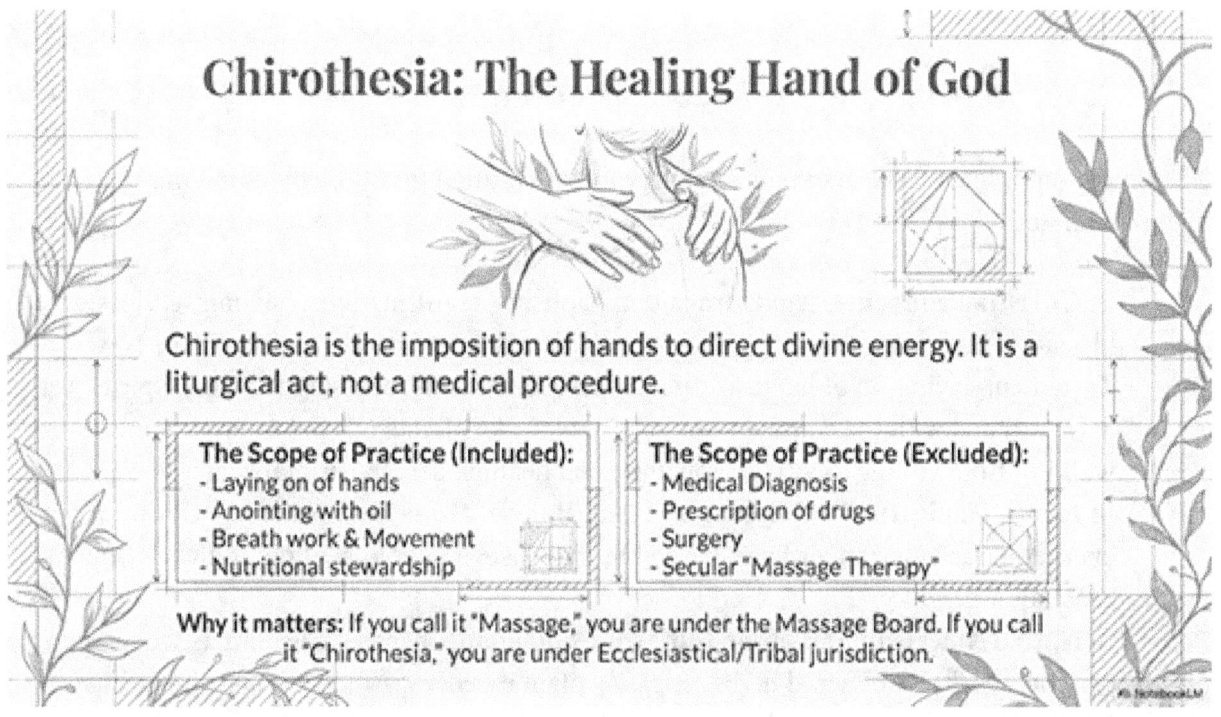

Chirothesia: The Healing Hand of God

Chirothesia is the imposition of hands to direct divine energy. It is a liturgical act, not a medical procedure.

The Scope of Practice (Included):
- Laying on of hands
- Anointing with oil
- Breath work & Movement
- Nutritional stewardship

The Scope of Practice (Excluded):
- Medical Diagnosis
- Prescription of drugs
- Surgery
- Secular "Massage Therapy"

Why it matters: If you call it "Massage," you are under the Massage Board. If you call it "Chirothesia," you are under Ecclesiastical/Tribal jurisdiction.

1. Etymology: What "Chirothesia" Means

The word **Chirothesia** is built from several Greek roots that together describe a sacred act.

- **Chi** (pronounced "ki") points to a place where God's law is taught, a sacred context of instruction and covenant.
- **Chiro** (from *cheir*, "hand") refers to the hand as the instrument of blessing: the literal laying on of hands, the imposition of hands to direct or deliver divine and healing energy.
- **Thesia** (from *thesis*) denotes a deliberate setting, placing, or doing, an intentional ritual action.
- **Theos** means "of or about God."

Taken together, **Chirothesia means "led by the healing hand of God."** It describes a ritual in which a minister's hands, guided by Spirit, become conduits for divine energy, *energia*, vital life force, Chi, Qi, Prana, Holy Spirit, breath, and related terms used across cultures. A Chirothesist is thus understood to be, in a real sense, the **hands of God** in the material world, administering healing as a religious act.

Chirothesia is a ritual in which divine or healing energy, awareness, consciousness, breath, and gentle pressure are passed to another as a religious or spiritual observance. It is not simply "touch"; it is ordered, intentional, and covenantal touch.

2. Hands-On Healing Across Traditions

The laying on of hands appears in almost every major spiritual tradition, though it may carry different names.

- In **Christian churches**, hands are laid in baptisms, confirmations, healing services, blessings, and ordinations of priests, elders, deacons, and other officers. In the New Testament, laying on of hands is directly associated with receiving the Holy Spirit (Acts 8:14–19) and with the commissioning of new leaders (Acts 6:5 & 6). Jesus' ministry of walking from village to village, touching and healing, sets the primal example.
- In **Islam, Hinduism, Buddhism, Sikhism, Baha'i, Huna, and other traditions**, touch, energetic transmission, or hand-based blessing also appear in healing, initiation, and protection rites.
- In **Native American and other Indigenous medicine**, hands-on healing is woven into ceremonies that use sacred herbs, oils, and plant essences. American Native spiritual leaders have long used touch as "Divine Touch" to accomplish healing, empowerment, and connection with the Creator.

Seen through the lens of Chirothesia, these practices share a common pattern: the healer's hands are placed on or near the recipient as an invocation of Spirit, not as a transactional bodywork service.

3. Theology and Duty of Chirothesia

From a Christian perspective, Jesus Christ is the archetypal Chirothesist. He heals by touch, commands his followers to lay hands on the sick, and establishes this gesture as a principle within the doctrine of Christ, listed alongside faith, repentance, baptisms, resurrection, and eternal judgment. The early church understood laying on of hands as an ordinance of the Lord, not an optional symbol.

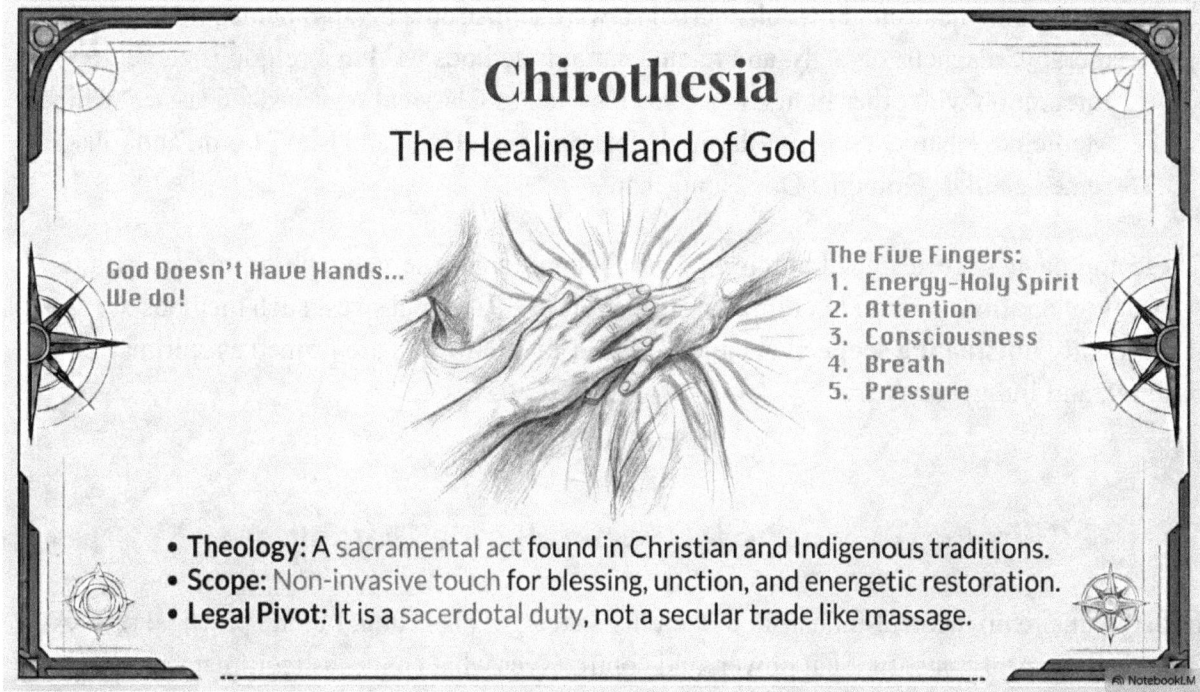

Chirothesia
The Healing Hand of God

God Doesn't Have Hands...
We do!

The Five Fingers:
1. Energy-Holy Spirit
2. Attention
3. Consciousness
4. Breath
5. Pressure

- **Theology:** A sacramental act found in Christian and Indigenous traditions.
- **Scope:** Non-invasive touch for blessing, unction, and energetic restoration.
- **Legal Pivot:** It is a sacerdotal duty, not a secular trade like massage.

Indigenous traditions tell a parallel story. Medicine people are recognized by their communities and elders as those who have a sacred duty to stand between their people and suffering, using touch, breath, song, and plant allies as directed by Spirit. NAIC explicitly treats Chirothesia (hands-on spiritual intervention) as a sacerdotal duty for authorized ministers and healers.

For the Chirothesist, then, laying on of hands is not a personal hobby; it is a **religious obligation** tied to ordination, calling, and lineage. To refuse to offer it when the Spirit leads and when the church or tribal authority has commissioned you can feel like failing your covenant.

4. Scope of Practice: What Chiropractors Actually Do

The NAIC/ACNM framework describes a Chirothesist's scope of practice as the evaluation and care of the human being, body, mind, and spirit, through religious therapeutics based on natural and spiritual laws, using non-invasive methods such as the laying on of hands, prayer, and traditional natural modalities.

When practiced by ordained, commissioned, or otherwise religiously authorized persons, Chirothesia-based Religious Therapeutics may include, for example:

- Sacred nutrition and dietary guidance, including fasting and food restrictions.
- Hands-on spiritual interventions: blessing touch, gentle pressure, and positional holds.
- Energy-based practices (polarity, somatics, Reiki, Chi Gung, Tai Chi, chakra work).
- Sound and breath work: mantra, chanting, prayer, sacred music, breath practices.

- Traditional naturopathic tools: herbal stewardship, aromatherapy, balneotherapy, light therapy, magnets, crystals, and related natural methods used in a religious context.
- Integration with other Indigenous systems such as Classical Ayurveda, Classical Chinese Medicine, Islamic Yunani, Filipino Hilot, Hawaiian Huna and Lomi Lomi, and folk remedies like "Grandma Doc" home care.

These approaches are designed to improve psychoemotional, energetic, physiological, and spiritual integration, leading to optimal wellness. As NAIC emphasizes, such methods are intentionally **outside the scope of secular licensed medicine** and are framed as spiritual, pastoral, and Indigenous care.

5. Chirothesia and the Medical-Industrial Paradigm

In the mainstream medical-industrial model, the stated goal is health, but the practical drivers often include profit, institutional power, and control over what counts as legitimate care. Medicine is often reduced to procedures, prescriptions, and standardized protocols delivered through insurance and regulatory systems.

Chirothesia stands in deliberate contrast. Its objectives are not corporate profit or social control, but deeper **oneness with Nature, Spirit, and God**, and the integration of all fractured parts of the sacred whole into a peaceful union marked by love, compassion, joy, and equanimity. Rather than isolating symptoms, it seeks to restore relationships, within the person, with their community, and with Creation.

This contrast does not mean Chirothesia is "anti-medicine"; it means it belongs to a different paradigm. You are not competing with hospitals; you are tending temples, human temples and ceremonial spaces, under a separate but complementary jurisdiction.

6. Not Practicing Medicine Under State Law

From the perspective of state medical boards, the practice of medicine is usually defined as diagnosing, treating, operating, or prescribing for human disease, pain, injury, deformity, or physical condition. Chirothesia, as framed here, explicitly **does not** include:

- Diagnosing or prescribing for medical or psychological conditions.
- Claiming to prevent, treat, mitigate, or cure such conditions as those terms are defined in secular practice acts.

- Using invasive techniques or potentially toxic drugs is reserved for licensed professionals.

Instead, Chirothesia is characterized as:

- A sacramental, non-invasive laying on of hands between minister and member.
- A set of natural and energetic modalities used as religious therapeutics and Indigenous medicine.
- A practice confined to private, ecclesiastical/tribal, and PMA domains, under church and tribal law rather than public commercial statutes.

By consistently using this language in your consent forms, membership agreements, and public communications, you help regulators see that your work belongs to the protected sphere of religious practice, not to the licensed practice of medicine or massage.

7. Learning and Community

Because Chirothesia is a sacramental science, it cannot be learned from random videos or weekend workshops alone. Organizations such as the Native American Indigenous Church and the American College of Natural Medicine offer structured training in Chirothesia-based ministries within broader programs in monastic, Christ-centered, and Native American traditional medicine.

Authorized NAIC memberships (such as Authorized Full Blessed Member status) and practitioner directories identify those who have been recognized to offer Chirothesia as part of an accountable religious and tribal framework. This communal recognition matters both spiritually and legally: it shows that your work is embedded in a living tradition rather than invented in isolation.

Chirothesia and Adoption of Religious Therapeutics from other Nations

Chirothesia protects practitioners using global modalities like Ayurveda and Traditional Thai Yoga by legally reclassifying these practices from "secular medicine" or "bodywork" to **"Religious Therapeutics."**

This reclassification moves the practice out of the public, commercial jurisdiction (governed by state medical and massage boards) and into the private, ecclesiastical, and tribal jurisdiction (protected by federal law).

Here is how Chirothesia provides this legal protection:

1. Theological Redefinition: From "Bodywork" to "Sacrament"

Legally, **Chirothesia** is defined as the "laying on of hands" or "Divine Touch," a ritual act where the practitioner serves as a conduit for healing energy. By framing modalities like Ayurveda or Thai Yoga as forms of Chirothesia, they become protected religious rites rather than regulated medical treatments.

- **Universal Anatomy:** The sources argue that the "Spirit Lines" of Native American medicine are functionally identical to the *Sen Lines* of Thai Medicine and the *Nadis* of Ayurveda. Therefore, manipulating these lines is not "massage" (a secular trade) but a spiritual act of clearing the "Spirit Anatomy" or "Hollow Bone".
- **Authorized Modalities:** The scope of practice for an ordained Chirothesist explicitly includes "Indigenous systems such as Ayurvedic Thai Yoga, Classical Ayurveda... and Traditional Thai Medicine".

2. Jurisdictional Shift: The "Four Umbrellas"

Chirothesia allows the practitioner to stand under specific legal "umbrellas" that state boards cannot easily penetrate, provided the practice is non-invasive and non-pharmaceutical.

- **Ecclesiastical Authority:** Under the First Amendment, churches have the autonomy to define their own ministries. If a bona fide church (like NAIC) defines Ayurveda as a sacrament of Chirothesia, the state is generally barred from regulating it as "unlicensed medicine," provided no harm is done.
- **Tribal Sovereignty & Federal Statutes:** The practice is bolstered by the **American Indian Religious Freedom Act (AIRFA)** and the **Religious Freedom Restoration Act (RFRA)**. These laws protect the right to exercise traditional religions. Since Native American Traditional Indigenous Medicine (NATIM) views healing and religion as inseparable, the "traditional rites" protected by AIRFA include healing ceremonies.

3. The L.C.H.T. License: Internal Credentialing

To operationalize this protection, organizations like the Native American Indigenous Church (NAIC) issue a specific credential: the **Licensed Commissioned Holistic Therapist (L.C.H.T.).**

- **Not a State License:** The L.C.H.T. is an ecclesiastical and tribal license, not a state license. It authorizes the holder to practice "Religious Therapeutics" and "Indigenous Healthcare" (IHSM).
- **Scope of Practice:** This license allows practitioners to offer Ayurveda, Thai Yoga, and hands-on healing legally, *as long as they serve only members* of the church/organization within a **Private Membership Association (PMA)** structure.

4. Semantic Defense: Avoiding "Forbidden Words"

Legal protection relies heavily on how the practice is described. Chirothesia protects the practitioner only if they strictly avoid secular medical terminology.

- **Forbidden Words:** Practitioners must **never** claim to "diagnose," "treat," "cure," or "prescribe" for any disease, nor call themselves "doctors" or "massage therapists" in a secular sense.
- **Protected Language:** Instead, practitioners must use religious descriptors. For example, instead of "Thai Massage," one should use terms like **"Indigenous Thai Yoga,"** **"Sacred Bodywork,"** or **"Religious Therapeutics"**. This signals to regulators that the work belongs to a religious framework, not the regulated field of massage therapy.

5. Integration of "Contentious" Modalities

The sources note that even "contentious" practices, such as the use of needles (acupuncture/dry needling), can be legally framed under this system if historical precedent exists.

- **Viddha Karma & Spirit Points:** The texts argue that ancient Ayurvedic needling (*Viddha Karma*) and Native American quill work are forms of "venting" bad energy. When practiced by a religiously authorized Chirothesist, these are not "medical acupuncture" but traditional rites for releasing spiritual stagnation.

Summary: Chirothesia protects the practitioner by defining the *intent* of the act as religious rather than medical. When an Ayurvedic practitioner touches a client, they are not "treating a patient" (public commerce); they are "ministering to a member" (private covenant), protected by the "ironclad triangle" of tribal sovereignty, church autonomy, and federal religious freedom laws.

Chapter 11 Conclusion – The Hands That Carry the Medicine

Chirothesia names what your hands already know how to do: bless, comfort, restore, and reconnect people with Creator and Creation. It places that knowing within a deep stream of Christian and Indigenous practice and within a modern legal vocabulary that can distinguish sacred touch from regulated secular therapies.

As you continue, remember that your hands do not belong to the medical-industrial system by default. Properly authorized and framed, they belong to the sanctuary, to the domain of churches, tribes, and private associations where Religious Therapeutics and Indigenous medicine can flourish lawfully.

In the next chapter, we broaden the view to the ceremonial landscape in which Chirothesia lives: the Indigenous rites of Birth, Breath, Pipe, Sacrament, Sweat Lodge, Vision Quest, and more that together form a protected ecosystem of healing.

LEARNING EXERCISE 11.1
Review & Application
Instructions: Select the best answer based on the reading.

1. What does "Chirothesia" literally convey?
   A) Legal authority
   B) Surgical incision
   C) Being led by the healing hand of God through intentional laying on of hands
   D) Physical therapy
   E) Massage with oil
   Correct Answer: C

2. Which statement best summarizes hands-on healing across traditions in this chapter?
   A) It is unique to Christianity
   B) It is only found in Asian religions
   C) Many traditions use touch, energetic transmission, or hand-based blessing as central healing or ordaining acts
   D) Only physicians may lay hands in healing
   E) It has disappeared in modern times
   Correct Answer: C

3. From the Christian perspective here, what is Jesus' role regarding Chirothesia?
   A) A critic of touch
   B) A neutral observer
   C) The archetypal Chirothesist whose ministry of touch sets the pattern for sacramental healing
   D) A secular physician
   E) A political leader only
   Correct Answer: C

4. Which of the following is within the described scope of Chirothesia-based Religious Therapeutics?
   A) Brain surgery
   B) Chemotherapy
   C) Non-invasive laying on of hands, sacred nutrition, breath work, sound, herbs, energy practices, and related natural modalities in a religious framework
   D) Controlled substance prescription
   E) Hospital administration
   Correct Answer: C

5. Why does the chapter insist Chirothesia is not "practicing medicine" as defined by state law?
   A) Because it never affects health
   B) Because it ignores safety
   C) Because it avoids diagnosing, prescribing, invasive techniques, and secular disease-treatment claims, and is confined to sacramental, non-invasive ministry
   D) Because it is purely symbolic
   E) Because it is always free of charge
   Correct Answer: C

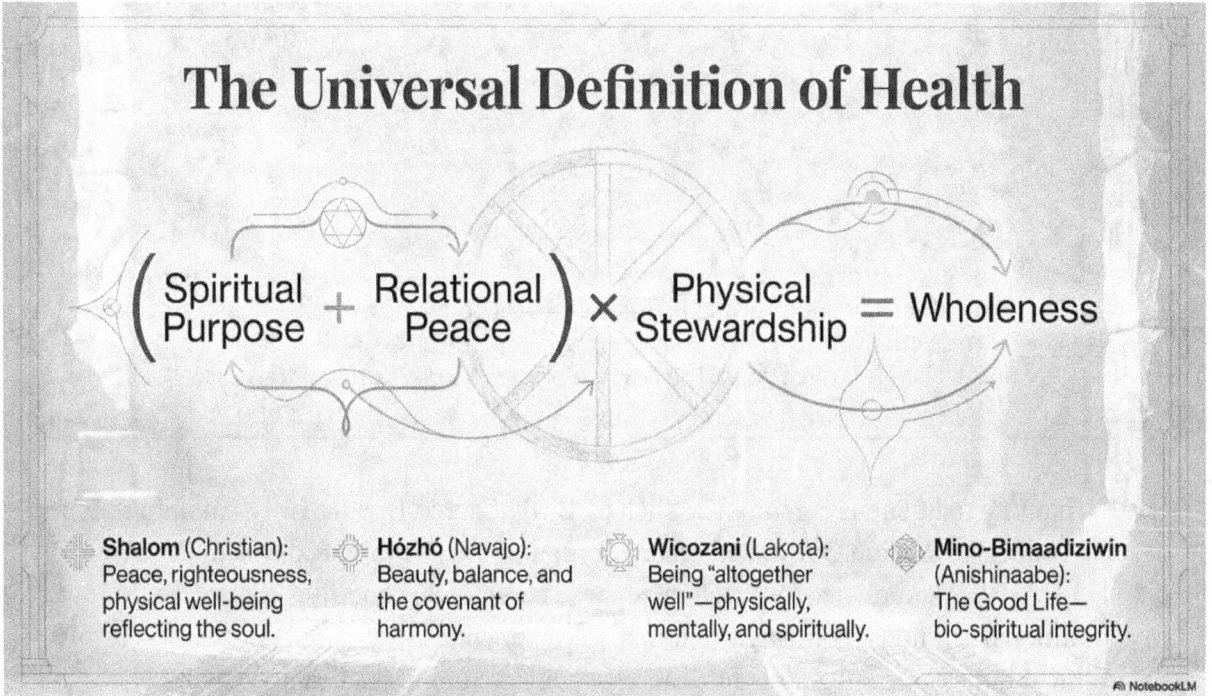

The Universal Definition of Health

$$\left(\begin{array}{c} \text{Spiritual} \\ \text{Purpose} \end{array} + \begin{array}{c} \text{Relational} \\ \text{Peace} \end{array} \right) \times \begin{array}{c} \text{Physical} \\ \text{Stewardship} \end{array} = \text{Wholeness}$$

Shalom (Christian): Peace, righteousness, physical well-being reflecting the soul.

Hózhó (Navajo): Beauty, balance, and the covenant of harmony.

Wicozani (Lakota): Being "altogether well"—physically, mentally, and spiritually.

Mino-Bimaadiziwin (Anishinaabe): The Good Life— bio-spiritual integrity.

NotebookLM

Chapter 12 – Indigenous Ceremonies and Protected Practices

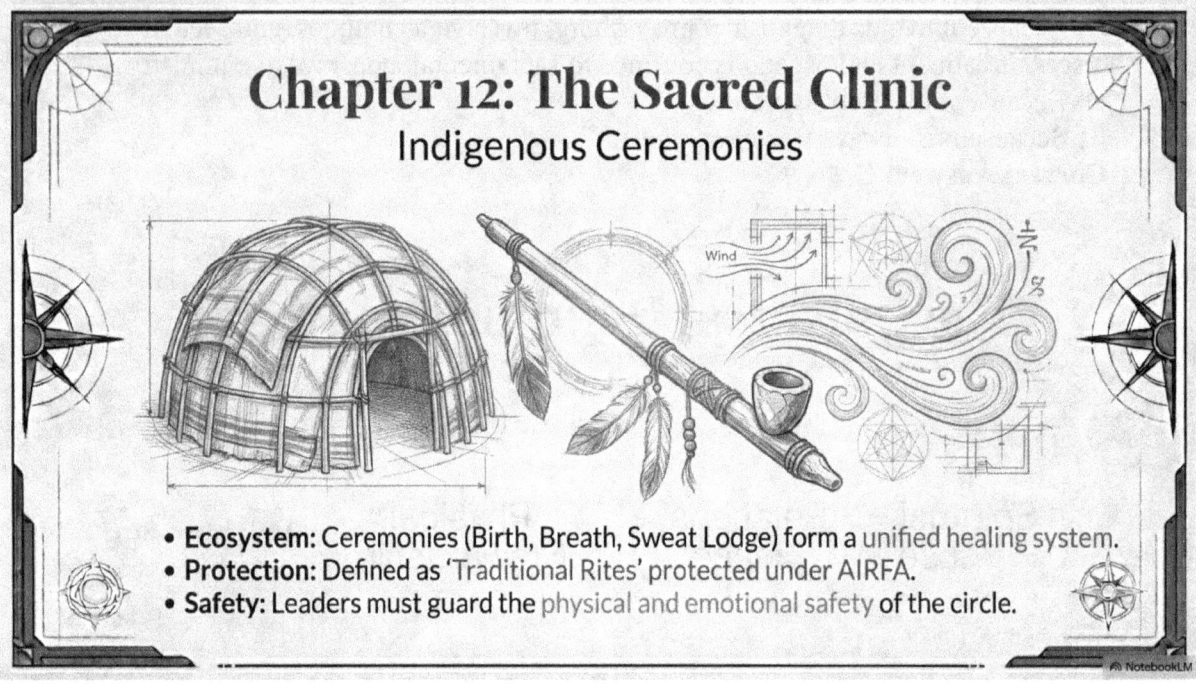

Chapter 12: The Sacred Clinic
Indigenous Ceremonies

- **Ecosystem:** Ceremonies (Birth, Breath, Sweat Lodge) form a unified healing system.
- **Protection:** Defined as 'Traditional Rites' protected under AIRFA.
- **Safety:** Leaders must guard the physical and emotional safety of the circle.

- ᔐ What key Indigenous ceremonies, such as Birth, Sacred Breath, Holy Anointing, Pipe, Sweat Lodge, Vision Quest, and others, form a unified healing ecosystem?
- ᔐ How AIRFA and related law recognize these ceremonials and rites as protected traditional religions, not fringe "alternative treatments."
- ᔐ Ethical duties and safeguards for leaders when ceremonies can catalyze "extreme" mental, emotional, or physical transformations.

Chirothesia is one thread in a much larger ceremonial fabric. Indigenous healing does not happen in isolated sessions; it unfolds within a cycle of **ceremonies** that mark every stage of life, from first breath to final passing. These ceremonies are simultaneously spiritual, communal, and therapeutic, and many are explicitly recognized in law as protected expressions of Native American religion.

This chapter revisits the core ceremonies described in your original materials, birth and death rites, Sacred Breath, Holy Anointing, Marriage Blanket, Potlach, Sacred Pipe, Sacrament, Spirit Dance, Sun Dance, Sweat Lodge, Vision Quest, and Bible-based natural healing, and views them as a unified Indigenous Religious Therapeutic system. We also note that NAIC's Code of Ethics highlights both its sacred power and its potential to bring profound transformation, which requires special care from leaders.

By the end, you will see not just a list of rituals, but a living ceremonial ecosystem that law has pledged, in part, to protect.

1. A Ceremonial Ecosystem of Healing

Indigenous teaching emphasizes that the Great Spirit gave human beings foundational ceremonies tied to the two substances that sustain life: **Air** (Father Sky) and **Food** (Mother Earth). From these roots, Sacred Breath and sacramental plants such as peyote, ayahuasca, San Pedro, tobacco, sweetgrass, sage, cannabis, and Yage gave rise to a diverse set of rituals addressing every aspect of human existence.

Over time, basic observances were elaborated into a full ceremonial calendar: rites of birth and naming, healing and reconciliation, marriage and communal sharing, purification and vision, sacrifice and thanksgiving, and passages into the next realm. Practicing these ceremonies regularly has been observed to cultivate faith, gratitude, humility, charity, respect, honor, forgiveness, and deep respect for "all our relations."

In this sense, Indigenous ceremonies are not occasional add-ons to life; they are the **community's primary healthcare system,** integrating spiritual, emotional, and physical well-being.

2. Key Ceremonies and Their Purposes

Based on the provided sources, the integration of **Chirothesia** (the Christian concept of laying on of hands) with **Native American Traditional Indigenous Medicine (NATIM)** and adopted global healing technologies represents a sophisticated, evolving "Whole Medical System." This synthesis is not merely an eclectic mix of techniques but a deliberate, religiously protected strategy to address the gaps in traditional knowledge caused by historical trauma and colonization.

The following sections detail how these practices are legitimately woven into modern Indigenous and Religious Therapeutics.

A. Chirothesia: The Universal "Hollow Bone" of Healing

The Christian concept of *Chirothesia*—defined as "the healing hand of God" or the transmission of divine energy through touch—aligns perfectly with the Indigenous concept of the healer as a "Hollow Bone". In this framework, the practitioner does not use their own energy but serves as a conduit for the Great Spirit or Holy Spirit to align the patient.

- **Integration with Global Modalities:** Because the "Spirit Lines" of Native American medicine (the pathways of the "Little People" or *Nilch'i*) are functionally identical to the *Sen Lines* of **Traditional Thai Medicine** and the *Nadis* of **Ayurveda**, adopting these foreign modalities is viewed as recovering lost "Spirit Anatomy" rather than appropriation.
- **Nuad Boran and Marma-Chikitsa:** Techniques such as **Nuad Boran** (Traditional Thai Massage) and **Marma-chikitsa** (Ayurvedic energy point therapy) are legally and theologically framed as forms of *Chirothesia*. They are used to physically "untie the knots" (trauma/blockages) in the body's fascia so that the spirit can flow freely. This allows a practitioner to perform physical alignment and energy balancing as a "sacramental act" under the church's legal umbrella, rather than as secular massage therapy.

B. Weaving Modalities into Sacred Ceremonies

The "Original Cure" outlines how natural and physical interventions are not separate from worship but are integral components of the "Ceremonial Ecosystem".

- **The Sweat Lodge (Inipi):** This purification ceremony is treated as "Clinical Hyperthermia" and a Naturopathic detoxification chamber. The intense heat mimics a fever, triggering an immune response (Heat Shock Proteins), while the spiritual context addresses the "Soul Wound." **Traditional Naturopathy** (hydrotherapy, heat) and **Homeopathy** (using remedies like *Sulphur* to stimulate pores) are often integrated to enhance the physical detoxification process within the spiritual container.

- **The Vision Quest (Hanblecheyapi):** This rite utilizes the Naturopathic principle of **Fasting** (metabolic reset) to induce *autophagy* (cellular cleaning) and clarity. It is framed as a "Neuro-Endocrine reset" that detoxifies the brain's dopamine receptors, curing the "spirit sickness" of addiction and lack of purpose.
- **Holy Anointing:** This ceremony is the direct application of *Chirothesia*. It legitimizes the use of **essential oils**, **salves**, and **herbal balms** (like CBD or Arnica) not just as chemical agents, but as "sacramentals" that carry the frequency of the plant spirit into the body through touch.
- **The Sacred Pipe (Chanupa):** Tobacco is used as a "bridge" between worlds. In a modern context, the Pipe ceremony serves as a form of **bio-energetic alignment**, where the collective intention (prayer) collapses quantum probabilities to manifest healing, supported by the "physics of prayer".

C. Wopela: Food as Medicine and Sacrament

The concept of **Wopela** (thanksgiving/gratitude) extends to the consumption of food, transforming eating into a medical intervention known as the "Wopila Effect," which is associated with the release of oxytocin and the reduction of cortisol.

- **Maize and First Foods:** The consumption of Native foods like **Non-GMO Corn (Maize)**, **Wild Rice**, and **Bison** is framed as "Nutritional Sovereignty." These are not just calories but "First Medicines" designed to treat the metabolic damage (diabetes/inflammation) caused by the "colonial diet" of flour and sugar.

- **The "De-Colonial Diet":** This protocol treats the "Three Sisters" (Corn, Beans, Squash) as a biochemical engine that provides complete proteins and prebiotic fiber. Preparing and eating these foods is a "Religious Therapeutic" act of restoring the body's ability to hold the spirit.
- **Sacred Sweetness:** Traditional sweeteners such as maple syrup and Raw Honey are valued for their mineral content and antimicrobial properties, in contrast to the "white death" of processed sugar.

D. Evolutionary Necessity: The Synthesis of Survival

The modern expression of this medicine is explicitly described as an **"evolving, elegant, and diverse expression"** necessitated by genocide and the suppression of culture.

- **Addressing Historical Gaps:** The text acknowledges that the "Code of Indian Offenses" (1883) and subsequent policies attempted to "kill the Medicine" to "kill the Indian". This forced medicine underground and fragmented knowledge.
- **The Innovator's Spirit:** To heal the "New Smallpox" (chronic disease, metabolic syndrome, despair), modern Indigenous healers act as "Innovators" rather than statues in a museum. They have adopted **Yoga Therapy**, **Homeopathy**, **Live Blood Analysis**, and **PEMF (Pulsed Electromagnetic Field)** technology because these tools align with the Indigenous worldview of energy and vibration.
- **Intertribal Exchange:** The adoption of Thai or Ayurvedic methods is framed as a continuation of the ancient "Intertribal Exchange," where tribes met to trade cures. Today, the trade is global. The "Medicine Man of the future" holds both the ancient pipe and the modern law (and science) to protect their people.

Conclusion: By categorizing these practices as **Religious Therapeutics**, practitioners create a protected legal and spiritual domain where **Traditional Naturopathy**, **Homeopathy**, and **physical therapies** (Yoga/Thai Massage) are not "unlicensed medicine" but are recognized as valid, traditional, and necessary forms of ministry and **Indigenous Healthcare (IHSM)**. This ecosystem restores the "Sacred Hoop" by treating the human being as a bio-psycho-socio-spiritual whole.

3. Legal Protection as Traditional Rites

The American Indian Religious Freedom Act and its amendments explicitly declare it U.S. policy to protect and preserve for Indigenous peoples their inherent right to believe, express, and **exercise** their traditional religions, including "access to sites, use and possession of sacred objects, and the freedom to worship through ceremonials and traditional rites." In Native American Traditional Indigenous Medicine, these ceremonials and rites are the healing system.

Because NATIM makes no separation between "religion" and "medicine," ceremonies like Sweat Lodge, Pipe, Sacrament, and Vision Quest are simultaneously worship and healthcare. When carried by federally recognized tribes or bona fide tribal religious organizations, such as

Native American churches and NAIC, they qualify as protected religious exercises under AIRFA and RFRA.

This does not put them above all law. Criminal statutes still apply, and contentious elements, such as Schedule I sacraments or physically demanding rites, attract additional scrutiny. Within those boundaries, the law acknowledges that these ceremonies are not merely cultural performances; they are core expressions of sovereign religious life.

4. Ethics, Extreme Transformations, and Duty of Care

NAIC's own Code of Ethics acknowledges that certain ceremonies, especially Birth, Sun Dance, Sweat Lodge, Vision Quest, and sacramental rites, can catalyze "extreme mental, emotional, and physical transformations." This recognition places a special duty of care on ceremonial leaders and Chirothesists.

Ethical practice requires, at a minimum:

- Clear, honest, **informed consent**, explaining the nature and potential intensity of the ceremony.
- Appropriate **screening**, especially for participants with physical or psychological vulnerabilities.
- Adherence to established **protocols** for safety, preparation, and integration.
- Willingness to say **"not now"** when Spirit or common sense indicates that the risk for a given person exceeds what is responsible.

By maintaining strong internal ethics and training standards, Indigenous churches demonstrate that their ceremonies are not reckless experiments, but disciplined, lineage-based practices aimed at healing and spiritual growth. This internal discipline strengthens both spiritual integrity and legal defensibility.

Chapter 12 Conclusion – Ceremonies as the Sacred Clinic

Taken together, these ceremonies form what might be called the **sacred clinic** of Indigenous life. They diagnose imbalance not through lab tests but through stories, dreams, and symptoms of disconnection; they treat not just the body, but the relationships and covenants that hold a person in place.

Under the law, they are protected as traditional rites when practiced by sovereign tribes and bona fide tribal religious organizations, subject to the same limits that apply to all religious exercise when public safety is at stake. In the eyes of Spirit, they remain the original medicine.

As you continue refining your practice, remember that you stand not as an isolated practitioner but inside this ceremonial house. The more faithfully you honor its ethics, protocols, and elders, the more clearly you can claim both the spiritual and legal protections that surround it.

LEARNING EXERCISE 12.1
Review & Application
Instructions: Select the best answer based on the reading.

1. How does the chapter describe Indigenous ceremonies as a whole?
   A) As isolated, unrelated rituals
   B) As entertainment events
   C) As a ceremonial ecosystem of healing that covers life from birth to death
   D) As purely political protests
   E) As modern inventions
   Correct Answer: C

2. Which of the following is *not* one of the "ALL protected practices" summarized?
   A) Birth Ceremony and Passing On of Spirit
   B) Sacred Breath and Holy Anointing
   C) Sacred Pipe, Sacrament, Sweat Lodge, Vision Quest
   D) Marriage Blanket and Potlach
   E) Robotic-assisted surgery
   Correct Answer: E

3. Why are these ceremonies treated as protected religious practices under AIRFA?
   A) Because they are secular cultural festivals
   B) Because NATIM does not distinguish between religion and medicine, ceremonies are core expressions of traditional religion
   C) Because they generate tourism income
   D) Because they use no physical elements
   E) Because they are scripted performances
   Correct Answer: B

4. What ethical concern does the NAIC Code of Ethics raise about certain ceremonies?
   A) They are always mild and risk-free
   B) They never affect emotions
   C) Some can produce "extreme" mental, emotional, and physical transformations, requiring special care and discernment
   D) They should be done without consent
   E) They must be recorded for social media
   Correct Answer: C

5. What is the metaphor used at the end of the chapter for these ceremonies?
   A) A business franchise
   B) A legal trap
   C) A "sacred clinic" diagnosing imbalance through stories and restoring covenant relationships
   D) A political manifesto
   E) A scientific laboratory
   Correct Answer: C

Chapter 13 – Religious Therapeutics, IHSM & Holistic Services Are NOT "Practicing Medicine"

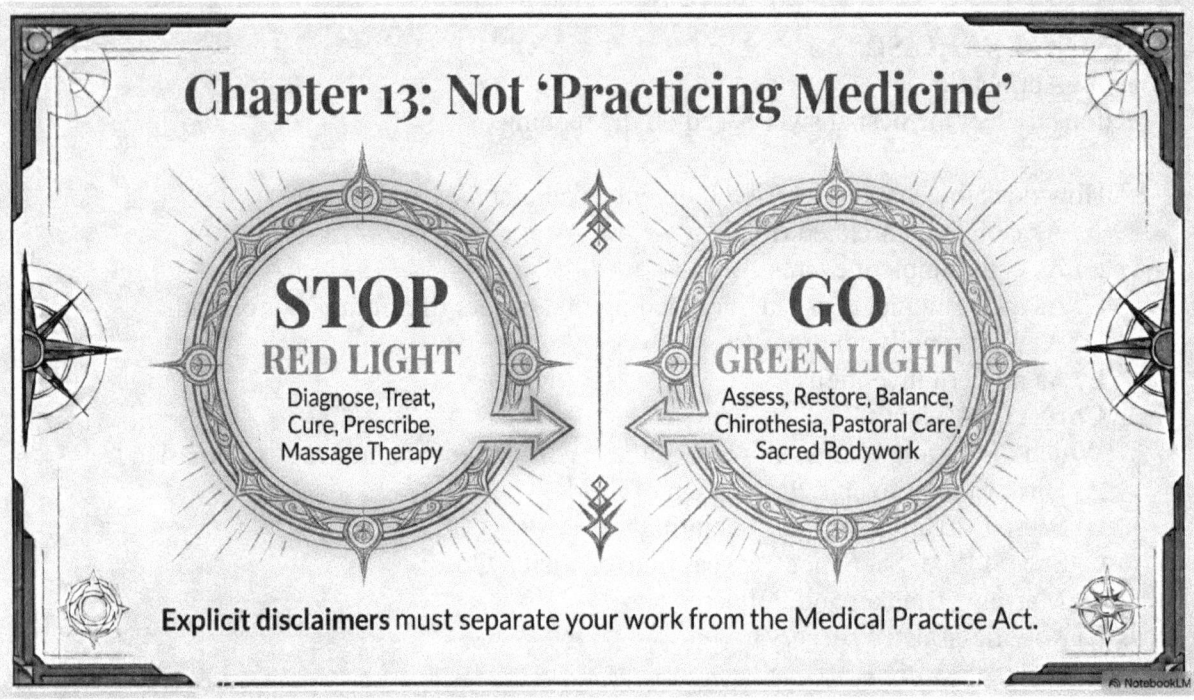

- ✏ How NAIC and similar bodies define CAM and Indigenous Healthcare (IHSM) as religious, non-medical practices.
- ✏ Defining IHSM, NATIM, and Holistic Services in a Religious Context.
- ✏ Examples of alternative modalities that fit within a non-diagnostic, non-prescribing religious scope.
- ✏ What careful language and explicit disclaimers keep your work outside statutory definitions of "practicing medicine"?

From the perspective of a state medical board, almost any conversation about diet, touch, herbs, or emotions can be recast as "nutrition counseling," "massage," "bodywork," or "psychotherapy". If you accept those labels, your work is immediately pulled into the regulatory orbit of secular licensure. Yet much of what you do as a Chirothesist or Indigenous healer is **not** the practice of medicine as the State defines it. It is Religious Therapeutics: spiritual, pastoral, and tribal care outside the statutory scope of licensed medicine.

This chapter clarifies that distinction. While there may be similarities in terminology or practice with "Complementary and Alternative Medicine" (CAM) or "Alternative Medicine," they are fundamentally distinct. We will first define IHSM, NATIM, and Holistic Services in a religious context, and then explain why they are intentionally excluded from the scope of secular medicine. We will review the legal language that explicitly separates religious therapeutics from "practicing medicine" and offer practical guidelines for describing your work accurately, so you do not accidentally step into regulated territory.

By the end, you should be able to say with confidence: "What I do is IHSM, NATIM, and Holistic service in a religious sense, but it is **not** the practice of medicine under state law".

1. Defining IHSM, NATIM, and Holistic Services in a Religious Context

In your source materials, "alternative medicine" or "spiritual medicine" is defined broadly as Religious Therapeutics, Traditional Chirothesia, spiritual, religious, energetic, vitality-based, pastoral, ministerial, clerical, tribal, Indigenous Native, familial, and related practices used by individuals for self-help and wellness. These practices are used either alone or alongside standard medical care and reflect Indigenous and Native cultures.

They are often grouped under terms such as:

- **IHSM:** Indigenous (clerical/pastoral/ministerial) Healthcare, Healing Science, Counseling, and Medicine.
- **NATIM:** Native American Traditional Indigenous Medicine.
- **Religious Therapeutics:** Principles and practices that support well-being by uniting health and religiousness.
- **Holistic Services:** Approach to integrate psycho-emotional, energetic, physiological, and spiritual components.

The NAIC/ACNM Chirothesia article emphasizes that these modalities are non-standard approaches "outside the scope of secular licensed medicine" and are rooted in natural and spiritual laws. Their purpose is to remedy and alleviate suffering and to enhance psycho-emotional, energetic, physiological, and spiritual integration, leading to optimal wellness, not to practice allopathic medicine.

2. Outside the Scope of Licensed Medicine

Your materials make a crucial legal and conceptual point: **"Religious Therapeutic, IHSM & Holistic Services are NOT the practice of medicine as defined by State Medical Practice Acts"**.

Why? Because they:

- **Do not** use invasive techniques (incisions, injections, surgical procedures).
- **Do not** use potentially dangerous drugs that are the province of licensed medicine.
- **Do not** claim to diagnose, prevent, treat, mitigate, or cure disease as those terms are defined in secular statutes.
-

Instead, they rely on:

- Non-invasive touch (Chirothesia, laying on of hands).
- Natural modalities (nutrition, herbs, aromatherapy, magnets, light, sound, crystals, somatics, etc.), expressly framed as spiritual and Indigenous.
- Prayer, ritual, confession, counsel, and other sacramental acts.

3. The Legal Statement: "We Do Not Practice Medicine."

To reinforce this separation, NAIC and similar organizations insist that Religious Therapeutic practitioners make certain statements, verbally and in writing:

- "[Practitioner/Member] does not diagnose or prescribe for either medical or psychological conditions nor claim to prevent, treat, mitigate, or cure such conditions (as defined by secular practice acts)".
- "[Practitioner/Member] does not provide diagnosis, care, treatment, or rehabilitation of individuals, nor apply medical, mental health, or human development principles (as defined by secular practice acts)".

These disclaimers are built into informed consent and membership documents to make the paradigm explicit: you are not acting as a secular health care provider; you are offering Religious Therapeutics, pastoral care, Indigenous ceremony, and spiritual counsel under ecclesiastical and tribal authority.

4. Examples of Non-Medical Alternative Practices

Appropriate modalities for ordained or religiously authorized Chirothesists include:

- Nutrition and sacred diets, including fasting and food restrictions.
- Homeopathy and traditional "Grandma Doc" remedies.
- Hands-on healing, magnetics, and biomagnetics.
- Sound therapy, mantra, chanting, sacred music.
- Polarity, somatics, energy therapies, Reiki, Chi Gung, Tai Chi.
- Reflexology (framed as sacred or religious, not as a secular therapy brand).
- Biofeedback, meditation, breath work, Pranayama.
- Herbology, aromatherapy, sacred incense, and smudging.
- Balneotherapy, light therapy, vibration, and crystal healing.
- Indigenous systems such as Ayurvedic Thai Yoga, Classical Ayurveda, Classical Chinese Medicine, Islamic Yunani, Filipino Hilot, Hawaiian Huna and Lomi Lomi, and Native American medicine.

5. Avoiding Trigger Words and Misclassification

Because secular boards regulate certain titles and verbs, the book warns strongly about "forbidden words": **diagnose, treat, prescribe, prevent, mitigate, cure**, when used in a secular medical sense. It also cautions against generic labels such as "massage," "massage therapy," "bodywork," "reflexology," and "yoga therapy," which are often defined in massage or allied-health statutes.

Instead, you are urged to use precise religious descriptors that signal your true scope and authority, such as:

- **SomaVeda® Integrated Traditional Therapies®:** Thai Yoga, Indigenous Thai Yoga Therapy.
- **Sacred Thai Bodywork**, Thai Yoga Religious Therapy, Thai Sacred Healing.
- **Religious Therapeutics**, Monastic Medicine, Pastoral Medicine, Pastoral Therapy.
- **Native American Indigenous Medicine** (with NAIC authorization).
- **Indigenous (clerical/pastoral/ministerial) Healthcare**, Healing Science, Counseling, and Medicine (IHSM).

6. Alternative ≠ Loophole

Legal exemptions for religious and tribal healers are **not loopholes**. A loophole is an ambiguity used to avoid the intent of a law; an exemption is a deliberately carved-out protection. AIRFA, RFRA, IHCIA, RLUIPA, and state statutes recognizing ecclesiastical and tribal healing are examples of the latter.

When you frame your practice correctly, clearly outside the statutory definition of medicine, firmly within a religious and tribal paradigm, and governed by codes of ethics and informed consent, you are exercising a recognized right to practice as part of the free exercise of religion.

Chapter 13 Conclusion – A Different Kind of "Practice"

Religious Therapeutics and Indigenous Healthcare is a distinct profession. Its tools may overlap with those used by secular systems—touch, herbs, breath, and counsel—but its purpose, authority, and legal framework are distinct.

As you continue through this book, keep refining how you talk about what you do. The more clearly you can explain that your work is ministry and ceremony, not diagnosis and treatment, the easier it will be to stand firmly inside your rights while honoring your responsibilities.

LEARNING EXERCISE 13.1

Review & Application

Instructions: Select the best answer based on the reading.

1. **How does this chapter distinguish Religious Therapeutics and IHSM from standard CAM or Alternative Medicine?**
   - A) They use more powerful pharmaceuticals.
   - B) They are fundamentally religious, pastoral, and tribal in nature, operating under a different legal and authority framework.
   - C) They are only practiced in hospitals.
   - D) There is no meaningful distinction.
   - **Correct Answer: B**
2. **What is the "core reason" Religious Therapeutic and IHSM services are not considered "practicing medicine"?**
   - A) They are provided for free.
   - B) They use only water-based remedies.
   - C) They avoid invasive techniques, dangerous drugs, and secular claims to diagnose, treat, or cure disease.
   - D) The Department of Transportation regulates them.
   - **Correct Answer: C**
3. **Which statement is required for Religious Therapeutic practitioners to maintain their non-medical paradigm?**
   - A) "I can cure any ailment using Indigenous herbs."
   - B) "I am a state-licensed physician specializing in religion."
   - C) "Practitioner does not diagnose or prescribe for medical/psychological conditions nor claim to prevent, treat, mitigate, or cure such conditions as defined by secular practice acts."
   - D) "Religious healing is a direct substitute for surgery."
   - **Correct Answer: C**
4. **Why is using accurate terminology like "Indigenous Thai Yoga Therapy" preferred over generic "Massage Therapy"?**
   - A) It sounds more exotic for marketing.
   - B) Generic terms are often defined in secular statutes and can pull religious ministry into regulated secular scopes.
   - C) The state trademarks generic terms.
   - D) It is a requirement for tithing.
   - **Correct Answer: B**
5. **What is the legal status of exemptions for religious and tribal healers?**
   - A) They are "loopholes" created by drafting errors.
   - B) They are temporary measures until all healers are licensed.
   - C) They are clear, intentional, and recognized protections written into federal and state law (e.g., AIRFA, RFRA).
   - D) They only apply on Sundays.
   - **Correct Answer: C**

Part IV – Ethics, Consent, and Professional Practice

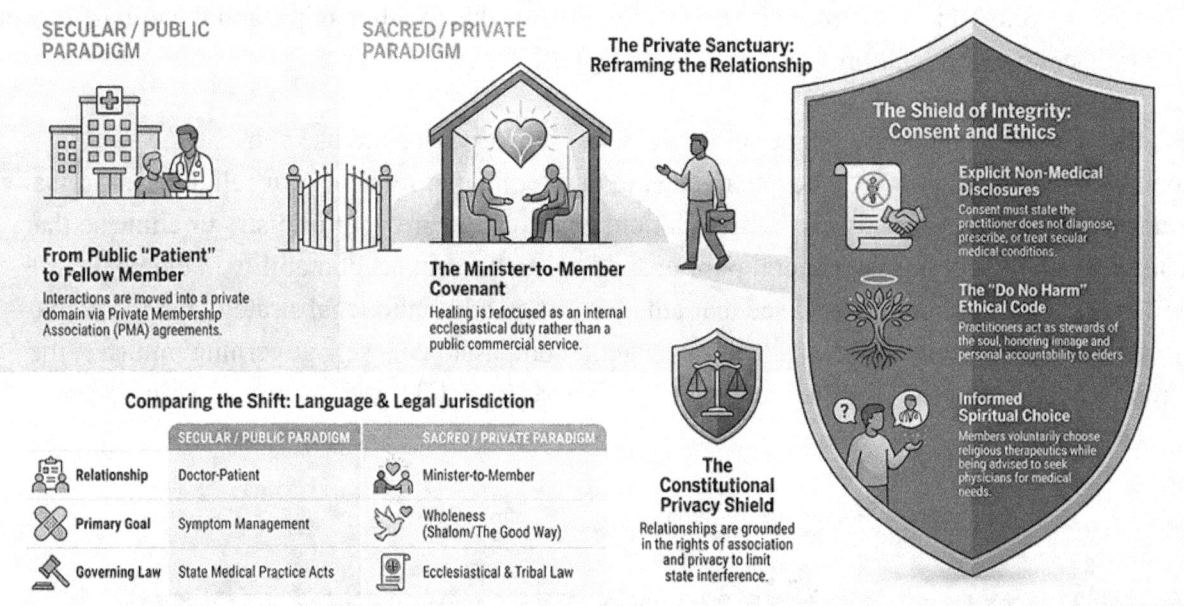

Part IV turns from "Can I do this?" to "How must I do this?" It gathers everything you have learned about sovereignty, exemptions, Religious Therapeutics, and Chirothesia, and translates it into the **day-to-day** ethics of a lawful, principled healing ministry. Here you will see that protection in law is tied to integrity in practice: codes of conduct, informed consent, boundaries, and honest language are as important as AIRFA, RFRA, or any court case nativefirechurch+1

The chapters in this Part begin with **concepts and philosophy**: what it has historically meant for healers and pastors to act as stewards rather than technicians. Christian and pastoral counseling traditions emphasize informed consent, confidentiality, and non-exploitation as basic duties of care. Indigenous healing systems, recognized by the NIH as holistic "whole medical systems," place equal weight on relational accountability to Creator, community, and elders as on technique. NAIC's own Code of Ethics distills this into a Chirothesia Practitioners' Code: do no harm, honor the communicant, work with consent, stay within your training, and remember that all work is an extension of Spirit and breath. These principles give theological and historical context for why an ethical framework is not optional but central to Religious Therapeutics and Native American medicine. nativefirechurch+5

From there, Part IV moves into **context and protected practices**. It shows how ethics, consent, and scope of practice apply not just to one-on-one sessions, but to the full range of protected

Indigenous and ecclesiastical practices you carry: sweat lodges, sacrament ceremonies, Birth and Passing-On rites, Vision Quests, pastoral counseling, and Chirothesia-based hands-on healing. You will learn how membership agreements and PMA language reframe your interactions as minister-to-member rather than doctor-to-patient; how informed-consent texts make clear that you do not diagnose, treat, or prescribe as defined in secular law; and how scopes of practice define which ceremonies and modalities you are authorized to lead. In parallel, we will draw on broader pastoral ethics literature on healthy boundaries, dual relationships, and the unique power dynamics in healing relationships.nativefirechurch+6

Finally, Part IV is intensely **practical**. It addresses how to write and use consent and membership forms; how to choose language in marketing that reflects your religious and tribal paradigm without triggering secular regulation; how to structure your ministry or clinic so that you serve members, not the general public; and how to live out accountability to elders, boards, and peers. Throughout, you will see that ethics is not an add-on to legal strategy but the core of it: the more your practice looks like a transparent, compassionate, self-governing ministry, the stronger your claim to the protections that Part II and Part III described.pmc.ncbi.nlm.nih+4

Standing Firm in the Sanctuary

The Mandate:
This is not a loophole; it is
a protected right.

Call to Action:
1. Structure your ministry.
2. Define your ethics.
3. Serve with integrity.
4. Practice without fear.

Sacred Hands, Secured Rights.

NotebookLM

Chapter 14 – Informed Consent, Membership, and the Private Relationship

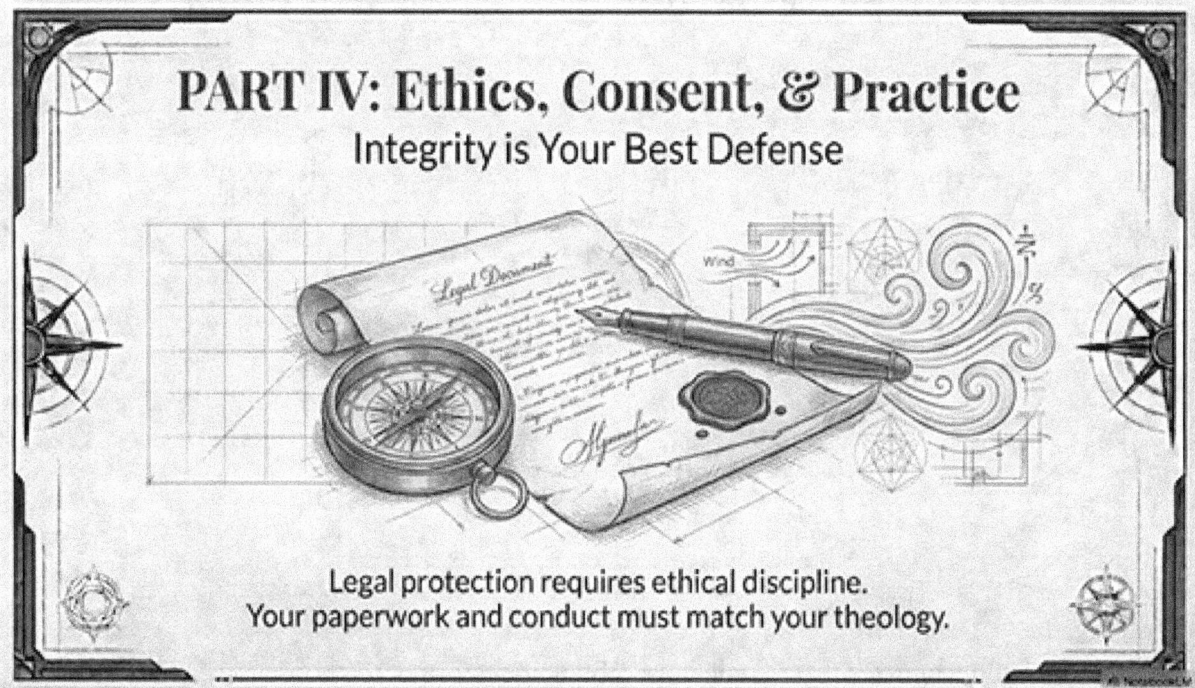

PART IV: Ethics, Consent, & Practice
Integrity is Your Best Defense

Legal protection requires ethical discipline.
Your paperwork and conduct must match your theology.

- How human-rights principles ground your members' right to choose Indigenous and religious modes of care.
- How membership and consent documents transform a "client" into a fellow member in a private ecclesiastical/tribal association.
- The key clauses that define your work as Religious Therapeutics and clarify that you do not diagnose or treat under secular law.

Every healer knows that trust is the first medicine. In the legal world, that trust is expressed, in part, through **informed consent**: a clear, honest agreement about what you are offering and what you are not. For Religious Therapeutics and Indigenous medicine, consent must also define another boundary: that your work occurs within a **private relationship** between members of a church or tribal organization, not as a public medical service.

This chapter explains how informed consent, membership agreements, and Private Membership Association (PMA) language work together to create that private ecclesiastical domain. We will draw on international human rights standards, NAIC's model consent forms, and key phrases that redefine the interaction as minister-to-member rather than doctor-to-patient.

By the end, you will see how a well-crafted consent and membership document not only protects you legally but also invites your clients, now fellow members, into a deeper, more conscious covenant around healing.

1. Human-Rights Foundations for Consent and Choice

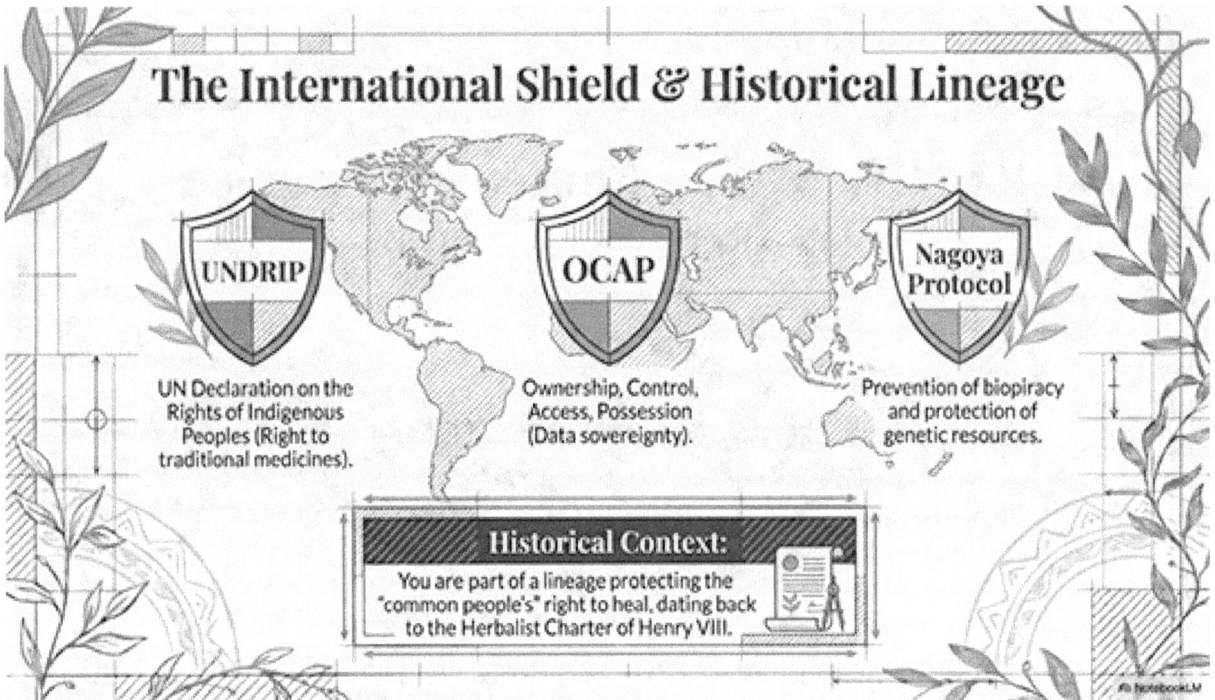

International law recognizes that people have a fundamental right to choose their beliefs and their modes of worship and practice.

- The **Universal Declaration of Human Rights (UDHR, Article 18)** affirms the right to freedom of thought, conscience, and religion, including the freedom to manifest religion or belief in teaching, practice, worship, and observance, alone or with others, in public or private. (https://www.un.org/en/udhrbook/pdf/udhr_booklet_en_web.pdf)
- The **American Declaration of the Rights and Duties of Man (Article III)** states that every person has the right freely to profess a religious faith and to manifest and practice it in public and in private. (https://www.oas.org/en/iachr/mandate/Basics/american-declaration-rights-duties-of-man.pdf)
- The **Declaration of Alma-Ata** frames health as a fundamental human right and emphasizes that people and communities must participate fully in their health care.

From these principles, NAIC and similar organizations conclude that individuals have the right to choose Indigenous, tribal, and religious therapeutics as modes of health support, provided they are not coerced and are fully informed. Informed consent in this context is not a mere legal formality; it is an expression of human dignity and religious freedom.

2. Reframing the Relationship: Member, Not "Patient."

NAIC's Participant Member Activity Consent, Disclosure, Waiver, and Disclaimer form offers a model for clearly defining the relationship. Key elements include:

- **Request for Religious Therapeutics & Definition of Health** – The member explicitly requests Native American and Biblical Religious Therapeutics and acknowledges that, in this jurisdiction, "health" is defined as *Shalom* (wholeness) and "The Good Way" (balance), a sacred integration of spirit, soul, and body.
- **Private Association & Jurisdiction** – The member acknowledges that the practitioner is an authorized NAIC minister/practitioner and that services are received strictly as a **fellow member**, not as a member of the public. The organization is described as a Tribal Organization and a private religious/church expressive association.
- **Disclaimer & Assumption of Responsibility** – The member affirms that Restorative Theology and Traditional Ecological Knowledge are not substitutes for regular medical care by a licensed physician, acknowledges being competent to make informed decisions, and voluntarily assumes responsibility for participation.

This language shifts the frame from "provider–patient" to "minister–member" inside a private, ecclesiastical, and tribal domain, where the primary law is church/tribal law, constrained by baseline civil and criminal protections.

3. The Core Informed-Consent Clauses

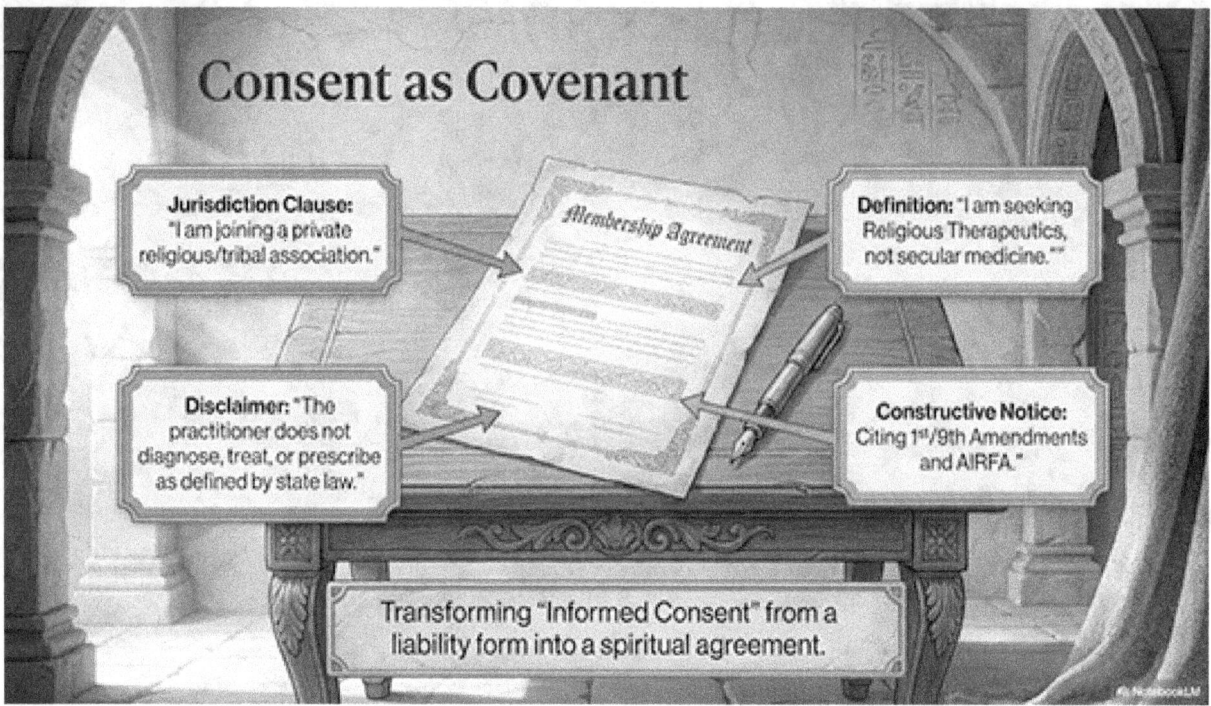

The standard informed-consent text NAIC recommends includes several clauses that are worth highlighting and adapting for your own practice:

1. **Non-Medical Scope**

   "The undersigned acknowledges that the practitioner does not diagnose or prescribe for medical or psychological conditions nor claim to prevent, treat, mitigate or cure such conditions, or to provide diagnosing, treating, operating or prescribing for any human disease, pain, injury, deformity or physical condition as defined in secular state medical practice acts."

2. **Religious Therapeutic Nature of Services**
   The practitioner "does not provide diagnosis, care, treatment, or rehabilitation of individuals, nor apply medical, mental health, or human development principles," but instead provides Religious Therapeutics (e.g., SomaVeda®), nutritional, mental, emotional, psychological, pastoral ministry, counseling, advisement, and consultation that may offer spiritual therapeutic benefit.

3. **Member's Informed Choice**
   The undersigned gives informed consent for the ministry, pastoral care, holistic services, sacred nutritional or other consultations and services to be provided and is advised to seek a physician if any medical condition is suspected.

4. **Use of Data for Research (Optional)**

   The member may consent to the anonymized use of information for research and publication.

Each clause helps align expectations: you are not a substitute for a physician, and the member is seeking spiritual and Indigenous support from you rather than regulated medical treatment.

4. The Private Membership Association Shield

The PMA framework is explicitly acknowledged in NAIC membership agreements. Members agree that:

- They are joining an Indigenous/Native American/Christian church and an expressive association for education and health care.
- They receive education and care from fellow members "in the capacity of a fellow member and not in the capacity of a secular or state-licensed health care provider."
- No doctor-patient relationship exists within the church association; rather, there is a private ecclesiastical/confessional/communicant relationship (often invoking the priest-penitent privilege).

They also acknowledge that the association is a private, religious/church-expressive membership organization under common law and tribal authority, dedicated to Indigenous, Traditional, and Native American medicine, Chirothesia, and related Religious Therapeutics. This language narrows the State's interest: what happens between members in this context is presumptively private, subject to ordinary criminal law but insulated from many regulatory controls intended for public commerce.

5. Constitutional Notice and Rights

NAIC's consent forms also provide **constructive notice** to any officials who might review them:

- They cite the **First and Ninth Amendments** and AIRFA, affirming the member's right to freedom of choice in health care, including diet, therapy, and spiritual regimens recommended by a fellow member/minister.
- They warn that anyone acting under color of law who interferes with the free exercise of these rights may implicate civil-rights statutes (e.g., 42 U.S.C. § 1983) and, in extreme cases involving conspiracies/threats, federal criminal provisions (e.g., 18 U.S.C. § 241). NOTE: As AIRFA was repealed and amended with the substitution of RLUIPA, AIRFA

is commonly characterized as a **policy** statement. Influential and important, yes, but NOT law. Do not overstate.

This notice does not guarantee that any official will never overstep, but it clarifies that the association is aware of its rights and prepared to assert them if necessary.

6. Why This Protects Both Sides

Well-crafted consent and membership documents protect **you** and **your members**.

For the member, they:

- Clarify whether they are seeking spiritual and Indigenous support, not secular diagnosis and treatment.
- Encourage responsible use of conventional medicine when appropriate.
- Ensure that participation is voluntary and informed.

For the practitioner and organization, they:

- Reduce misunderstandings and unrealistic expectations.
- Demonstrate to regulators that your practice is transparent and well-defined.
- Strengthen the argument that your work belongs in the private, religious domain, under church and tribal exemptions, rather than in the public regulatory domain.

Chapter 14 Conclusion – Consent as Covenant

Informed consent and membership agreements are more than legal paperwork; they are modern covenants. They say, "Here is who I am, here is what I can and cannot offer, and here is how we will walk together." That clarity honors the member's freedom, and you're calling as a healer-minister.

By consistently using this language, you reinforce the reality that your work is Religious Therapeutics within a private association of believers, not unlicensed public medicine. In the next chapter, we will extend these ethical foundations into codes of conduct and scopes of practice, showing how a clear internal discipline further strengthens both your spiritual integrity and your legal protection.

LEARNING EXERCISE 14.1
Review & Application
Instructions: Select the best answer based on the reading.

1. What human-rights principle undergirds informed consent in this chapter?
   A) Health is a privilege for professionals
   B) Religion must stay private
   C) People have a right to choose their beliefs and modes of worship and practice, including health-care approaches
   D) Only states can decide on health care
   E) Communities must surrender all traditions
   Correct Answer: C

2. What is the key relationship shift created by NAIC membership agreements?
   A) From minister to state employee
   B) From client to hospital patient
   C) From public "patient" to fellow member in a private religious/tribal association
   D) From citizen to foreign national
   E) From adult to dependent
   Correct Answer: C

3. Which clause type is *central* in the NAIC informed-consent text?
   A) Mandatory use of insurance
   B) Requirement to reject conventional medicine
   C) Explicit statement that the practitioner does not diagnose or treat medical/psychological conditions as defined by secular law
   D) Agreement never to seek legal advice
   E) Waiver of religious freedom
   Correct Answer: C

4. How does the PMA framework protect ministry activities?
   A) By banning all secular law
   B) By placing all disputes in criminal court
   C) By defining services as private, expressive, and religious activities among members, narrowing the State's regulatory interest
   D) By avoiding written agreements
   E) By granting political immunity
   Correct Answer: C

5. Why do consent and membership documents protect both sides?
   A) They guarantee specific outcomes
   B) They replace all other contracts
   C) They clarify expectations, preserve member choice, and show regulators that the practice is transparent and well-defined
   D) They eliminate ethical responsibilities
   E) They transfer all liability to the State
   Correct Answer: C

Figure 4, A strong Medicine Woman stands behind a table with both traditional native medicine and modern evolving tools in a natural surrounding.

Chapter 15 – Codes of Ethics and Scope of Practice

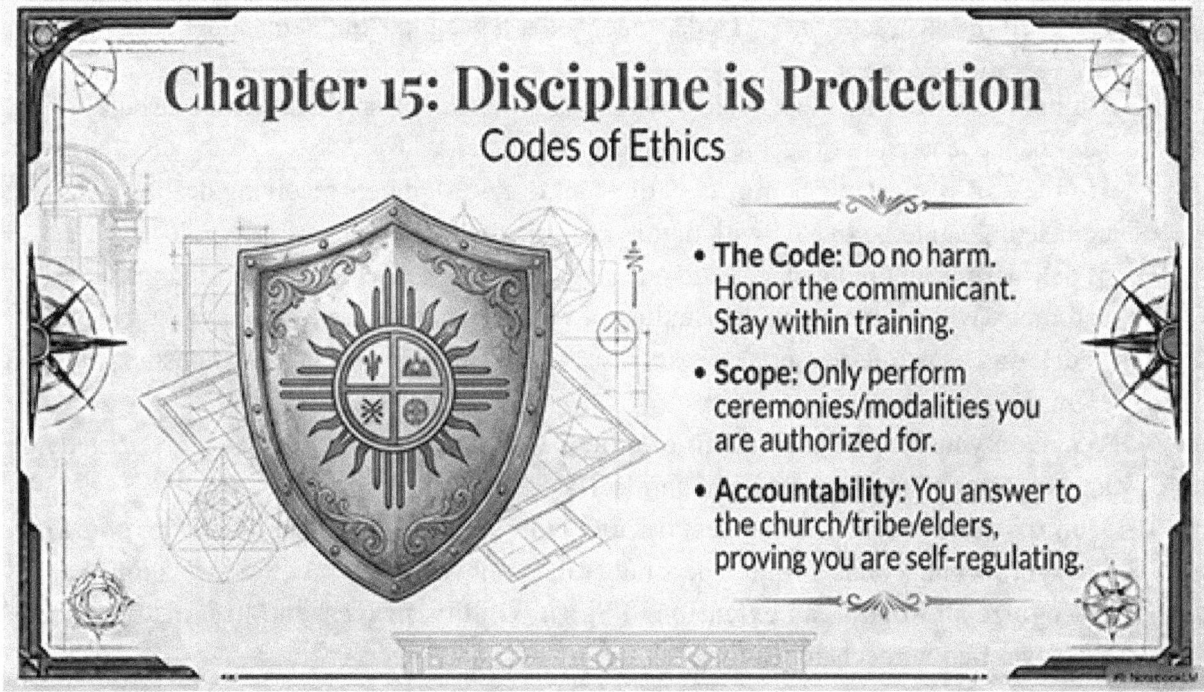

Chapter 15: Discipline is Protection
Codes of Ethics

- **The Code:** Do no harm. Honor the communicant. Stay within training.
- **Scope:** Only perform ceremonies/modalities you are authorized for.
- **Accountability:** You answer to the church/tribe/elders, proving you are self-regulating.

- The core commitments of the NAIC/Chirothesia ethical code and why internal discipline matters legally.
- How to define a realistic, non-medical scope of practice for ministers and healers, and why staying inside it protects you.
- How ethics and scope operate differently, but complementarily, for "everyday" modalities and contentious practices.

The legal structures you have built, tribal sovereignty, church autonomy, and PMA membership, are only as strong as the **ethics** that animate them. Courts and communities alike look for evidence that your ministry is disciplined, compassionate, and self-regulating, not a free-for-all hidden behind religious language. Codes of ethics and clearly defined scopes of practice are how you demonstrate that discipline.

This chapter brings together NAIC's Code of Ethics, Chirothesia principles, and Legal Shield guidance to show what ethical practice looks like for Religious Therapeutics and Indigenous medicine. We will outline core ethical commitments, define a realistic scope of practice for ministers and healers, and explain how staying within that scope strengthens both your spiritual integrity and your legal protection.

1. NAIC's Ethical Core

The NAIC Chirothesia Practitioners' Code centers on a few simple but demanding commitments:

- **Do no harm.** Healers must avoid physical, emotional, and spiritual harm caused by negligence, coercion, or reckless practices.
- **Honor and respect the communicant at all times.** Members receiving healing or counseling are to be treated with dignity, confidentiality, and compassion.
- **Work with informed consent.** No one should be touched, counseled, or led into a ceremony without a clear understanding of what is being offered and the right to say no.
- **Work on the whole person.** Care addresses body, mind, spirit, and relationships, not just symptoms.
- **Work on yourself for the benefit of others.** Ongoing personal practice, prayer, study, and supervision are expected, not optional.
- **Honor your predecessors, ancestors, and elders.** Practitioners are to remain rooted in lineage, seeking counsel from elders rather than reinventing practices in isolation.
- **Recognize all work as an extension of Spirit, vitality, prayer, and breath.** Techniques are never purely mechanical; they are sacramental acts.

The NAIC Code of Ethics explicitly notes that ceremonies such as Birth, Sun Dance, Sweat Lodge, Vision Quest, and Chirothesia-based healing "may carry extreme mental, emotional, and physical transformations," and therefore require special awareness and responsibility from leaders.

2. Scope of Practice: What You Are Authorized to Do

A **scope of practice** defines what you are trained and authorized to do within your religious and tribal role. In the NAIC/ACNM framework, an ordained or commissioned minister/healer may:

- Offer Religious Therapeutics, Chirothesia (laying on of hands), prayer, and anointing as sacramental acts between members.
- Lead or assist in authorized ceremonies (Birth, Sacred Breath, Holy Anointing, Pipe, Sacrament, Sweat Lodge, Vision Quest, etc.) according to their level of training and blessing.
- Provide Indigenous and pastoral counseling, restorative theology, and moral/spiritual guidance.
- Use non-invasive natural modalities (nutrition, herbs, aromatherapy, biomagnetics, somatics, breath, sound, movement, etc.) as religious therapeutics, not as secular medical treatments.

At the same time, the scope explicitly excludes:

- Diagnosing or prescribing for medical or psychological conditions.
- Claiming to prevent, treat, mitigate, or cure disease as defined in state medical practice acts.
- Invasive procedures and potentially toxic pharmaceuticals are reserved for licensed medicine.

NAIC Legal Shield materials stress that "ministerial, pastoral, clerical massage (Chirothesia, Anointing) and/or religious… hands-on healing is by definition the practice of Chirothesia… and in no way refers to the secular practice of 'Massage' or 'Massage Therapy' as defined by various state laws." Staying within that definition is central to your protection.

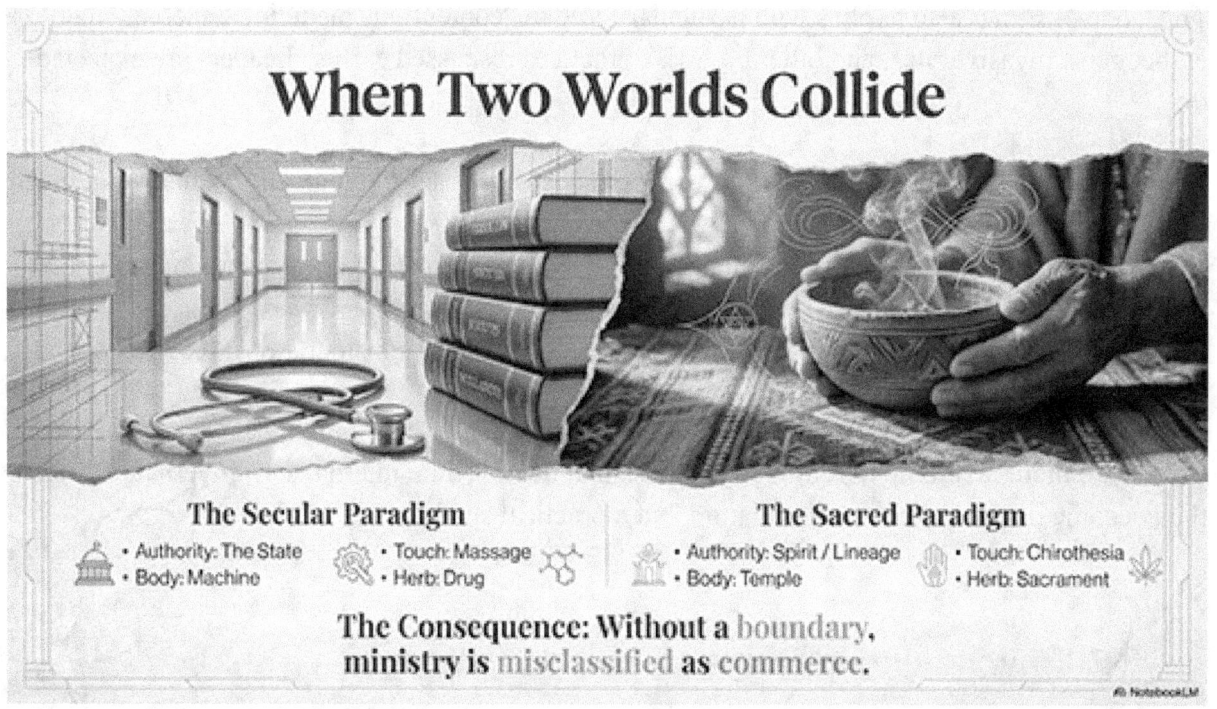

3. Conditions of Practice Under Ecclesiastical Exemptions

If you intend to rely on ecclesiastical or tribal exemptions from medical licensing, several conditions apply:

- You must join and maintain an active membership in a bona fide church or tribal organization (such as NAIC/SMOKH/First Nations Medical Board-FNMB).
- Your training and scope of practice must be defined and overseen by that body through licenses, commissions, ordinations, or similar credentials.

- Your ministry must remain accountable to the church/tribal authority for as long as you practice.
- Those you serve must themselves be members of the church/tribal organization or sign appropriate membership/consent forms, bringing the relationship into the private domain.

Authorization is **not** a "get out of jail free" card. Your practice must be an authentic representation of your church's doctrines and your firmly held beliefs; otherwise, the exemption is at risk of being treated as a pretext.

4. Ethics, Risk, and Controversial Practices

The Code of Ethics also applies with particular force to "contentious medicine", sacramental entheogens, invasive rites, and other high-risk practices discussed earlier. Leaders are expected to:

- Recognize when a ceremony may be too physically or psychologically intense for a given participant.
- Obtain robust informed consent and explain that participation is voluntary and can be stopped at any time.
- Stay within both traditional protocols and modern safety considerations; reckless improvisation is unethical.

Courts are more favorable to religious practices that demonstrate internal self-governance. Ethics thus become not just a spiritual obligation, but a practical shield.

5. Why Staying in Scope Matters Legally

When you adhere to your defined scope of practice and ethical code, you:

- Show regulators that your work is **non-medical** and religious by design.
- Reduce the likelihood that a disgruntled member can plausibly claim you promised secular medical outcomes.
- Strengthen your claim to exemptions in statutes that distinguish "practice of the religious tenets of any church" from secular health-care practice.

If you exceed your scope by using reserved medical titles, performing invasive procedures, or making disease claims, you risk collapsing your religious protections and stepping into regulated territory.

Chapter 15 Conclusion – Discipline as Protection

Ethics and scope of practice are not bureaucratic burdens; they are how you embody your calling and protect your community. They tell the world that your work is serious, accountable, and rooted in a coherent theology and tradition, not in personal whim.

The stronger your internal discipline, the more credible your claim to external freedom. In the next chapter, we turn to the language you use in public, on websites, brochures, and social media, and show how words can either reinforce or unravel the protections you have worked so hard to build.

LEARNING EXERCISE 15.1
Review & Application
Instructions: Select the best answer based on the reading.

1. What is a core commitment of the NAIC Chirothesia Practitioners' Code of Ethics?
   A) Maximize income
   B) Avoid informed consent to preserve spontaneity
   C) Do no harm and honor the communicant at all times
   D) Delegate all decisions to boards
   E) Focus only on physical symptoms
   Correct Answer: C
2. Why is a clearly defined scope of practice so important?
   A) It increases billing codes
   B) It reduces the need for training
   C) It sets realistic boundaries for what you are authorized to do and strengthens legal protection when you remain within them
   D) It is required only for physicians
   E) It replaces ethics codes
   Correct Answer: C
3. Which of the following is *excluded* from the NAIC minister/healer scope?
   A) Prayer and anointing
   B) Indigenous ceremonies
   C) Nutritional and herbal guidance
   D) Invasive procedures and potentially toxic pharmaceuticals are reserved for licensed medicine
   E) Pastoral counseling
   Correct Answer: D
4. How do ecclesiastical exemptions typically function under state law?
   A) They exempt any activity done for money
   B) They cover all commercial clinics
   C) They carve out space for "the practice of the religious tenets of any church" when ministers act within their regular ministerial scope

D) They override criminal law

E) They are purely symbolic

Correct Answer: C

5. What ethical duty is emphasized for "contentious medicine" in this chapter?

   A) Ignore risks if participants consent

   B) Keep protocols secret

   C) Apply heightened caution, consent, screening, and adherence to tradition and safety

   D) Allow minors without conditions

   E) Avoid documentation

   Correct Answer: C

Chapter 16 – Language, Marketing, and the "Forbidden Words"

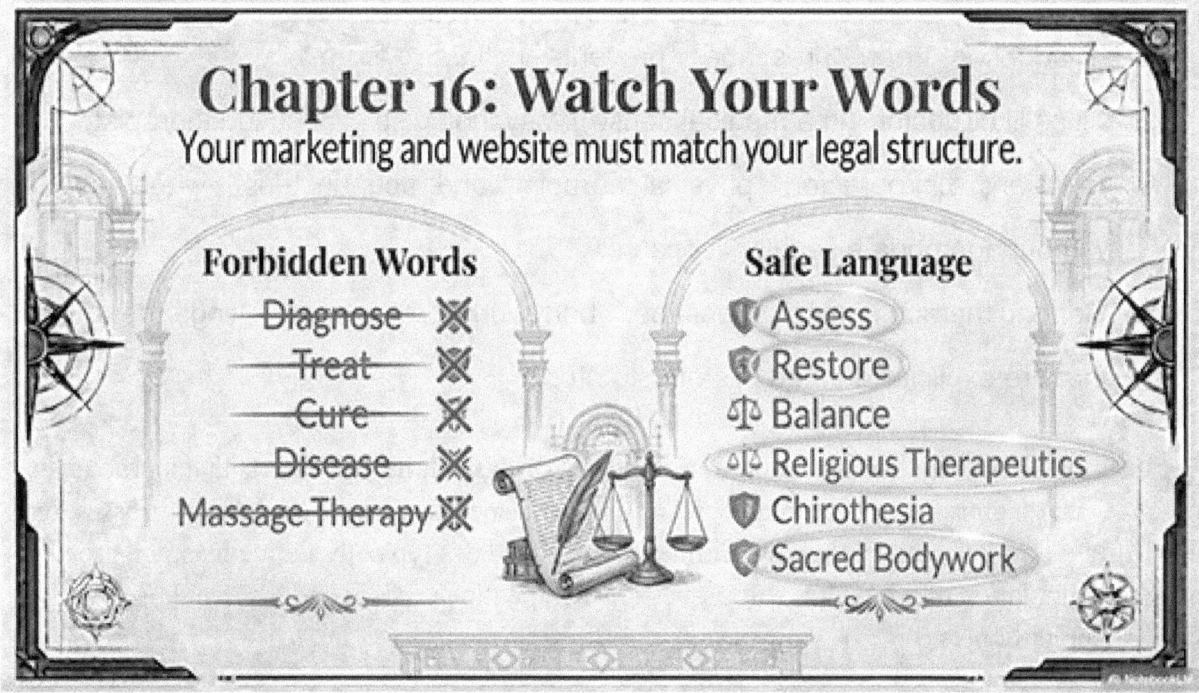

- Why certain verbs and titles ("diagnose," "treat," "massage," "bodywork") trigger regulation and board jurisdiction.
- Safer lineage-specific and religious descriptors you can use in websites, brochures, and social media.
- How DSHEA "structure/function" language and careful online presentation keep your outreach aligned with your legal framework.

You can have perfect ethics and a clean scope of practice and still create legal trouble with your **words**. Regulators do not attend your ceremonies; they review your website, business card, intake forms, and social media posts. If what they see looks like secular medicine or massage, they will treat you that way.

This chapter explains why certain words and phrases are "forbidden" or high-risk in marketing, how FDA and state standards interpret disease claims, and how to choose safer language that still truthfully describes your Religious Therapeutics and Indigenous medicine. We will contrast generic, regulated labels with NAIC-approved descriptors and show how consistent language can keep you inside the private, religious domain.

1. Why Words Trigger Regulation

Medical and allied-health boards typically define their jurisdiction partly by **terms of art**:

- "Diagnose," "treat," "prescribe," "prevent," "mitigate," "cure."

- Titles like "doctor" (in a medical sense), "psychologist," "massage therapist," "dietitian," "chiropractor," "physical therapist," and "acupuncturist," when used without appropriate secular licensure.

- Generic therapy names ("massage," "bodywork," "reflexology," "yoga therapy") that are explicitly defined in state statutes.

For example, FDA regulations treat a statement as a **disease claim** if it asserts that a product or practice can diagnose, mitigate, treat, cure, or prevent a specific disease or class of diseases, or is a substitute for a recognized therapy. Similarly, massage laws typically define massage broadly as the manipulation of the body's soft tissues for therapeutic purposes and reserve those terms for licensed practitioners.

If you use this language in a secular, public-facing way, you invite agencies to regulate you, even if your actual work is religious.

2. The "Forbidden Words."

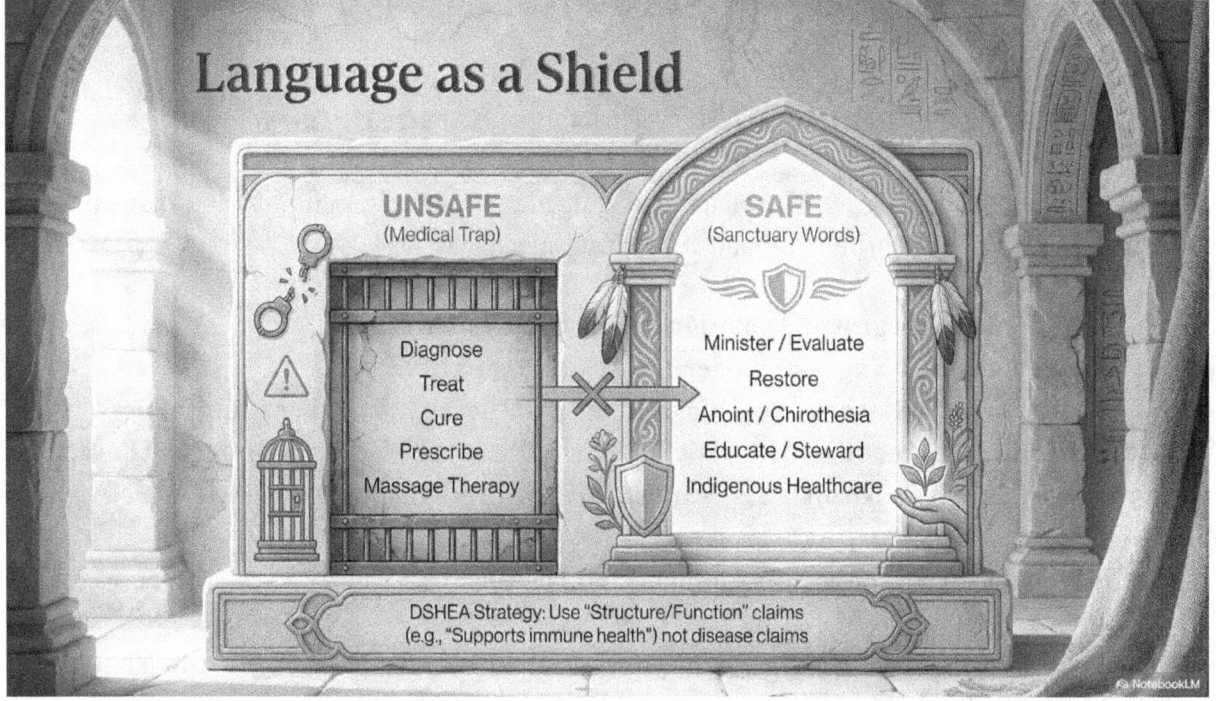

Based on NAIC legal guidance, you should avoid using the following terms in marketing or public communications **unless** they are clearly situated within an ecclesiastical/religious context and you are willing to defend that usage:

- Diagnose
- Prescribe
- Treat (especially in connection with massage or manual therapy)
- Prevent
- Mitigate
- Cure

In addition, generic therapy labels are risky, particularly when used alone without religious qualifiers:

- Massage, Massage Therapy
- Bodywork, Bodywork Therapy
- Thai Massage, Thai Yoga Therapy, Thai Bodywork
- Reflexology (in a secular, standalone sense)
- "Yoga Therapy" in jurisdictions moving toward yoga licensing.

NAIC explicitly advises: "Let's be clear. If the term of medical practice is defined and limited by a State Medical Board… refrain from using it!"

3. Safer Descriptions for Religious Therapeutics

Instead of regulated generic terms, you are encouraged to use precise religious and Indigenous descriptors that reflect your training and authorization, such as:

- **SomaVeda® Integrated Traditional Therapies®: Thai Yoga**
- **Indigenous Thai Yoga** or **Indigenous Traditional Thai Yoga**
- **Thai Sacred Bodywork, Thai Yoga Religious Therapy, Thai Sacred Healing**
- **Religious Therapeutics, Monastic Medicine, Pastoral Medicine, Pastoral Therapy**
- **Native American Medicine** or **Native American Indigenous Medicine** (with NAIC authorization).
- **Indigenous (clerical/pastoral/ministerial) Healthcare, Healing Science, Counseling, and Medicine (IHSM)**
- **Ayurveda Wellness Counseling, Ayurveda Health Consultant, Ayurveda Yoga Therapist** for those with appropriate ecclesiastical credentials.

These terms signal that your work is:

- Rooted in a particular lineage (SomaVeda®, NAIC, SMOKH, etc.).
- Religious/pastoral in nature, not generic clinical services.
- Carried out within church/tribal and PMA frameworks, not as public commerce.

4. DSHEA and Structure/Function Language

If you recommend herbs, supplements, or nutritional approaches, you should follow the Dietary Supplement Health and Education Act (DSHEA) pattern:

- Use **structure/function** language ("supports immune function," "helps maintain joint flexibility," "promotes relaxation") rather than disease claims ("treats arthritis," "cures depression").
- Include disclaimers such as: "The Food and Drug Administration has not evaluated these statements. This product (or service) is not intended to diagnose, treat, cure, or prevent any disease."

When combined with your ecclesiastical framing ("Religious Therapeutics," "Indigenous Healthcare") and membership-only context, this language helps show that you are not marketing unapproved medical treatments but offering spiritual and wellness support consistent with federal guidelines.

5. Internet Presence and Meta-Language

Your online presence is often the first and only thing regulators see. NAIC recommends:

- Keeping overt marketing and practice information on a **"fan page"** or organizational page clearly branded with church/tribal identity (NAIC, SMOKH, Priory, ACNM).
- Using **cross-links** to official NAIC and ACNM sites (NativeFireChurch.org, naic.edu.org, thaiyogacenter.com, etc.) to contextualize your work.
- Avoiding risky meta-tags and hidden text (e.g., stuffing "cure cancer" into page metadata), which can be used as evidence of intent to market medical services.

The goal is not to hide what you do, but to describe it truthfully within its proper religious and tribal paradigm.

6. Distinguishing Dual Roles

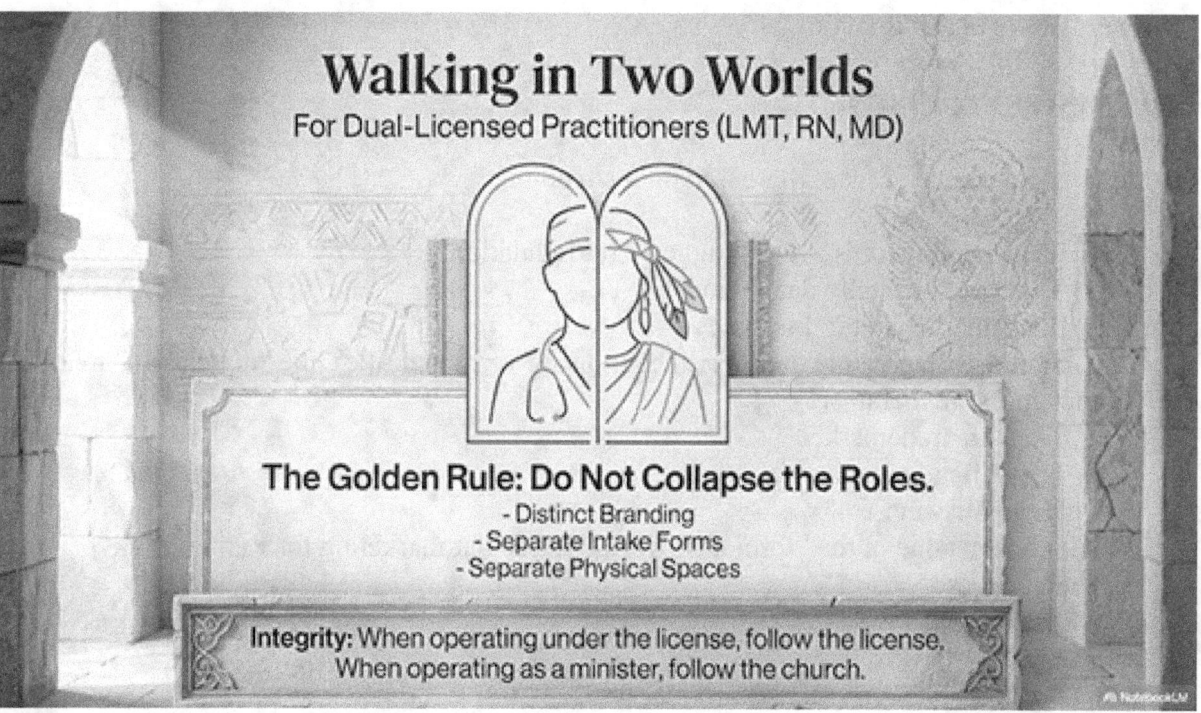

Walking in Two Worlds
For Dual-Licensed Practitioners (LMT, RN, MD)

The Golden Rule: Do Not Collapse the Roles.
- Distinct Branding
- Separate Intake Forms
- Separate Physical Spaces

Integrity: When operating under the license, follow the license. When operating as a minister, follow the church.

If you also hold secular licenses (LMT, RN, counselor, etc.), it is crucial not to collapse your **licensed** role and your **religious** role in your language. You should:

- Maintain clear separation of business names, websites, and marketing between secular practice and ecclesiastical/PMA practice.
- Avoid implying that your secular license covers your religious work or vice versa.
- Be prepared to explain, if asked, which hat you are wearing in any given context.

NAIC often counsels dual-role practitioners individually on how to design strategies that preserve both roles without confusing boards and clients.

Chapter 16 Conclusion – Speaking the Language of Your Sanctuary

Language is one of your most powerful tools. Used carelessly, it can drag your ministry into systems it was never meant to inhabit; used wisely, it can clarify that you live and work in a different legal and spiritual neighborhood.

By avoiding forbidden words, choosing lineage-specific and religious descriptors, and aligning your public communications with your actual ethical scope, you help everyone, members, regulators, and yourself, see your work for what it truly is: Indigenous Religious Therapeutics, not unlicensed secular medicine. In the next chapter, we will explore how to structure your ministry or tribal clinic so that your physical spaces and daily operations match the sanctuary your words have begun to build.

LEARNING EXERCISE 16.1
Review & Application
Instructions: Select the best answer based on the reading.

1. Why do certain words act as "triggers" for regulation?
   A) They are spiritually dangerous
   B) They are difficult to translate
   C) Statutes often define their jurisdiction using verbs and titles like "diagnose," "treat," and "massage therapist."
   D) They are trademarked
   E) They offend patients
   Correct Answer: C
2. Which is *not* one of the "forbidden words" in secular marketing for Religious Therapeutics?
   A) Diagnose
   B) Treat
   C) Prevent
   D) Cure

E) Bless
Correct Answer: E

3. What is the main advantage of using lineage-specific and religious descriptors (e.g., "SomaVeda® Thai Yoga Religious Therapy")?
   A) They guarantee better SEO
   B) They automatically grant licensure
   C) They signal that your work belongs to a specific religious/Indigenous framework rather than generic, regulated clinical categories
   D) They are legally required in all states
   E) They avoid all scrutiny
   Correct Answer: C

4. How does DSHEA-style "structure/function" language help when talking about herbs or nutrition?
   A) It allows disease-treatment claims
   B) It removes the need for disclaimers
   C) It frames support in terms of body functions ("supports immune function") rather than claims to treat diseases
   D) It applies only to prescription drugs
   E) It is required only for physicians
   Correct Answer: C

5. What guidance is given for online presence?
   A) Mix all roles and brands on one page
   B) Use disease names heavily in meta-tags
   C) Clearly brand ministry pages as church/tribal/PMA, avoid regulated terms, and link to official NAIC/ACNM resources for context
   D) Avoid referencing any legal framework
   E) Hide all contact information
   Correct Answer: C

Chapter 17 – Structuring Your Ministry or Tribal Clinic

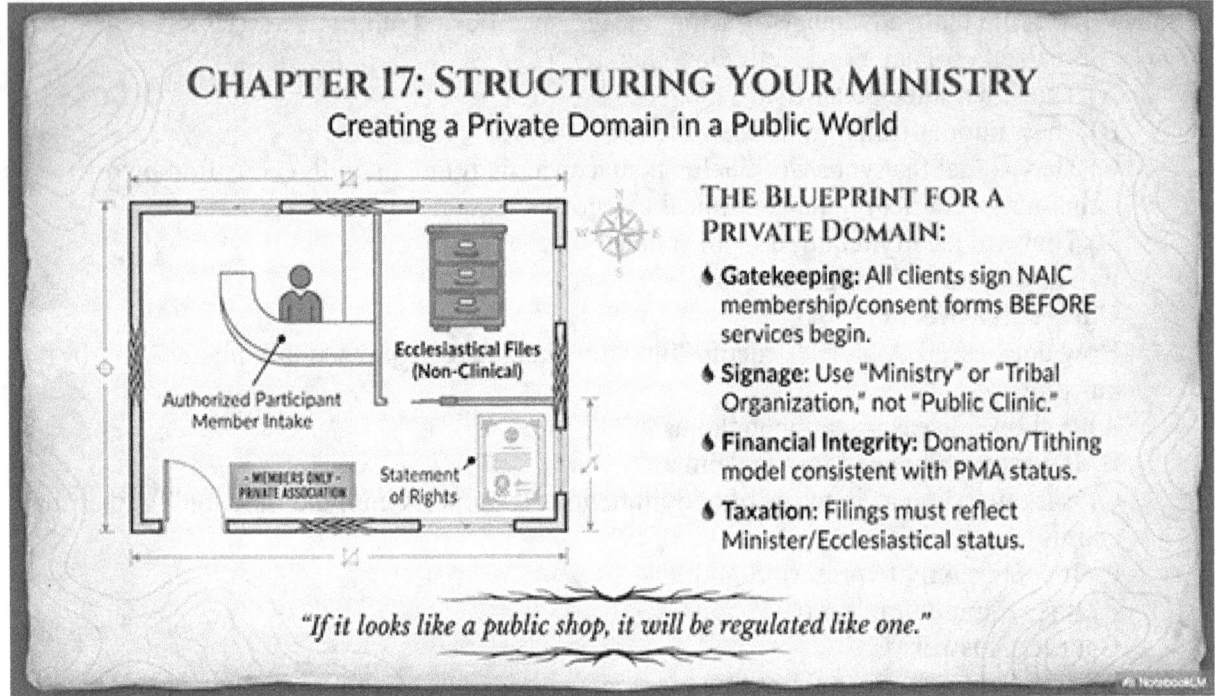

CHAPTER 17: STRUCTURING YOUR MINISTRY
Creating a Private Domain in a Public World

Authorized Participant Member Intake

Ecclesiastical Files (Non-Clinical)

- MEMBERS ONLY - PRIVATE ASSOCIATION

Statement of Rights

THE BLUEPRINT FOR A PRIVATE DOMAIN:

- **Gatekeeping:** All clients sign NAIC membership/consent forms BEFORE services begin.
- **Signage:** Use "Ministry" or "Tribal Organization," not "Public Clinic."
- **Financial Integrity:** Donation/Tithing model consistent with PMA status.
- **Taxation:** Filings must reflect Minister/Ecclesiastical status.

"If it looks like a public shop, it will be regulated like one."

- Practical steps for organizing a home office, shared space, or full clinic so it looks and functions like a ministry, not a public shop.
- How membership-only policies, PMA structures, and (when needed) RLUIPA notices create a real private domain.
- How to keep ecclesiastical/tribal work distinct from any secular practice that shares your name or building.

Your theology and legal theory only come alive when they are built into the **structure** of your day-to-day work. Whether you serve from a spare room in your home, a shared office, or a full tribal clinic, the way you organize membership, space, paperwork, and authority determines whether your practice looks like public commerce or protected ministry. This chapter shows how to design your ministry or clinic so that every element, door sign, intake process, website, and accounting, points clearly to the ecclesiastical, tribal, and PMA umbrellas you have chosen.

We will begin with the core rule for NAIC and similar structures: you serve only members/communicants and work only on members/communicants. From there, we will look at concrete steps for structuring a home-based ministry, shared space, or larger clinic, including membership enrollment, informed consent processes, and when and how to notify local zoning authorities under RLUIPA. Finally, we will touch on branch churches and integrated auxiliaries for those who feel called to build full tribal clinics under NAIC and Priory of Saving Grace.

1. Members First, Members Only

The "Sacred Hands, Secured Rights" Legal Guidelines lay out a simple but non-negotiable foundation for structuring a Religious Therapeutics practice:

1. All clients join NAIC (and/or an NAIC Authorized Independent Branch) as Authorized Participant Members (APM) or equivalent (FNMB, Nemenha Band, SMOKH, Gold Care Wellness etc.)
2. You serve only member communicants and work only with them.
3. If a member of the public seeks help, they must either join the church/PMA or sign the appropriate NAIC membership and consent forms (APM, AFM) before receiving services.

By doing this, you move the interaction out of the public marketplace and into the **private, ecclesiastical, and tribal domain** of a First and Fourteenth Amendment association. Members acknowledge that you are an authorized NAIC minister/practitioner and that they receive services as fellow members, not as public patients of a secular clinic.

2. Home Offices, Shared Spaces, and RLUIPA

The Guidelines make clear that you have the right as a minister to express, practice, and share your healing work "anywhere a minister of any religion can go": in a home office, shared office space, hospital, or other venues where ministry is welcomed. At the same time, practical and legal considerations apply:

- **Home Office:** You may need a professional home-office rider from your homeowner's insurance to cover ministry activities.
- **Zoning and Special Exceptions:** While the Religious Land Use and Institutionalized Persons Act of 2000 (RLUIPA) establishes your right to conduct and practice ceremonies and healing without discriminatory burdens, it can still be wise to notify your county or city that you are operating a religious or pastoral ministry from a given address. They cannot lawfully deny you the right to practice your ministry, but you may need to file for a "religious exception" or similar designation to avoid misunderstandings. The "equal terms" concept appears in § 2000cc(b)(1) ("less than equal terms with a nonreligious assembly or institution").
- **Shared Offices and Institutional Settings:** You can share office space or see members in hospitals and other facilities, provided you remain clear that you are operating as a minister, not under any secular clinical license that those institutions may host.

RLUIPA gives you leverage if a locality tries to single you out or impose burdens not placed on comparable secular uses. Still, it is always better to build cooperative, informed relationships where possible.

3. Branch Churches and Tribal Clinics

If you feel called to expand beyond a solo ministry, NAIC provides a path for creating a more formal structure:

- You may apply for an **NAIC Branch** to serve as an integrated auxiliary, independent affiliate of NAIC, functioning as a local church or tribal organization.
- For full clinics, especially those integrating secular services under supervision, NAIC recommends applying for a Branch. Several state-certified medical clinics are already operating under this layered ecclesiastical and tribal supervision.

Regardless of scale, the same principles apply: clear membership, internal governance, adherence to the NAIC Code of Ethics, and a defined scope of practice that remains within Religious Therapeutics and Indigenous medicine.

4. Keeping Ministry and Secular Work Distinct

Many practitioners are already licensed in secular professions (massage therapy, nursing, counseling, etc.). The Guidelines warn that it is "vitally important that you do not collapse" your NAIC Religious Therapeutics work with your secular therapy practice. You must:

- Create clear **distinctions** between your healing ministry and any state-licensed services.
- Use separate branding, paperwork, and (ideally) scheduling systems when acting as a licensed provider versus as an NAIC minister.
- Be ready to explain, if asked, under which authority you were acting in any given interaction.

In practice, it is often safest to keep your NAIC work within the PMA/church framework and avoid mixing it with insurance-billed or employer-controlled clinical services.

5. Financial Structure: Ministers Can Make a Living

The Guidelines make an important point: **for licensing purposes, it does not matter whether you charge or how much you charge.** All ministers can make a living. What matters is how you define and structure the work.

- Tithes, offerings, suggested donations, and set fees can all support the ministry, provided they are consistent with church/tribal policies.
- NAIC suggests tithing (e.g., 10% of net income) to support the tribal organization's offices, infrastructure, and expansion, as most churches request from ministers.
- Filing your taxes as a **minister** further supports the claim that this is your primary vocational identity.

As long as your practice is genuine ministry within scope, charging for services does not turn it into secular medicine or massage.

Structuring the Sanctuary: Essential Paperwork

Documentation is the evidence of your sanctuary.

Membership Agreement

Establishes the Private Membership Association (PMA).

Explicitly states: "I am not a patient; I am a member."

Informed Consent

Explicit Disclaimers. "I do not diagnose or treat medical conditions." Member assumes assumes responsibility.

Code of Ethics

Demonstrates self-regulation. Do no harm, honor the communicant, stay within scope.

Wilson's Practical Parallels

Dr. Lawrence Wilson's *Legal Guidelines for Unlicensed Practitioners* reaches many of the same conclusions about structure that this chapter does, but from a general legal-risk perspective. He emphasizes that how you **present** your work, your titles, signage, paperwork, and corporate form often matters as much as what you actually do. If you describe yourself as "treating disease," call your space a "medical office," and use medical language in advertising, courts and boards will tend to interpret your work as practicing medicine regardless of your inner intentions.

Wilson recommends several safeguards that mirror NAIC's structural approach:

- Use **clear titles and descriptions**, avoiding medical jargon and instead emphasizing education, consultation, and support.
- Choose a **legal form** that fits your purpose, church, association, or other entity, rather than operating as a lone individual, and keep your activities clearly within that entity's stated purposes.
- Maintain simple, accurate **records** and clear office policies that show you stay within your declared scope and refer out when issues exceed it.

NAIC's layered umbrella, church/tribal organization, plus PMA, implements these same principles in a Native and religious key. By building your ministry or clinic inside that framework and using NAIC-style language and forms, you are essentially doing what Wilson advises holistic practitioners to do everywhere: align your structure, words, and deeds so regulators see a consistent, non-medical helping role rather than a shadow medical practice.

Chapter 17 Conclusion – Making Your Structure Match Your Calling

A ministry or tribal clinic that is structured as a public wellness shop will be treated like one, regardless of your inner intentions. But when your membership procedures, locations, branding, and governance all align with your ecclesiastical and tribal umbrellas, your outer form matches your inner call.

Structuring your practice well is not bureaucracy; it is part of your stewardship. It tells your people, and any outsider who looks in, that you know who you are, whom you serve, and under whose authority you heal.

LEARNING EXERCISE 17.1
Review & Application
Instructions: Select the best answer based on the reading.

1. What is the "core rule" for NAIC-style ministry or clinic structure?
   A) Serve anyone who walks in
   B) Only serve minors
   C) Only and exclusively serve members/communicants, and only work on members/communicants
   D) Avoid written agreements
   E) Operate only online
   Correct Answer: C
2. How does RLUIPA support home or small-scale ministries?
   A) By funding building projects
   B) By forbidding any zoning regulation
   C) By requiring strict scrutiny when land-use rules substantially burden religious exercise
   D) By licensing counselors
   E) By setting fee schedules
   Correct Answer: C
3. Why is it vital not to "collapse" NAIC Religious Therapeutics with secular therapy practice for dual-licensed practitioners?
   A) It reduces income
   B) It confuses friends and family
   C) It can blur legal boundaries, inviting boards to treat religious work as regulated practice
   D) It prevents the use of herbs
   E) It invalidates ordination
   Correct Answer: C

4. What structural choice best signals that a practice is a ministry rather than a public shop?
   A) Walk-in hours posted on a street sign
   B) Insurance billing for all services
   C) Membership-only intake, NAIC/tribal branding, consent forms, and ecclesiastical governance
   D) Use of hospital gowns
   E) Display of pharmaceutical samples
   Correct Answer: C
5. What does the chapter say about ministers and income?
   A) Ministers must work for free
   B) Ministers can never accept donations
   C) Ministers can make a living from their ministry; what matters is how the work is defined and structured, not whether money changes hands
   D) Ministers must work only in hospitals
   E) Ministers must be paid only by the State
   Correct Answer: C

Figure 5, Crow Adoption Ceremony. Dr. Anthony B. James Adopted by Crow Tribe, Whisling Water Clan, Realbird Family, Chief Floyd Realbird, Chief Charlie Realbird. 1992 Medicine Tail Coulee, on the banks of the Little Big Horn River

Chapter 18 – Licensure, Insurance, and Interaction with Regulators

CHAPTER 18: LICENSURE & REGULATORS
Standing Calm at the Door

DON'T	DO
♦ Panic or ask boards for permission.	♦ Identify as Authorized NAIC Minister.
♦ Pre-emptively ask "Am I legal?"	♦ Point to PMA Membership & Consent forms.
♦ Imply secular insurance covers religious acts.	♦ Distinguish *Mala in se* (Evil) vs. *Mala prohibita* (Regulatory).
	♦ Assert Ecclesiastical Jurisdiction.

"You are not sneaking around the law; you are standing in a doorway the law carved for religious healing."

> ᐅ When secular licenses are appropriate, when ecclesiastical/tribal exemptions apply, and how they differ.
> ᐅ How liability and insurance look inside a private religious association versus in public secular practice.
> ᐅ Dos and don'ts for responding to boards or investigators without panic or "sovereign citizen" rhetoric.

Even in the best-structured ministry, questions arise: "Do I need a state license?" "Should I carry liability insurance?" "What do I do if a board or investigator contacts me?" This chapter addresses those questions from the standpoint laid out in the Guidelines: your work is Religious Therapeutics and Indigenous medicine, not secular health care, and exemptions are **not** loopholes but explicitly recognized exceptions in law.

We will first clarify when secular licenses are helpful, when they are irrelevant, and when they can actually complicate your religious practice. We will then examine the role of liability insurance in a private ecclesiastical context. Finally, we will outline practical advice for responding to regulators or law enforcement officers, grounded in the NAIC legal framework and case-law distinctions between mala in se and mala prohibita.

1. When Licensure Applies, and When It Does Not

The Guidelines identify four legal systems under which CAM and natural medicine can be practiced: secular licensure, religious/ecclesiastical authority, Native American/tribal jurisdiction, and expressive Private Membership Associations. Your need for a **secular** license depends on which umbrella you stand under:

- If your practice is secular, corporate, and aimed at the general public, you belong under the **secular umbrella** and must comply with state medical, massage, or allied-health licensing.
- If your practice is spiritual, religious, Indigenous, and based on faith in the unseen and sacred texts, you are directed to go **ecclesiastical and/or tribal**, where exemptions from state medical licensing exist by statute and precedent.
- PMAs add a shield but are safest when nested within ecclesiastical and tribal structures, not used alone.

Under many state statutes, activities that qualify as "the practice of the religious tenets of any church" and that are performed under the auspices of an established church, with accountability to that church, are **explicitly exempt** from medical or psychology licensing. Florida, for example, exempts clergy performing duties within their regular ministerial scope (with no separate charge) or under church auspices from psychological and medical practice statutes. (**Fla. Stat. § 490.014(1)(f)** "under the auspices… of an established and legally cognizable church," and "remains accountable").)

If you are ordained or commissioned by an established and legally cognizable church or tribal organization (e.g., NAIC, Priory of Saving Grace, SMOKH), and your services stay within your defined religious scope, you may be exempt from state and federal medical licensing requirements, including massage laws.

2. Exemptions Are Not Loopholes

The Guidelines emphasize that "legal exemptions are not loopholes." A loophole exploits ambiguity; an exemption is a **clear, intentional exception** built into law:

- AIRFA and RFRA create broad protections for Indigenous and religious practices.
- State statutes carve out exceptions for "the practice of the religious tenets of any church."
- Federal FMLA guidance and IHCIA provisions recognize traditional healers as health care providers and legitimate participants in care.

When you operate openly as a minister or medicine person under a bona fide tribal/church structure, and within your defined scope, you are not evading the law; you are exercising a right the law intentionally preserves.

3. Liability Insurance in a Private Religious Context

Because your services are not secular "massage" or "medicine," the Guidelines argue that you are not engaged in a high-risk, invasive profession that routinely requires liability insurance. They note that "no one has ever died from receiving SomaVeda® Therapies… ever," and that work occurs only with NAIC members who have agreed to private jurisdiction and internal arbitration.

Key points:

- NAIC members agree in advance that services are private, privileged, and under church jurisdiction, and that any claims of injury will be handled through the church's arbitration process.
- As long as your practice is genuine and within scope, and you follow NAIC's Code of Ethics and consent procedures, you are "protected from liability" within this private, ecclesiastical framework.
- If, despite this, you still wish to obtain a policy, NAIC can recommend insurers that have already recognized SomaVeda® Thai Yoga as a Yoga/Yoga Therapy-type somatic practice.

Insurance can be a personal prudential choice, but it is not legally mandated in the same way it is for many secular professions, because your practice exists in a different legal and risk category.

4. Interaction with Regulators: Do's and Don'ts

The Guidelines offer several practical cautions about regulators:

- **Do not pre-emptively contact massage or medical boards "to see if you are legal."** These boards know little or nothing about Religious Therapeutics, Chirothesia, Indigenous medicine, or tribal law, and their mandate is to regulate secular practice, not to advise churches.
- If contacted by a board or agency, your **primary defense** is that you are an Authorized NAIC Minister (or equivalent) practicing a healing ministry, religious therapy, based on your education and authorization from the church/tribal organization.

- You can point to your structure: PMA membership, informed-consent forms, NAIC Articles of Religious Practice, and the clear statement that you do not practice medicine as defined by state acts.
- Remember the distinction between **mala in se** and **mala prohibita**: your authorized religious acts, when non-harmful and within scope, are at worst mala prohibita and are explicitly exempted by federal and state statute when properly structured. Criminal acts that are mala in se (violence, abuse, exploitation) are never protected.

If a situation escalates beyond simple clarification, the Guidelines strongly recommend consulting an attorney familiar with federal Indian law, constitutional law, and your state's medical and allied-health statutes.

5. Dual-Licensed Practitioners

For those who are already licensed (LMTs, RNs, counselors, etc.), the text stresses that you must not **collapse** NAIC, Church, Ministry, or Inter-tribal based Religious Therapeutics with secular practice:

- Keep your NAIC, Church, Ministry, or Inter-tribal-based Religious Therapeutics work distinct in branding, paperwork, and context.
- Do not imply that your state license covers your religious services or that your religious status alters the scope of your secular license.
- Seek individualized guidance from NAIC/Legal Shield if you intend to maintain both types of work.

Done well, dual roles can complement each other; done carelessly, they can undermine both your secular standing and your ecclesiastical protections.

Special Notes: Licensure, Insurance, and Interaction with Regulators

Wilson's Insights on Avoiding Legal Trouble

Wilson's manual is written for "unlicensed practitioners," but much of his advice applies equally to religious and Indigenous healers, and even to licensed professionals who also offer non-medical services. He stresses three themes that echo this chapter:

1. **Words matter.**

   Wilson explains that statutes often hinge on verbs like "diagnose," "treat," "prescribe," and phrases like "practicing any system or mode of treating the sick." Courts look at how you describe your work to decide whether you fall under a medical practice act. NAIC's insistence that you avoid those words in a secular sense and instead speak of "Religious Therapeutics," "counsel," "education," and "ceremony" is a direct application of this principle.

2. **Consent, disclaimer, and disclosure.**

   Wilson devotes an entire chapter to well-drafted consent, disclaimer, and disclosure statements as a key line of defense, both ethically and legally. He recommends telling clients plainly what you do, what you do not do, and urging them to seek licensed medical care as needed. NAIC's membership and informed-consent forms, stating that you do not diagnose or treat, that your work is spiritual and Indigenous, and that members retain full freedom to use conventional care, embody this same approach in a church/tribal format.

3. **Professional demeanor and cooperation.**

   Wilson cautions that, should authorities ever inquire, practitioners who are calm, respectful, and clear about their non-medical role fare better than those who are evasive or hostile. This aligns with the guidance here: if regulators contact you, you respond as an authorized minister/medicine person, explain your ecclesiastical and tribal scope, and, when necessary, refer questions to your organization's leadership or counsel, never claiming to be "above" the law, but protected *by* specific laws.

Read alongside this chapter, Wilson's book confirms that NAIC's Legal Shield model is not an eccentric invention; it is a careful, Indigenous-context adaptation of best practices that many holistic and unlicensed practitioners have used successfully for years.

Chapter 18 Conclusion – Standing Calm at the Door

Licensure, insurance, and regulators can feel intimidating, especially for those who have seen colleagues harassed or misunderstood. But when you understand where secular licensing truly applies, how your exemptions work, and how to present your ministry as what it is, much of the fear drains away.

You are not sneaking around the edges of the law; you are standing in a doorway the law itself has carved for religious and Indigenous healing. With clear structure, honest consent, sound ethics, and steady communication, you can meet regulators without panic, knowing both your rights and your responsibilities.

LEARNING EXERCISE 18.1
Review & Application
Instructions: Select the best answer based on the reading.

1. When is secular licensure the appropriate umbrella?
    A) When all work is purely sacramental
    B) When practice is secular, corporate, aimed at the general public, and fits regulated scopes like medicine, massage, or psychology
    C) When no money is charged
    D) When services are only online
    E) When practice occurs on tribal land
    Correct Answer: B

2. How do ecclesiastical and tribal exemptions differ from "loopholes"?
    A) They are secret tricks
    B) They exploit drafting errors
    C) They are intentional, written-in exceptions recognizing religious and Indigenous practice
    D) They are temporary until regulations tighten
    E) They are unenforceable
    Correct Answer: C

3. What does the chapter say about liability insurance for NAIC-style religious practice?
    A) It is always required by law
    B) It is illegal
    C) It may be less central in a non-invasive, member-only, ecclesiastical context governed by internal arbitration, though some may still choose it
    D) It guarantees immunity
    E) It replaces ethics
    Correct Answer: C

4. What is advised regarding contacting boards preemptively about Religious Therapeutics?
    A) Always ask boards to approve your theology
    B) Send them your ceremony calendar
    C) Do not rely on boards for guidance about ecclesiastical/tribal work, as they are mandated to regulate secular practice and know little about religious frameworks
    D) Request that they regulate your church
    E) Ask them to ordain you
    Correct Answer: C

5. For dual-licensed practitioners, what is the key recommendation?
    A) Use one title for everything
    B) Blend all roles in one chart
    C) Keep NAIC/church/tribal Religious Therapeutics distinct from secular licensed services in branding, paperwork, and context
    D) Surrender all secular licenses
    E) Avoid all documentation
    Correct Answer: C

PART V- Global Context and Historical Roots

The legal and ecclesiastical structures you have studied so far do not exist in a vacuum. They are part of a much larger story in which nations, churches, Indigenous peoples, and international bodies have wrestled with a simple but revolutionary idea: **health is a human right, and traditional, familial, and faith-based medicines are part of that right, not an exception to it.** This Part traces that wider horizon so you can see your own Religious Therapeutics and Indigenous practice not as a private workaround but as a legitimate expression of global principles that have emerged for centuries.

PART V
GLOBAL CONTEXT & HISTORICAL ROOTS
HEALTH AS A HUMAN RIGHT & THE INTERNATIONAL SHIELD

• Validating practice through International Law
• Health beyond the biological model
• Protection against biopiracy

We begin with the modern human rights framework and primary health care movements, documents such as the Universal Declaration of Human Rights and the Declaration of Alma-Ata, that declare health and well-being a universal right and affirm the role of communities and cultures in defining and delivering care. These texts opened philosophical and legal space for non-biomedical approaches, especially at the community level, long before "CAM" became a marketing label. They help explain why the WHO and many national systems now take seriously the integration of traditional and complementary medicine rather than erasing it.

From there, we turn to specifically Indigenous instruments, UNDRIP, the OCAP® principles, and the Nagoya Protocol, that address who owns traditional medicines, who controls data about Indigenous peoples, and who benefits when tribal knowledge is commercialized. These documents form what this book calls an "international shield" around your ceremonies, plants, and knowledge, insisting that Indigenous healing is not a relic but a sovereign science to be respected and protected.

Finally, we look back to European and common-law history, to the Herbalist Charter of Henry VIII and similar moments when the law explicitly protected lay herbalists and folk practitioners against emerging medical monopolies. By linking that history to today's debates about iatrogenic harm, scientism, and overregulation, Part V shows that your insistence on low-tech, non-invasive, spiritually grounded care has deep precedents.

Taken together, these chapters give you a wide-angle lens: they show that when you stand as an NAIC minister, Indigenous healer, or traditional naturopath under a lawful ecclesiastical and tribal umbrella, you are not hiding from the modern world. You are standing inside a global and historical current that has long recognized the right of peoples to care for their own, in their own way, with their own sacred medicines.

Chapter 19 – Health as a Human Right: Alma-Ata and Beyond

CHAPTER 19: HEALTH AS A HUMAN RIGHT
The Mandate for Community Care

1948 - Universal Declaration of Human Rights.
Health is a fundamental right.

1978 - Declaration of Alma-Ata.
Primary Health Care must be socially acceptable & include community participation.

TODAY - Modern Indigenous Healthcare.
Fulfilling the global mandate.

THE GLOBAL CONSENSUS:

WHO Definition: Health is complete physical, mental, and social well-being, not just absence of disease.
Your Practice: Family remedies and tribal ceremonies are legitimate expressions of this human right.

"No government holds a monopoly on how people care for one another."

- ﾞ What international human-rights instruments and WHO policies define health as a fundamental right tied to community participation?
- ﾞ How primary health care and "health for all" frameworks implicitly support community healers and non-biomedical approaches.
- ﾞ Why your Religious Therapeutics practice fits within, not outside, this global right-to-health horizon.

When you insist that your people have a right to their own medicine, you are not speaking only from scripture or tradition; you are standing inside a global human-rights consensus. International declarations and covenants, along with WHO policy, *"affirm that health is a fundamental human right, that people must participate in decisions about their own care, and that primary health care includes community-based, culturally grounded approaches, not just hospital medicine."* This chapter traces that thread from the Universal Declaration of Human Rights through the Alma-Ata Declaration and later instruments that support Indigenous and family-based healing. (https://www.who.int/publications/i/item/9789241506096)

We will begin with the **Universal Declaration of Human Rights** and related covenants that establish a right to an adequate standard of health and well-being. We then turn to the **1978 Alma-Ata Declaration**, in which many WHO member states agreed that health is a human right and that primary health care, delivered with community participation and self-determination, is the path toward "health for all." Finally, we will look at how these global frameworks support community healers, "Grandma Doc" remedies, and non-standard, non-allopathic practices as legitimate components of the right to health, including in the United States. (https://www.who.int/publications/i/item/declaration-of-alma-ata)

1. Human Rights Foundations: UDHR and Beyond

Article 25 of the **Universal Declaration of Human Rights (UDHR)** states that "everyone has the right to a standard of living adequate for the health and well-being of himself and of his family, including food, clothing, housing, and medical care…" and necessary social services. The latter **International Covenant on Economic, Social and Cultural Rights (ICESCR)**, Article 12, goes further, recognizing "the right of everyone to the enjoyment of the highest attainable standard of physical and mental health," and obligating states to take steps for disease prevention, environmental hygiene, and access to medical services when sick. [We are citing the ICESCR text from OHCHR, and, when you interpret the scope (determinants of health; not limited to healthcare) and the **CESCR General Comment No. 14** as the authoritative interpretive document.]

Regional instruments, such as the African Charter on Human and Peoples' Rights, echo this language, affirming every individual's right to "the best attainable state of physical and mental health." (https://achpr.au.int/en/node/641)

These documents are not limited to one model of medicine. They speak of **conditions** that enable health and access to care, but do not prescribe that care as exclusively biomedical or state-delivered. They create space for a plurality of systems, public, private, traditional, and religious, so long as people can achieve adequate health and well-being and are not denied care due to discrimination. This broad framing is the first legal doorway through which Indigenous and religious therapeutics walk.

2. Alma-Ata: Primary Health Care and Self-Determination

The **Declaration of Alma-Ata** (1978), endorsed by the WHO/UNICEF, explicitly affirms that "health… is a fundamental human right" and that the attainment of the highest possible level of health is "a most important worldwide social goal." Alma-Ata defines **primary health care (PHC)** as essential health care based on practical, scientifically sound, and socially acceptable methods and technology, made universally accessible to individuals and families in the community "through their full participation and at a cost that the community and country can afford… in the spirit of self-reliance and self-determination."

Subsequent analysis notes that Alma-Ata expanded the approach to health "from the focus on doctors, hospitals and biomedical advances to include human rights, concern for equity and community participation." In other words, PHC is not just a lower tier of biomedicine; it is a **philosophy** that centers communities, recognizes social determinants, and affirms that people have both a right and a duty to participate individually and collectively in planning and implementing their own health care.

For Indigenous and religious healers, this is a direct affirmation: community-based, culturally specific care, including traditional medicine, family remedies, and parish or tribal healing ministries, is consistent with, not opposed to, the global right-to-health framework.

3. Traditional and Complementary Medicine in WHO Policy

WHO's current **Traditional, Complementary and Integrative Medicine (TCI) strategies** further acknowledge that many people worldwide rely on traditional and familial health practices. The strategy emphasizes principles such as holism and health, Indigenous peoples' rights, culture and health, people-centered care, and community engagement. It seeks to integrate traditional and complementary medicine into health systems in ways that are evidence-based, culturally respectful, and aligned with the right to health and autonomy.

This is an important shift: rather than dismissing traditional medicine as unscientific, the WHO now emphasizes protecting traditional knowledge, supporting the responsible use of natural resources, and recognizing the role of Indigenous and local practices in achieving health equity. Scholarly reviews of Indigenous Native American healing traditions likewise stress that such systems are holistic, community-anchored, and often effective in addressing spiritual and emotional dimensions of illness that biomedicine neglects.

In practice, this means that **Grandma Doc** remedies, family herbalism, and tribal ceremonies are no longer merely tolerated; they are increasingly recognized as part of how communities exercise their right to health in culturally coherent ways.

4. Implications for Religious and Indigenous Therapeutics

For a Religious Therapeutics and Chirothesia-based ministry, these international frameworks offer several points of support:

- They affirm that **health is a human right**, not a privilege reserved for those who can access high-tech hospitals.

169

- They emphasize **community participation and self-determination**, aligning with tribal sovereignty and church autonomy in deciding how to care for their members.
- They recognize **traditional and complementary medicine** as legitimate components of health systems, especially when integrated ethically and with attention to safety and evidence.

When you, as a minister or medicine person, offer non-invasive, natural, and ceremonial healing in the context of a community that has chosen you, you are not acting outside the human-rights vision of health. You are one of the intended actors in that vision. The rest of this Part will show how more specific instruments, UNDRIP, OCAP, and the Nagoya Protocol, protect the **knowledge** and **resources** that make your medicine possible.

Chapter 19 Conclusion – Claiming the Human Rights You Already Live

When Alma-Ata declared that "health… is a fundamental human right," it put into modern policy language what Indigenous and faith communities have lived by for millennia: that no government, profession, or corporation holds a monopoly on the ways people care for one another. By insisting on primary health care that is "socially acceptable," rooted in community participation, and achievable through self-reliance and self-determination, the declaration quietly affirmed that family remedies, tribal ceremonies, parish healing services, and traditional practitioners have a rightful place in the world's health landscape.

For a Religious Therapeutics and Native American medicine practitioner, this means your work is not simply "outside the system"; it is one of the forms of care Alma-Ata was meant to protect and empower. When you sit with a member and pray, when you lay on hands, when you ceremonially share herbs or Thai Yoga, you are acting out a vision of health as wholeness that is fully compatible with health as a human right, so long as you practice transparently, ethically, and within a lawful umbrella.

The task now is not to beg for permission to exist, but to structure your ministry and clinic so that its human-rights foundations are visible: clear membership, informed consent, honest scope statements, and an unapologetic affirmation that your people have the right to define and pursue health in ways that honor their Creator and their ancestors. In doing this, you do not reject hospitals or antibiotics; you refuse to let them be the whole story. You take your rightful place as one of the many hands the world needs if "health for all" is to become more than a slogan.

LEARNING EXERCISE 19.1
Review & Application
Instructions: Select the best answer based on the reading.

1. What does the Universal Declaration of Human Rights say about health?
   A) It is a privilege for citizens only
   B) It is unrelated to human rights
   C) Everyone has a right to a standard of living adequate for health and well-being, including medical care and social services
   D) Only states have health rights
   E) Health is defined solely as the absence of disease
   Correct Answer: C

2. How did the Alma-Ata Declaration redefine "primary health care"?
   A) As high-tech hospital care only
   B) As a physician,-only care
   C) As essential health care based on practical, socially acceptable methods with community participation and self-determination
   D) As emergency care only
   E) As purely pharmaceutical care
   Correct Answer: C

3. How do the WHO's Traditional, Complementary, and Integrative Medicine strategies regard traditional practices?
   A) As obsolete
   B) As illegal
   C) As important components of people-centered, culturally respectful health systems
   D) As a purely placebo
   E) As restricted to research labs
   Correct Answer: C

4. What does this chapter suggest about your Religious Therapeutics practice in light of these frameworks?
   A) It conflicts with human rights
   B) It belongs only in private
   C) It fits within the global movement recognizing health as a human right and validating community-based, cultural approaches
   D) It must be standardized globally
   E) It should replace all biomedical care
   Correct Answer: C

5. What is a key implication of Alma-Ata's emphasis on community participation?
   A) Only governments deliver care
   B) Communities must abandon local healers
   C) Family remedies, tribal ceremonies, and parish healing services are legitimate ways communities exercise their right to health
   D) Only NGOs have authority
   E) Health is purely economic
   Correct Answer: C

Chapter 20 – UNDRIP, OCAP, and the Nagoya Protocol

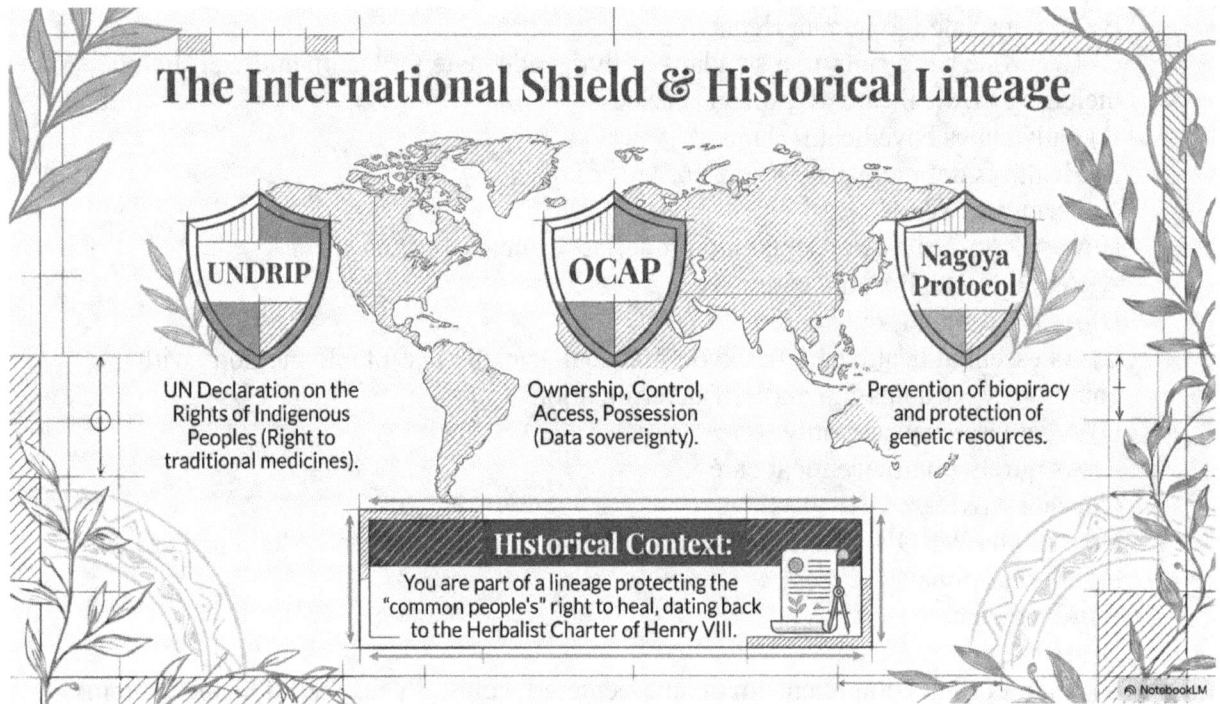

The International Shield & Historical Lineage

UNDRIP
UN Declaration on the Rights of Indigenous Peoples (Right to traditional medicines).

OCAP
Ownership, Control, Access, Possession (Data sovereignty).

Nagoya Protocol
Prevention of biopiracy and protection of genetic resources.

Historical Context:
You are part of a lineage protecting the "common people's" right to heal, dating back to the Herbalist Charter of Henry VIII.

- How UNDRIP affirms Indigenous peoples' right to their medicines, ceremonies, and health practices.
- How OCAP and the Nagoya Protocol protect Indigenous data and plant knowledge from extraction and biopiracy.
- What these instruments mean for how you share, document, and safeguard your medicine today.

If the Alma-Ata Declaration and the right-to-health documents indicate that communities have a right to access health care, instruments such as UNDRIP, OCAP, and the Nagoya Protocol indicate that Indigenous peoples also have a right to **define, control, and benefit from** their own medicines and knowledge. Together, they address a long history of suppression and exploitation: ceremonies banned, plant medicines outlawed or stolen, data extracted and used without consent.

This chapter introduces three key tools in what your text calls the "international shield": the **United Nations Declaration on the Rights of Indigenous Peoples (UNDRIP)**, the **First Nations Principles of OCAP®**, and the **Nagoya Protocol** on Access to Genetic Resources and the Fair and Equitable Sharing of Benefits. We will examine how each contributes to medical and data sovereignty and to protection against biopiracy, and how they reinforce the argument that Indigenous and religious therapeutics are not only permitted but also **protected** globally.

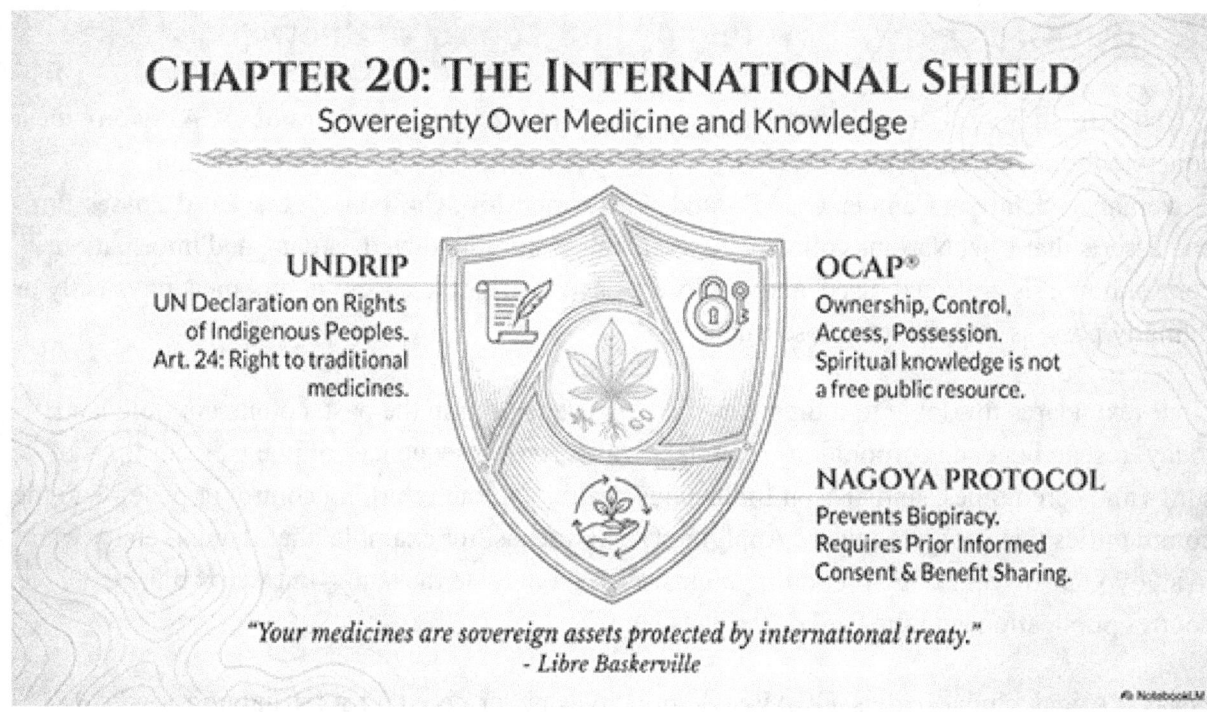

CHAPTER 20: THE INTERNATIONAL SHIELD
Sovereignty Over Medicine and Knowledge

UNDRIP
UN Declaration on Rights of Indigenous Peoples. Art. 24: Right to traditional medicines.

OCAP®
Ownership, Control, Access, Possession. Spiritual knowledge is not a free public resource.

NAGOYA PROTOCOL
Prevents Biopiracy. Requires Prior Informed Consent & Benefit Sharing.

"Your medicines are sovereign assets protected by international treaty."
- Libre Baskerville

1. UNDRIP: Medical Sovereignty and Traditional Medicines

The **United Nations Declaration on the Rights of Indigenous Peoples (UNDRIP)** is a non-binding but authoritative human rights standard adopted by the UN General Assembly. Article 24 is especially important for medicine; it affirms that Indigenous peoples have the right to their traditional medicines and to maintain their health practices, including the conservation of their vital medicinal plants, animals, and minerals. Article 31 further recognizes their right to maintain, control, protect, and develop their cultural heritage, traditional knowledge, and traditional cultural expressions, explicitly including traditional knowledge associated with genetic resources.

Commentary in medical and legal literature notes that UNDRIP recognizes access to and use of traditional medicines and practices as a **fundamental right**, underpinning Indigenous definitions of health and wellness. It reinforces that each Nation has unique health-related values tied to its traditions, lands, and laws, and that cultural and traditional wellness practices provide the foundation for Indigenous health.

In your context, UNDRIP supports the claim that Native American Traditional Indigenous Medicine, ceremonies, sacraments, herbs, and Chirothesia-based healing are not optional add-ons, but core components of an internationally recognized right to health and culture.

2. OCAP®: Data Sovereignty and Control of Knowledge

If UNDRIP addresses rights in broad strokes, the **First Nations Principles of OCAP®** provide a concrete framework for data sovereignty. Developed by the First Nations Information Governance Centre in Canada, OCAP stands for **Ownership, Control, Access, and Possession**, and asserts that First Nations collectively own their cultural knowledge, data, and information; control how it is collected, used, and disclosed; have the right to access it; and must physically or digitally possess it to enforce those rights.

Your text adapts this logic to Indigenous medicine generally: in the past, colonizers stole land; today, researchers and corporations often take **data**, genetic sequences of plants, recordings of songs and ceremonies, statistics on Indigenous health, without returning control or benefits to the communities that generated them. Applying OCAP means, for example, that if a university wants to study your Sweat Lodge program, you insist: "You may do the study, but we own the data, we control publication, and the hard drive stays here."

For NAIC and similar bodies, OCAP-style principles underscore that **spiritual and medical knowledge is not a free public resource**. It first belongs to the people and organizations that carry it; any outside use must be negotiated on terms that respect that ownership and control.

3. The Nagoya Protocol: Stopping Biopiracy

The **Nagoya Protocol on Access to Genetic Resources and the Fair and Equitable Sharing of Benefits** is a supplementary agreement to the Convention on Biological Diversity (CBD). Its purpose is to implement one of the CBD's core objectives: fair and equitable sharing of benefits arising from the utilization of genetic resources, including those associated with traditional knowledge.

Under Nagoya, parties must:

- Require **prior informed consent (PIC)** from provider countries, and, where applicable, Indigenous and local communities, before accessing genetic resources or associated traditional knowledge.
- Establish **mutually agreed terms (MAT)** that specify how benefits (profits, royalties, technology, etc.) will be shared.
- Ensure that their nationals comply with the access and benefit-sharing laws of the provider countries, including those related to traditional knowledge.

Your text uses a vivid example: if a company develops a billion-dollar drug from a Cherokee remedy, the Nagoya framework provides a legal basis to require that a portion of those benefits be returned to the Cherokee Nation to fund hospitals and schools. In this sense, Nagoya operationalizes UNDRIP's recognition of Indigenous rights to their medicinal plants and knowledge, turning moral claims into contract and enforcement mechanisms.

4. The International Shield and Your Practice

Together, UNDRIP, OCAP, and Nagoya form what your materials call an **"international shield"** around Indigenous medicine and knowledge.

- UNDRIP affirms the **right to practice and develop traditional medicine**, and to control related knowledge and resources.
- OCAP provides a practical framework for asserting **data sovereignty**, ensuring that research and documentation do not become new forms of colonial extraction.
- Nagoya sets out enforceable rules to prevent **biopiracy** and ensure benefit sharing when traditional knowledge leads to commercial products.

For your Religious Therapeutics and Chirothesia-based ministry, this means your right to heal and your right to guard your knowledge are recognized not only in U.S. domestic law (AIRFA, RFRA, IHCIA) but also in global human rights and environmental law. When you insist on private membership, informed consent, internal ethics, and careful relations with researchers and corporations, you are not being difficult; you are acting in accordance with the best international standards for Indigenous health and knowledge governance.

Chapter 20 Conclusion – A Fortress, Not a Loophole

UNDRIP, OCAP, and the Nagoya Protocol show that the world has begun, however imperfectly, to recognize Indigenous medicine as a **sovereign science to be respected**, not a relic to be harvested. They affirm that your ceremonies, plants, data, and stories belong first to your people, and that any state or institution that seeks to regulate or use them must do so with consent, respect, and fair return.

As you continue to develop your ministry or tribal clinic, these instruments remind you that you stand inside a fortress built from both domestic and international law. Your task is not to sneak through loopholes, but to inhabit that fortress with integrity: practicing your medicine in a good way, protecting your knowledge, and welcoming partners who are willing to honor the rights that these documents so clearly proclaim.

175

LEARNING EXERCISE 20.1
Review & Application
Instructions: Select the best answer based on the reading.

1. What does UNDRIP Article 24 affirm for Indigenous peoples?
   A) Only a right to education
   B) Only land rights
   C) The right to their traditional medicines and to maintain their health practices
   D) The right to emigrate
   E) The right to vote in UN elections
   Correct Answer: C

2. What is the central idea of the OCAP® principles?
   A) States own all Indigenous data
   B) Corporations own genetic resources
   C) Indigenous communities have Ownership, Control, Access, and Possession of their data and knowledge
   D) Data must be in the public domain
   E) Only universities may manage data
   Correct Answer: C

3. What is the primary purpose of the Nagoya Protocol?
   A) To ban traditional medicine
   B) To liberalize biotech patents
   C) To ensure fair and equitable sharing of benefits from genetic resources and associated traditional knowledge, based on prior informed consent and mutually agreed terms
   D) To regulate hospitals
   E) To privatize water
   Correct Answer: C

4. How do these instruments together form an "international shield"?
   A) By isolating Indigenous communities from the world
   B) By banning ceremonies
   C) By recognizing rights to practice traditional medicine, control knowledge, and prevent biopiracy without benefit-sharing
   D) By standardizing Western medicine globally
   E) By funding pharmaceutical monopolies
   Correct Answer: C

5. What practical stance do these tools support for your ministry?
   A) Give away knowledge freely to any researcher
   B) Avoid documenting anything
   C) Share medicine and knowledge only under terms that respect Indigenous and religious ownership, control, and fair benefit
   D) Reject all collaboration
   E) Seek patents on all ceremonies
   Correct Answer: C

Chapter 21 – The Herbalist Charter and Common-Law Protections

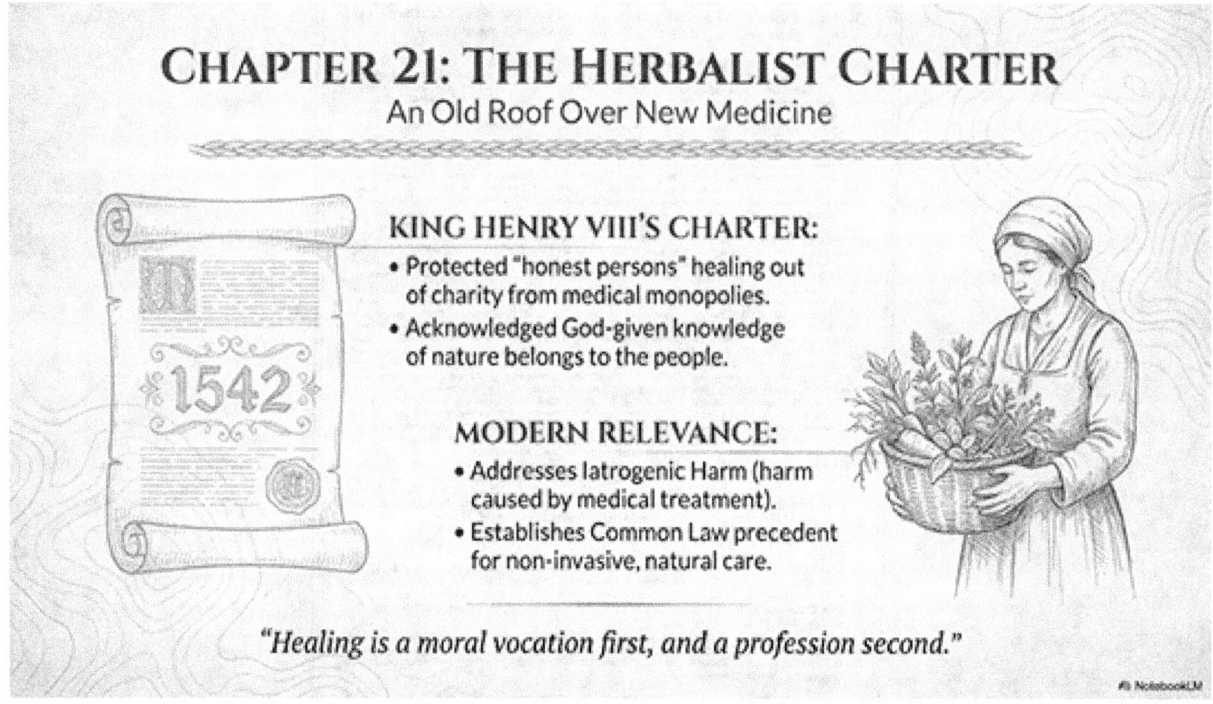

CHAPTER 21: THE HERBALIST CHARTER
An Old Roof Over New Medicine

KING HENRY VIII'S CHARTER:
- Protected "honest persons" healing out of charity from medical monopolies.
- Acknowledged God-given knowledge of nature belongs to the people.

MODERN RELEVANCE:
- Addresses Iatrogenic Harm (harm caused by medical treatment).
- Establishes Common Law precedent for non-invasive, natural care.

"Healing is a moral vocation first, and a profession second."

> ✌ The story of Henry VIII's "Herbalist Charter" and how it defended lay healers against early medical monopolies.
> ✌ How do echoes of that Charter appear in modern exemptions and the common-law space for herbal and traditional practice?
> ✌ How concerns about iatrogenic harm and scientism underscore the ongoing need for low-tech, spiritually grounded care.

Long before modern licensing boards, a very different law was written to shield community healers from professional harassment. In 1542–1543, under King Henry VIII, Parliament enacted "An Act That Persons, Being No Common Surgeons, May Administer Outward Medicines, " which later herbalists would call the **Herbalist Charter**. It condemned London surgeons for "minding only their own lucre's" and explicitly legalized the work of "divers' honest persons, as well men as women," whom God had endowed with knowledge of herbs, roots, and waters, and who ministered to the sick "for neighborhood and God's sake."

This chapter revisits that act as an early declaration of sovereignty for natural medicine, affirming that lay and familial healers have a legitimate place alongside learned physicians, and traces how its spirit has echoed into modern common-law protections for herbalism and holistic practice. We will examine the controversy that led to its passage, its later reception in England and the colonies, and its contemporary relevance in a world where biomedicine is powerful but also deeply implicated in iatrogenic harm.

THE HERBALIST IS ALLOWED TO PRACTICE BY THIS
ACT AND IT HAS NEVER BEEN REPEALED. 1512 AD

Herbalist's Charter
of Henry the VIII

Annis Tricesimo Quarto and Tricesimo Quinto, Henric VIII
Regis. Cap. VIII. An Act That Persons, Being No Common
Surgeons, May Administer Outward Medicines

WHERE in the Parliament holden at Westminster in the third Year of the King's most gracious Reign, amongst other Things, for the avoiding of Sorceries, Witchcrafts, and other Inconveniences, it was enacted, that no Person within the City of London, nor within Seven Miles of the same, should take upon him to exercise and occupy as Physician or Surgeon, except he be first examined, approved, and admitted by the Bishop of London and other, under and upon certain Pains and Penalties in the same Act mentioned: Either in the making of which said Act, the Company and Fellowship of Surgeons of London, minding only their own Lucres, and nothing the Profit or ease of the Diseased or Patient, have sued, troubled, and vexed divers honest Persons, as well Men as Women, whom God hath endued with the Knowledge of the Nature, Kind and Operation of certain Herbs, Roots, and Waters, and the using and ministring of them to such as been pained with customable Diseases, as Women's Breast's being sore, a Pin and the Web in the Eye, Uncomes of Hands, Burnings, Scaldings, Sore Mouths, the Stone, Strangury, Saucelim, and Morphew, and such other like Diseases; and yet the said Persons have not taken anything for their Pains or Cunning, but have ministred the same to poor People only for Neighbourhood and God's sake, and of Pity and Charity: And it is now well known that the Surgeons admitted will do no Cure to any Person but where they shall be rewarded with a greater Sum or Reward than the Cure extendeth unto; for in case they would minister their Cunning unto sore People unrewarded, there should not so many rot and perish to death for Lack or Help of Surgery as daily do; but the greatest part of Surgeons admitted been much more to be blamed than those Persons that they troubled, for although the most Part of the Persons of the said Craft of Surgeons have small Cunning yet they will take great sums of Money, and do little therefore, and by Reason thereof they do oftentimes impair and hurt their Patients, rather than do them good. In consideration whereof, and for the Ease, Comfort, Succour, Help, Relief, and Health of the King's poor Subjects, Inhabitants of this Realm, now pained or diseased: Be it ordained, established, and enacted, by Authority of this present Parliament, That at all Time from henceforth it shall be lawful to every Person being the King's subject, having Knowledge and Experience of the Nature of Herbs, Roots, and Waters, or of the Operation of the same, by Speculation or Practice, within any part of the Realm of England, or within any other the King's Dominions, to practice, use, and minister in and to any outward Sore, Uncome Wound, Apostemations, outward Swelling or Disease, any Herb or Herbs, Ointments, Baths, Pultess, and Emplaisters, according to their Cunning, Experience, and Knowledge in any of the Diseases, Sores, and Maladies beforesaid, and all other like to the same, or Drinks for the Stone, Strangury, or Agues, without suit, vexation, trouble, penalty, or loss of their goods; the foresaid Statute in the foresaid Third Year of the King's most gracious Reign, or any other Act, Ordinance, or Statutes to the contrary heretofore made in anywise, notwithstanding.

1. Why Henry VIII Stepped In

By the early 1500s, the English Crown and Parliament had begun to formalize medical professions, creating charters and statutes for physicians, surgeons, and apothecaries, and restricting practice in London and surrounding areas to those examined and approved by ecclesiastical or collegiate authorities. The 3 Henry VIII statute required examination and admission before anyone could "exercise and occupy as physician or surgeon" in London or within seven miles, under penalties for violators.

Yet, despite these measures, a robust culture of lay healers persisted, midwives, wise women, clergy, and household herbalists, who treated burns, wounds, eye problems, stones, fevers, and "such other like diseases" using herbs, ointments, baths, and plasters, often without charge. According to contemporary accounts, the Company of Surgeons used the earlier statute to **"sue, trouble, and vex"** these healers, prioritizing their own profits over "the ease of the diseased or patient."

The 1542–1543 Act was Parliament's response: a corrective aimed at restoring balance between professional medicine and popular, herbal practice.

178

2. What the Herbalist Charter Actually Did

The Act (34 & 35 Henry VIII, cap. 8) did not abolish the regulation of physicians and surgeons; it carved out a **broad exemption** for others. In essence, it declared that:

- Any of the King's subjects, "having knowledge and experience of the nature of herbs, roots, and waters," could practice and minister outward remedies, herbs, ointments, baths, poultices, and plasters, for a wide range of external sores and ailments.
- They could also provide drinks for conditions such as "the stone, strangury, or agues," without fear of "suit, vexation, trouble, penalty, or loss of goods," notwithstanding the earlier restrictive statute.

Scholars of medical history note that this effectively legalized lay herbalism across England and recognized that herbal medicine "still flourished" and could treat a wide range of diseases, some life-threatening. Barbara Griggs, in *Green Pharmacy: A History of Herbal Medicine*, describes it as a "flimsy legal roof" under which the profession of herbal medicine has sheltered and flourished to this day in Britain.

Your own text points out that, under the general laws of the colonies inherited by the United States, these kinds of common-law protections were never expressly repealed in the original thirteen states, and thus still form part of the legal backdrop for herbal and natural practice.

3. Common-Law Exemptions in the Modern Era

Modern regulation has tightened around pharmaceuticals and standardized medicinal products, but echoes of the Herbalist Charter remain, especially in common-law jurisdictions. In the United Kingdom, for example, when the 1968 Medicines Act significantly tightened medicine regulation, herbalists mobilized and secured special provisions:

- Section 12(1) exempts from licensing any herbal medicine made up for a particular patient after a one-to-one consultation.
- Section 12(2) exempted certain over-the-counter herbal remedies prepared through non-industrial methods, provided labels did not make specific medicinal claims.

Socio-legal studies note that these exemptions created "a relatively open space for herbal practice," allowing homegrown and imported traditions (Ayurveda, TCM, etc.) to thrive under lighter regulation, even as pharmaceuticals faced stricter controls. Another analysis describes how, in England, herbalists have benefited from a "common-law exemption to make herbal medicines," though newer EU-derived directives now contest the boundaries.

The pattern is familiar: whenever law seeks to centralize and standardize medicine, countervailing pressures emerge to protect local, herbal, and traditional practitioners, often by reviving or reinventing the spirit of the Herbalist Charter.

4. Herbalism, Safety, and Iatrogenic Harm

One reason the Herbalist Charter remains morally compelling is that **modern medicine is not risk-free**. Contemporary research on iatrogenesis, the harm caused by medical treatment, highlights the scale of the problem. A review of adverse drug reactions (ADRs) and medical error reports indicates that millions of people each year experience serious drug-related harm, and that, in some analyses, government-sanctioned medicine in the U.S. has been implicated as a leading cause of death. WHO has also estimated that around half of all medicines are prescribed or used inappropriately, and that a substantial proportion of patients do not take them correctly.

In the UK, concern over repeated clinical errors and iatrogenic injuries led to what one historian calls the "moment of patient safety" around 2000, when patient safety became a central policy concern, and hospital errors undermined public trust. These findings do not negate the life-saving power of biomedicine. Still, they expose the limits of a system that often equates "licensed" with "safe" and discredits traditional practices regardless of their track record at the household and community level.

Herbal and natural medicine are not free of risk. Still, many of the **familial and community-based practices**, "Grandma Doc" remedies, kitchen herbals, and non-invasive plant-based therapies have historically offered low-tech, low-toxicity options for everyday ailments, long before modern pharmacovigilance existed. The Herbalist Charter's critique, that some licensed professionals "mind only their own lucre's" and that people "rot and perish" for lack of accessible care, still resonates in an era of expensive, sometimes harmful, over-medicalization.

5. Scientism, Regulation, and the Marginalization of Tradition

Today's regulatory environment is often driven less by genuine science than by **scientism**, a belief that only randomized, industrial-scale, pharmacological interventions are "real" medicine, and by economic, bureaucratic, or political interests that shape what evidence is generated and trusted. Scholars examining the regulation of herbal medicines argue that law has "reshaped herbal medicines in the UK, rewriting their histories and potential futures" by embedding narrow definitions of "tradition" and imposing industrial standards unsuited to small-scale practice.

Similar dynamics are evident globally: traditional medicines are sometimes rebranded as "complementary" or "alternative" and tightly controlled, even as high-risk pharmaceuticals are aggressively marketed. The Herbalist Charter reminds us that this tension is not new: in every era, power struggles between elite and popular healers, between centralized and local knowledge, and between profit and neighborly care shape what counts as legitimate healing.

Your work situates Religious Therapeutics and Native American medicine as **heirs** to this older, community-anchored stream of healing, updated with clear ethics, informed consent, and an explicit non-medical scope of practice. In that sense, you are not rejecting science; you are rejecting the idea that only one, state-licensed form of science may exist, even when its own record includes serious iatrogenic harm.

For a deeper dive into the issue of "Scientism's" role in the marginalization of traditional, indigenous, and religious/ spiritually based medicine and healing practices, read "Decoding AI Bias" by this author. This insightful and powerful revealing book is available on Amazon.com (https://beardedmedia.com/product/decoding-ai-bias-in-medicine-how-artificial-intelligence-ignores-traditional-indigenous-and-holistic-healing/)

6. The Herbalist Charter's Legacy in Your Context

Your own materials treat the Herbalist Charter as part of the common-law backdrop that still informs exemptions and exceptions for natural and religious healing today. The logic is consistent:

- Common-law and statutory **exemptions** protect those who practice under the tenets of a church or within tribal traditions.
- AIRFA, RFRA, IHCIA, UNDRIP, and human-rights instruments recognize Indigenous and religious medicine as legitimate expressions of health and culture.
- Modern herbal and traditional practitioners continue to negotiate regulatory space, through PMAs, ecclesiastical licenses, and tribal organizations, much as their predecessors did through the Herbalist Charter.

For NAIC and similar bodies, the Charter functions as both a historical precedent and a metaphor: a reminder that law **can** step in to restrain professional monopolies and to protect the right of ordinary people, endowed with knowledge by God and tradition, to minister to their neighbors with herbs, hands, and prayer.

Chapter 21 Conclusion – An Old Roof Over New Medicine

The deeper lesson of the Herbalist Charter is that law can recognize healing as a **moral vocation** first, and a profession second. When Parliament defended "honest persons… whom God hath endued with the knowledge of the nature, kind and operation of certain herbs, roots, and waters," it was acknowledging what your framework calls Religious Therapeutics: people called by God and community to tend the sick with natural, non-invasive means as an expression of faith. That same logic undergirds your ministry today, where herbs, hands-on prayer, ceremony, counseling, breath work, and other gentle modalities are offered under church, tribal, and PMA authority, not as commercial "services" but as sacramental duties.

For a modern religious therapeutic ministry or tribal clinic, the Charter's principles translate into three practical supports. First, they reinforce the idea of a **non-monopoly** on care: just as Henry VIII's Act limited surgeons' ability to harass lay herbalists, contemporary exemptions (AIRFA, RFRA, IHCIA, state religious-practice carve-outs) limit medical boards' claims to exclusive jurisdiction over all forms of "helping the sick." Second, they affirm the legitimacy of **local, relational knowledge**, the "Grandma Doc," family herbalist, or medicine person whose wisdom is tested in homes and circles, not only in laboratories, so long as that knowledge is now carried within a disciplined, accountable framework like NAIC, a church, or an inter-tribal organization. Third, they support a **plural vision of health**, in which herbalism, Chirothesia, counseling, ceremony, and other non-invasive practices are recognized as lawful expressions of ministry and Native American medicine, not as unauthorized imitations of biomedicine.

This inheritance is not limited to herbs. The same common-law and statutory reasoning that once sheltered ointments and poultices can shelter the full spectrum of gentle, non-invasive Religious Therapeutics: laying on of hands, anointing, movement and breath practices, somatic prayer, Indigenous ceremonies, and pastoral counseling, provided they are clearly framed as spiritual, non-medical acts. When such work is carried out under the regulatory and supervisory functions of a bona fide church, PMA, or intertribal body, with codes of ethics, informed consent, defined scopes of practice, and internal accountability, it falls squarely within the protected space the Charter prefigured and modern law has expanded. In this way, your ministry is not asking for special favors; it is stepping into a long legal and moral tradition that says communities have the right to care for their own, with their own medicines and sacraments, in natural, non-invasive ways, and to be answerable to both Spirit and law.

LEARNING EXERCISE 21.1
Review & Application
Instructions: Select the best answer based on the reading.

1. What problem did the 1542–1543 Herbalist Charter address?
   A) Lack of pharmacies
   B) Overregulation of physicians
   C) "Common surgeons" harassing lay herbalists and prioritizing profit over patients
   D) Shortage of herbs
   E) Excessive public trust in herbalists
   Correct Answer: C

2. What did the Charter effectively legalize?
   A) All surgery
   B) Only physician practice
   C) The work of "divers' honest persons" using herbs, roots, waters, baths, and plasters for many ailments without fear of punishment
   D) Only licensed apothecaries
   E) Only midwives
   Correct Answer: C

3. How has the spirit of the Charter reappeared in modern UK law?
   A) Through bans on herbs
   B) Through the criminalization of lay healers
   C) Through exemptions in the Medicines Act, allowing certain herbal medicines to be prepared for individual patients, or through non-industrial methods
   D) Through the mandatory medicalization of all remedies
   E) Through the prohibition of midwifery
   Correct Answer: C

4. Why does the chapter discuss iatrogenic harm in relation to herbalism?
   A) To show that conventional medicine is always dangerous
   B) To prove herbs are risk-free
   C) To highlight that licensed systems also cause harm, so claims that only regulated biomedicine is "safe" are incomplete
   D) To discourage hospital use
   E) To demand the abolition of licensing
   Correct Answer: C

5. What broader principle does the Herbalist Charter support for today's Religious Therapeutics?
   A) Monopoly of care
   B) Centralization of all practice
   C) Recognition that communities have a right to care for their own with natural, non-invasive means under accountable frameworks
   D) Replacement of all doctors with herbalists
   E) Privatization of all health care
   Correct Answer: C

Part VI – Implementation, Resources, and Next Steps

Sacred Hands, Secured Rights: From Calling to Compliance

A practical, step-by-step roadmap for practitioners to implement a legally sheltered and ethically sound healing ministry.

SECULAR / STATE JURISDICTION
(Licensed Professional)

SACRED / ECCLESIASTICAL JURISDICTION
(Healing Ministry)

PHASE 1: NAVIGATING THE "TWO ROADS"
(Dual Role Management)

Establish Jurisdictional Separation

- ☑ Maintain separate branding, websites,
- ☑ intake forms, and
- ☑ scheduling.

Formalize Ecclesiastical Alliances

- ☑ Join bona fide oversight body (e.g.,
- ☑ NAIC or FNMB) for
- ☑ training, ethics codes, and licensure.

PHASE 2: STRUCTURAL IMPLEMENTATION & STEWARDSHIP

Know Which "Hat" You Are Wearing

Ensure language and behavior match specific legal umbrella (state license) at time of service.

Prioritize the Stricter Standard

When acting under state license, religious status never justifies falling below clinical standards of care.

Implement a Member-Only Model

Private Membership Association (PMA)

Reframe all interactions as "minister-to-member" via PMA agreements and informed consent.

Audit Your Professional Language

Religious Therapeutics
Chirothesia
SomaVeda
Naturopathic

Medical

Replace "forbidden" medical verbs like diagnose or treat with approved terms.

ESSENTIAL DOCUMENTATION FOR A LEGALLY SHELTERED MINISTRY

Statement of Sacred Conviction

Defines practitioner's theology of health as spirit, soul, and body.

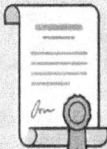

Participant Member Agreement

Moves interactions from public marketplace into private religious domain.

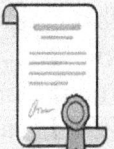

Religious Therapeutic Consent

Clarifies work is non-medical and does not diagnose or cure disease.

NotebookLM

The final part of this book brings everything down to earth. Law, theology, and history are only useful if they translate into daily decisions: how you describe yourself, how you organize your practice, which organizations you align with, and how you respond when challenges arise. Part VI is your field manual for living out the rights and responsibilities you have just studied.

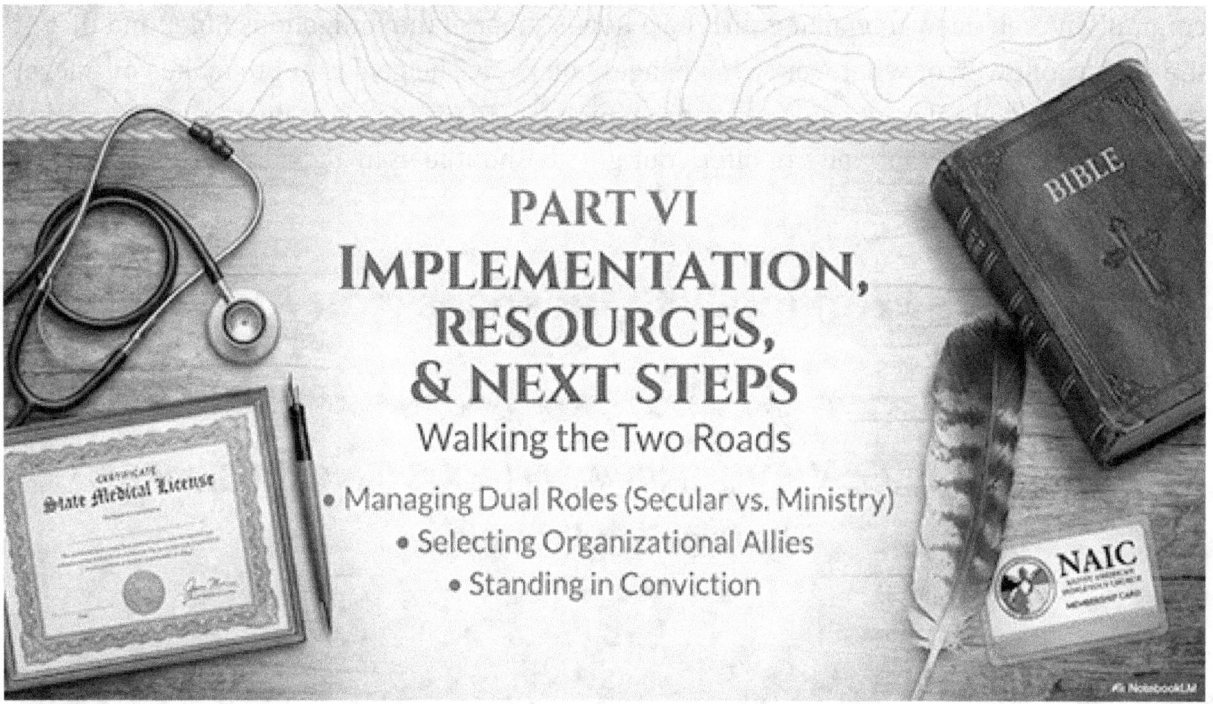

We begin by looking at the licenses and roles you may already hold, such as massage therapist, nurse, counselor, social worker, or other secular credentials, and how they intersect with your religious practice. You will learn why it is crucial not to collapse these identities, and how to create clean boundaries so that what you do as a state-licensed professional remains distinct from what you do as an ordained minister, medicine person, or tribal practitioner. We will offer practical strategies for documentation, scheduling, and communication that keep these lanes clear.

Next, we survey organizational allies: churches, tribal organizations, and boards that recognize Indigenous and holistic medicine as legitimate forms of religious therapy. You will read about examples such as the Native American Indigenous Church, the Priory of Saving Grace, SMOCH, the First Nations Medical Board, and others, not as exclusive channels, but as illustrations of what a robust ecclesiastical or tribal structure can look like. We will also share criteria you can use to discern whether any organization you join truly supports your rights and responsibilities.

We then turn to practical questions of sustainability and protection: tithe and donation models, tax treatment for ministers, potential liability insurance options, and simple internal policies that reduce misunderstandings before they start. You will see how member education, clear agreements, and a consistent code of ethics can resolve many conflicts before any lawyer or regulator is involved.

Part VI closes by returning to where we began: you're calling. You will be invited to craft your own Statement of Sacred Conviction in light of everything you have learned, and to commit yourself anew to walking the "Two Roads", that of the Indigenous Elder and that of the Christ-follower, or whatever twin lineages you bear. The goal is not to make you a legal technician, but a healer who understands enough law to protect your people, your practice, and your prayers, so that you can offer your gifts without fear, in a good way.

Chapter 22 – Working with Licenses You Already Hold

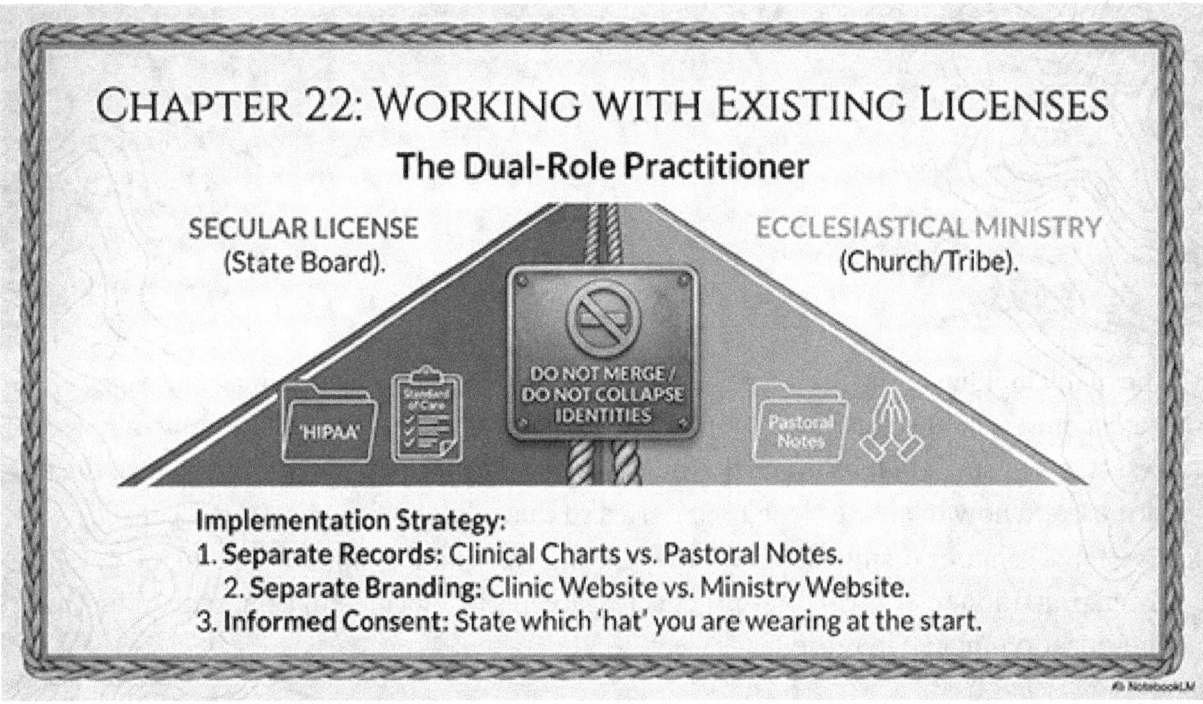

- How to distinguish and ethically inhabit your two jurisdictions: state-licensed professional and ecclesiastical/tribal healer.
- Practical models for separating or carefully integrating your secular and religious roles without collapsing either.
- Concrete safeguards, language, documentation, and boundaries that help you "walk in both worlds" with integrity.

Many who feel called to Religious Therapeutics, Chirothesia, or Native American medicine already hold secular licenses, such as massage therapist, nurse, counselor, physician, social worker, psychologist, dietitian, or similar. Those licenses carry their own statutes, ethics codes, and standards of care. At the same time, you retain an independent constitutional and statutory right to practice the tenets of your religion without government interference, including Indigenous and church-based healing.

Many of you reading this already hold secular licenses, such as massage therapist, nurse, chiropractor, counselor, physician, social worker, physical therapist, or acupuncturist, or you hold certifications in modalities such as Thai Yoga, yoga teaching, Reiki, nutrition, or coaching. At the same time, you are drawn to practice Native American medicine, SomaVeda® Thai Yoga, Religious Therapeutics, or other Indigenous/faith-based healing under a church, tribal, or PMA umbrella. The question is: **How do you walk in both worlds without violating either?**

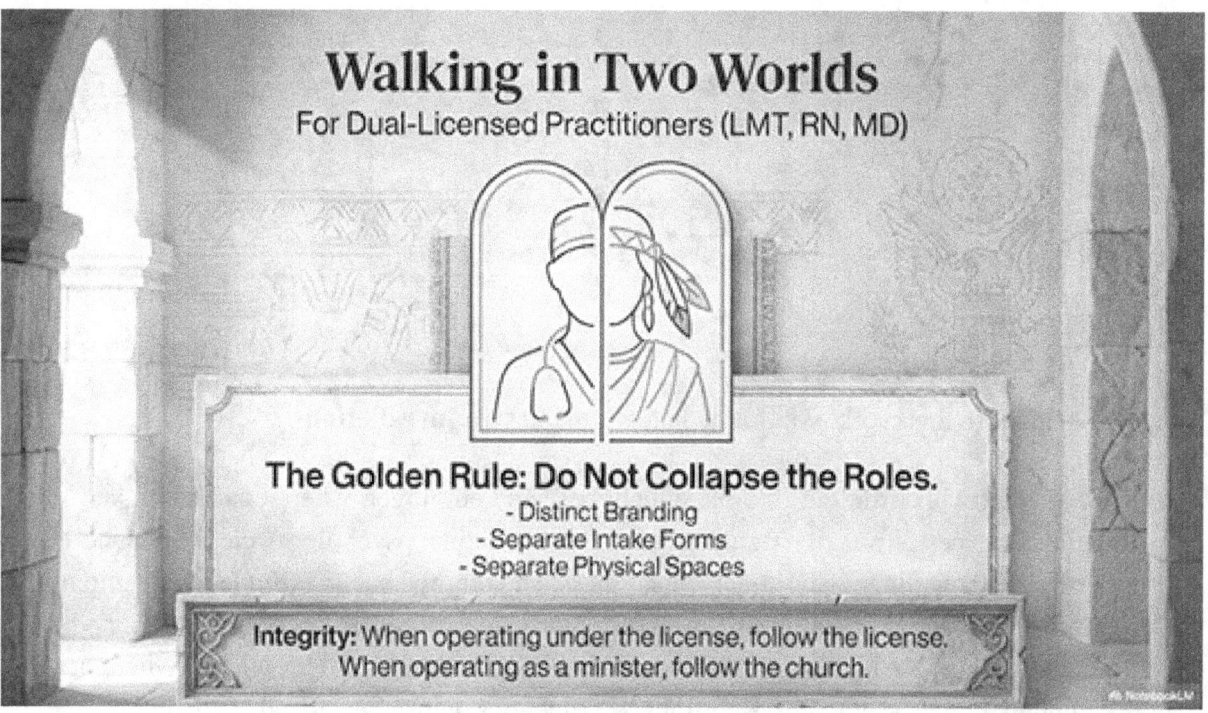

This chapter addresses a practical question: **How can you walk in both worlds, licensed professional and religious healer, ethically and lawfully?** We will first identify the two jurisdictions in which you live, then outline concrete models and safeguards to reconcile them. Throughout, remember: your right to religious exercise does not vanish when you obtain a license, but it is not a permit to ignore the ethical and legal obligations you voluntarily accepted in that licensed role. There must be a **cogent, rational, and legally coherent way** to hold both.

This chapter answers that question by weaving together three strands: (1) a clear distinction between secular **licensing**, private **certification**, and ecclesiastical/tribal **licensure**, (2) the dual-role guidance from previous chapters, and (3) lessons from Dr. Lawrence Wilson's *Legal Guidelines for Unlicensed Practitioners* and the ThaiYogaCenter legal articles on Thai Yoga and

Thai massage. The aim is to give you a practical roadmap for honoring your religious and Indigenous calling while remaining ethical and coherent in respect to any state licenses you hold.

1. Two Jurisdictions, Two Sets of Duties, Two Identities

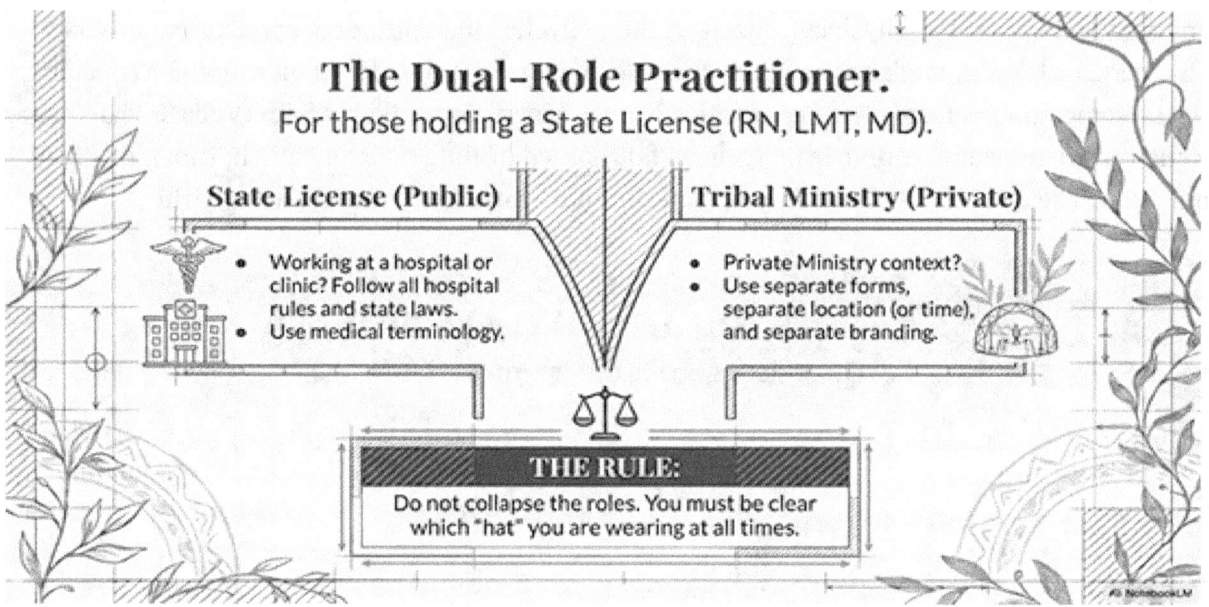

When you step into this work, you immediately inhabit **two jurisdictions**:

- The **secular jurisdiction** of your state license and employer, where boards regulate defined scopes of practice (massage, nursing, medicine, psychology, etc.), and where language like "diagnose," "treat," and "massage therapy" has specific legal meanings.
- The **ecclesiastical/tribal jurisdiction** of a bona fide church, tribal organization, and PMA (such as NAIC, Priory of Saving Grace, SMOCH/SMOKH, FNMB), where healing is understood as sacrament, Religious Therapeutics, Chirothesia, and Indigenous medicine, and where AIRFA, RFRA, IHCIA, RLUIPA, UNDRIP, and related instruments protect religious and Indigenous practice.

The core rule is simple but non-negotiable: **you must know which hat you are wearing, and your behavior, language, paperwork, and setting must match that hat.** If you present as a licensed massage therapist to the general public, use "massage therapy" language, and bill as such, you are under the massage board. If you present as an NAIC minister, serving only NAIC members in Religious Therapeutics, under church/tribal auspices, you are under ecclesiastical and tribal law.

When you hold a state license, you stand under **two** overlapping authorities:

- The **State's licensing regime**, which governs what you may do when you present yourself and bill as a nurse, LMT, counselor, physician, etc. It defines the scope of practice, standard of care, documentation, informed consent, and discipline.
- Your **church/tribal/PMA jurisdiction**, which governs what you may do as an ordained/commissioned minister, medicine person, or religious therapeutic practitioner under ecclesiastical and Indigenous law.

Federal protections like the American Indian Religious Freedom Act (AIRFA), RFRA, and IHCIA confirm that Indigenous religion and traditional medicine are legitimate forms of religious exercise and health care. But those same laws do not automatically erase your duties when you are acting in a licensed capacity. The key is to **know which hat you are wearing, and when.**

2. Licensing vs Certification vs Ecclesiastical Licensure

Dr. Lawrence Wilson's *Legal Guidelines for Unlicensed Practitioners* and Dr. James's ThaiYogaCenter articles hammer home a distinction that most practitioners overlook: **licensing is different from certification**, and neither is the same as ecclesiastical/tribal licensure.

A. Secular licensing

- **Licensing** is a government-granted privilege. It allows you to perform certain acts that would otherwise be legally restricted, such as practicing medicine, nursing, massage therapy, psychology, or other regulated professions, as those acts are defined in statutes.
- Your state license comes with a codified scope of practice, mandatory standards of care, documentation requirements, continuing education, and disciplinary oversight.

When you function **in that licensed role**, you must comply fully with those laws, and you cannot use your religious status to loosen the standard of care.

B. Certification

- **Certification** is recognition by a **private school or association** that you have completed a course of study and met their standards in a particular modality (e.g., Thai Yoga, Reiki, health coaching, herbalism).
- Certification, by itself, does **not** grant any legal right to practice a regulated profession to the public. Wilson is explicit: "Certification does not automatically give you the legal right to practice ANY healing, medical, or therapeutic art."

The ThaiYogaCenter articles on Thai Yoga and Thai massage make this concrete:

- Your Thai Yoga / SomaVeda® certificate proves you have been trained; it does not make Thai Yoga "legal" massage under a massage act, nor does it substitute for a state license.
- If you call what you do "massage" or "massage therapy" in a state where that term is regulated, you have effectively placed yourself under the massage practice act and will be judged by that standard.

C. Ecclesiastical/tribal licensure and commissions

In this course, a third category is crucial: **ecclesiastical and tribal licensure**, such as:

- NAIC Licensed Commissioned Holistic Therapist (L.C.H.T.) and related pastoral/clinical licenses.
- FNMB Indigenous Medicine licenses.
- SMOCH/SMOKH priest,-physician, or monastic medical commissions.

These are not state licenses. They function as **internal authorizations** within church, tribal, and PMA jurisdiction, indicating that you are trained, accountable, and permitted to practice Religious Therapeutics, Chirothesia, Indigenous medicine, and related non-invasive holistic services **for members**, as an expression of religious and Indigenous rights.

In practice, this means:

- Your Thai Yoga and Ayurveda **certificates** qualify you for ecclesiastical/tribal licensure (e.g., L.C.H.T.), but they do not, on their own, authorize anything in secular law.
- Once you hold an NAIC/tribal **license or commission**, you may lawfully practice those modalities as Religious Therapeutics and Indigenous Healthcare **within** the private domain of NAIC/church/PMA membership and under AIRFA/RFRA/IHCIA and parallel state exemptions.

In the language of this book: **certification proves competence; secular licensing gives public permission; ecclesiastical/tribal licensure defines and protects religious practice.** You need to be clear which you are invoking at any given time.

Models for Working with Licenses You Already Hold

With these distinctions in mind, there are several practical ways to integrate your existing licenses with your Religious Therapeutics and Indigenous work.

3. Model One – Clean Separation of Roles and Structures

In this model, you keep your **licensed** and **ecclesiastical/tribal** practices as separate as possible.

The simplest and often safest approach is to **separate your licensed work and your religious therapeutic work as clearly as possible.**

In this model:

- You maintain a conventional practice (or employment) where you function strictly under your state license, e.g., "John Smith, LMT" at a spa or clinic. You use standard forms, chart as required, and bill as a massage therapist, nurse, physician, or counselor.
- Outside that context, you operate a distinct **NAIC/tribal ministry**:
    - Only NAIC or church/PMA members are served.
    - All services are framed as Religious Therapeutics, Chirothesia, Indigenous medicine, or pastoral care, not as licensed massage or medicine.
    - Separate websites, logos, intake forms, and record systems are used.

- You maintain a secular practice (or job) where you function **fully under your license**. You follow the state scope of practice and professional ethics, use conventional informed-consent forms, chart appropriately, and bill as required by law and your employer.
- Outside that setting, you operate a **distinct ministry or tribal clinic** under NAIC or a similar body, with its own branding, membership, consent, and internal governance.

This is the most conservative approach; it minimizes confusion for clients, boards, and courts and aligns closely with the guidance from both Wilson and NAIC: don't mix categories, and don't let your certification-based or ecclesiastical work be mistaken for unlicensed medical or massage practice.

Key features:

1. **Different legal umbrellas.**
    - Secular clinic/employment: under state board, employer policies, malpractice standards.
    - Religious practice: under church/tribal/PMA authority, within the explicit Religious Therapeutics/Native American medicine scope.
2. **Distinct language and paperwork.**
    - Licensed side uses standard professional terminology and avoids implying that services are religious sacraments.

- Ministry side uses NAIC-style language: Religious Therapeutics, Chirothesia, Indigenous Healthcare (IHSM); explicit statements that you **do not diagnose, treat, or prescribe** as defined by state acts; membership and informed-consent forms that frame all services as minister-to-member.

3. **Separate marketing and online presence.**
   - One website/page for your licensed practice; another, clearly church/tribal branded, for NAIC-type ministry.
   - No implication that your license "covers" your religious services, or that your ministry is part of a state-regulated clinic.

4. **Time and place boundaries.**
   - Religious Therapeutics is offered only in designated times and spaces, not while you are "on duty" in your licensed employer's facility (unless you have explicit written permission and a clear policy).

Advantages:

- Minimizes confusion for clients, boards, and courts.
- Makes it easy to show that NAIC-type work occurs **outside** the licensed arena.

4. Model Two – Ethically Integrated Roles (When Allowed)

In some fields, especially counseling and psychotherapy, codes of ethics recognize that practitioners may also be clergy or spiritually oriented, particularly in small or faith communities. In such cases, a **carefully integrated role** may be possible, but it demands high ethical discipline.

Core principles from counseling and pastoral-ethics literature include:

- **Avoid harmful dual relationships.** A dual role (therapist + pastor; clinician + fellow congregant) is not inherently unethical, but it becomes so when it impairs objectivity, increases the risk of exploitation, or clouds judgment.
- **Radical transparency and informed consent.** At intake, disclose your dual identity (e.g., licensed counselor and ordained minister), discuss boundaries, and clarify what role you are in when you meet. Document that discussion.
- **Prioritize the stricter standard.** When acting under your license, you must meet or exceed your profession's standard of care; religious commitments cannot be used to justify substandard clinical decisions.

- **Be willing to refer or switch hats.** If a relationship becomes too spiritually enmeshed for objective clinical work or too clinically complex for brief pastoral care, ethical practice may require referral to another caregiver.

In practical terms, this model might look like:

- Using spiritual language, prayer, or scripture **within** therapy sessions, but still charting and intervening according to clinical standards. i.e., offer spiritually integrated counseling **within** your licensed role, documenting according to professional standards while making your religious perspective clear in informed consent.
- Limiting "church-only" sacramental work (e.g., intensive deliverance, high-risk ceremonies) to settings and relationships clearly outside your clinical caseload. Offer more explicitly sacramental or Indigenous work **outside** formal counseling hours and roles, under church/tribal auspices, when appropriate, with clear disclosures and boundaries.
- Creating written policies for yourself and your organization about when you will or will not see congregants as therapy clients, and vice versa.

This model is more complex and not suitable for everyone. It requires careful consultation with supervisors, elders, and, at times, legal counsel.

Wilson's repeated warning is that dual roles become dangerous when boundaries blur: when your counseling client becomes your parishioner, and your parishioner becomes your therapy patient without clarity or documentation. The ethical literature echoes this: dual relationships must be managed or avoided to prevent harm and conflicts of interest.

5. Model Three – Licensed Professional, Unlicensed Ministry

A third pattern is common among Indigenous and Native practitioners: maintaining a secular license as one aspect of their vocation while **keeping Native American Traditional Indigenous Medicine (NATIM) entirely within tribal and church jurisdiction.**

Here, federal law adds specific protections:

- **AIRFA (42 U.S.C. § 1996)** declares that it is U.S. policy to protect the inherent right of American Indians and related peoples to believe, express, and exercise their traditional religions, including access to sacred sites, use of sacred objects, and worship through **ceremonials and traditional rites.**
- **IHCIA (25 U.S.C. § 1680u)**

1) "Traditional health care practices" is codified at 25 U.S.C. § 1680u

This section exists and is explicitly titled "Traditional health care practices." It authorizes the promotion of traditional practices consistent with Service standards and includes a federal liability limitation/savings clause (useful for your "boundary" messaging).

2) "Promote traditional health care practices" appears in an operational program section (25 U.S.C. § 1616)

Section 1616 (Community Health Representative Program) directs the Service to "promote traditional health care practices of the Indian tribes served" consistent with Service standards for health care, promotion, and prevention. This is strong support for "integration/recognition,"

- Case law such as *United States v. Boyll* recognizes that protections for Native American Church practices are grounded in religion, not race; sincere participants, Native and non-Native, may be covered when acting within bona fide NAC/tribal structures.

Under this model:

- When you work as, say, an RN or MD in a hospital, you abide fully by professional and institutional standards; NAC or NAIC membership does not excuse you from charting, medication protocols, or mandatory reporting duties in that role.
- When you function as a **traditional healer or NAIC minister**, you do so in separate spaces and times, under clear tribal/church auspices, with members who understand they are in a religious-ceremonial context, not receiving licensed medical services.
- High-risk or "contentious" practices (e.g., sacramental entheogens, invasive rites) are kept well away from your licensed work and conducted only within the strict protocols and safeguards of the tribal/church framework, if at all.

This is especially appropriate when you are dealing with **contentious medicine** (sweat lodges, sacraments, or advanced ceremonies) that should never be confused with hospital work. It allows you to honor both sets of obligations without collapsing them.

This allows you to "walk in two worlds": one as a licensed professional in mainstream systems; the other as a traditional or ecclesiastical healer under Indigenous and religious rights.

6. Practical Safeguards for Walking in Both Worlds

A. Watch your words

- Avoid using reserved medical and massage terms, diagnose, treat, prescribe, cure, massage therapy, except when you are clearly acting **within** your state license and willing to meet that standard.

- In your religious/tribal role, use accurate NAIC-style language: Religious Therapeutics, Chirothesia, Indigenous Thai Yoga Therapy (*Ryksaa Thang Nuad Phaen Boran Thai*) "*Marma Chikitsa*", Ayurveda, pastoral counseling, spiritual direction, Indigenous medicine, etc.

ThaiYogaCenter emphasizes that most legal issues in Thai Yoga and Thai massage arise from ambiguous language, with people calling everything "massage" or "therapy" even when they intend to do spiritual/yogic work.

B. Informed consent and disclosure

Both Wilson and NAIC/ThaiYogaCenter insist on **robust informed consent**:

- Spell out in writing what you do and what you do **not** do, and that you are not providing medical diagnosis or treatment as defined by state law when in your ecclesiastical role.
- Advise members/clients to maintain and seek licensed medical care as needed.
- Identify your role clearly: "I am serving you as an NAIC minister / L.C.H.T.," or "I am serving you as a licensed counselor," and document that conversation.

NAIC's Participant Member Consent and Membership Agreements operationalize this, placing your services firmly in a private religious/tribal domain.

C. Structure and setting

ThaiYogaCenter advises that if you want to avoid being treated as a public massage clinic, you **must not look like one**:

- Do not advertise generic "Thai Massage" to the public if you intend to operate as an ecclesiastical/tribal Thai Yoga ministry.
- Use clearly religious/tribal branding, membership-only language, and private-association framing (PMA) to show that your work is internal to a church/tribal community.

Wilson says something similar more generally: your business form, records, and advertising should all point in the same direction: education and support, and the licensed practice of a regulated profession.

7. Standing in Your Conviction While Honoring Both Roads

The thread running through every part of this book is that **conviction must be lived, not only claimed**. You have a right, under the Constitution, AIRFA, RFRA, IHCIA, RLUIPA, UNDRIP, and parallel state exemptions, to practice Indigenous and religious medicine; that right does not evaporate when you obtain a secular license.

But standing in your conviction does not mean ignoring the obligations you voluntarily accepted as a licensed professional. It means:

- Being ruthlessly honest about which role you are in at any given moment.
- Allowing your state license to inform your ethics and your sense of red-flag situations, even when you are in your ecclesiastical role.
- Allowing your ecclesiastical/tribal commitments to prevent you from collapsing everything into a secular model that denies spirit and community.

Wilson's book and the ThaiYogaCenter legal articles show that many practitioners have navigated this terrain successfully by respecting the distinctions among licensing, certification, and ecclesiastical/tribal licensure, speaking carefully, and structuring their work intelligently.

If you build on that foundation, you can practice as a **legitimate religious health minister and Indigenous healer** while still acting ethically and lawfully with the licenses you already hold. You will not be trying to escape the law; you will be walking the two roads in full daylight, pipe and smudge in one hand, briefcase of rights in the other, doing in public what you know in your heart you were called to do.

Regardless of which model fits you best, several **practical safeguards** help you remain ethical and legally coherent:

1. **Clarity of self-presentation.**
   Always make it clear in writing and in speech **who you are in that moment**: "I am serving you as an NAIC minister in a private religious capacity," or "I am serving you as a licensed counselor in my clinical role."
2. **Accurate scope statements.**
   In your ministry context, repeat and document NAIC-style scope limits: you do **not** diagnose, treat, or prescribe for medical or psychological conditions as defined by state law; you provide Religious Therapeutics, Indigenous ceremonies, and pastoral care.
3. **Separate records.**
   Do not mix clinical charts with ministry notes. Clinical records must meet board and legal standards; ministry notes are ecclesiastical and should be held under church/PMA privacy rules.
4. **Informed consent everywhere.**
   - In clinical work, standard informed-consent forms cover risks, benefits, confidentiality, and your religious orientation, where relevant.

- In ministry: NAIC-style membership and consent forms defining Religious Therapeutics, private association, and constitutional/ AIRFA rights.

5. **Supervision and consultation.**

   Regularly consult with elders, supervisors, or ethics mentors on both sides, clinical and ecclesiastical, especially when roles begin to overlap.

6. **Know your board's rules.**

   Many boards allow respectful integration of spirituality but prohibit certain dual relationships and deceptive advertising. Know where your board draws the lines so you can honor them while still asserting your religious rights outside that context.

SPECIAL NOTES: Working with Licenses You Already Hold

Wilson's Guidance for Certified but Unlicensed (and Dual-Role) Practitioners

Several professional associations and training bodies recommend Wilson's *Legal Guidelines* to their certified members who are not state-licensed or who hold a license in one field but also offer services outside that license. His advice reinforces many of the dual-role principles in this chapter:

- **Know what your license actually covers.**

  Wilson notes the crucial distinction between **licensing** (a government privilege to do what would otherwise be prohibited) and **certification** (a private or organizational recognition of training in an area that may already be lawful to practice). This mirrors the NAIC distinction between state licenses and ecclesiastical/tribal licenses (L.C.H.T., pastoral counseling licenses, FNMB Indigenous Medicine licenses), and why you must not assume that one automatically extends the other.

- **Stay within each role's limits.**

  Wilson repeatedly warns that trouble begins when a practitioner overreaches their role, e.g., a certified coach "treating depression," or an unlicensed helper using language that sounds like a medical diagnosis. For dual-role practitioners under NAIC, this is exactly why you keep your licensed practice, and your Religious Therapeutics practice distinct, and why you must be able to say, at any moment, "Right now I am acting as a licensed _____," or "Right now I am acting solely as an NAIC minister/medicine person."

- **Present yourself honestly and refer appropriately.**

  Wilson encourages certified/unlicensed practitioners to build honest referral relationships with licensed providers, to avoid claiming to "treat" conditions outside their remit, and to be scrupulously honest in advertising. This dovetails with NAIC's guidance that you:
  - Advertise your ministry as a ministry, not as an alternative medical clinic.
  - Refer members to physicians, therapists, or emergency services when signs of serious pathology appear.

o Use your secular training as a safety net and discernment tool, not as a secret expansion of your ecclesiastical scope.

When students read Wilson's manual together with this chapter, they see the same message from two angles: one general (for any unlicensed or hybrid practitioner) and one specifically Indigenous and ecclesiastical (NAIC/Legal Shield). Both urge you to walk the two roads with clarity, never pretending to be a doctor when you are a minister and never hiding your sincere religious and Indigenous identity behind clinical jargon.

IMPLEMENTATION CHECKLIST

Here is a practical, implementation-focused checklist you can use or adapt for managing **dual roles** as a counselor (licensed or otherwise) and a religious/Native American therapeutic minister.

1. Self-Assessment and Role Clarity

- Define in writing your **two roles**:
    - o Role A: Licensed counselor/therapist (scope, setting, population, laws, board).
    - o Role B: Minister/medicine person/Religious Therapeutics practitioner under NAIC or another church/tribal authority
- Write a short statement for each role: "When I am in this role, I am accountable to…" (board vs. church/tribal/PMA).
- Identify **where** you are likely to encounter overlap (e.g., counseling congregants, counseling NAIC members, seeing therapy clients who later join your ministry).
- Decide in advance which **hat has priority** if there is a conflict (e.g., mandatory reporting vs. pastoral confidentiality) and seek consultation about those edge cases.

2. Structural Separation

- Maintain **separate structures** for each role whenever possible:
    - o Separate business entities or at least clearly separate "programs."
    - o Distinct websites or pages: one clearly clinical, one clearly ecclesiastical/tribal (NAIC, church, or PMA-branded).
- Use **different paperwork**:
    - o Clinical: standard counseling intake, informed consent, HIPAA/record policies.
    - o Ministry: NAIC-style membership agreement, Participant Member Consent/Disclosure/Waiver with Religious Therapeutics language and AIRFA/First Amendment notices

- Keep **physical and time boundaries**:
  - Designated hours/locations for licensed work.
  - Designated hours/locations for ministry/ceremonial work.

3. Role Disclosure and Informed Consent

- At first contact with any person, decide: **Am I meeting them as a counselor, a minister (or both)?**
- In clinical settings, your consent form should:
  - Disclose that you are a person of faith and/or ordained, *if* that will be visible in the work.
  - Clarify that counseling services follow the standards and laws of your profession and are not a substitute for medical care.
- In ministry settings, your NAIC/tribal consent form should:
  - Clearly state you are **not** diagnosing, prescribing, treating, or curing medical/psychological conditions as defined by secular law
  - Define "health" in theological terms (Shalom / The Good Way/wholeness) and describe services as Religious Therapeutics, pastoral care, Indigenous ceremony, and Chirothesia.
  - State that services occur in a **private religious domain** between members of a church/PMA/tribal organization.
- Verbally review the role you are in at the start of each new work relationship and **document** that conversation.

4. Boundary Management and Dual-Relationship Controls

- Adopt a written **dual-role policy** for yourself (and your organization), addressing:
  - Whether you will see congregants/NAIC members as clinical clients.
  - Whether you will provide pastoral or ceremonial services to current therapy clients.
- When dual roles are unavoidable (e.g., small communities):
  - Discuss risks/benefits with the person at intake.
  - Document their understanding and your boundary plan (e.g., no social media "friendship," limits on social contact, a clear endpoint for therapy vs. ministry).
- Be prepared to **refer**:
  - If clinical needs escalate beyond what is appropriate for a pastoral setting.
  - If the depth of spiritual involvement makes clinical neutrality unrealistic.

5. Documentation and Records

- Maintain **separate records**:
    - Clinical files: diagnostic impressions (if licensed to diagnose), treatment plans, progress notes, risk assessments, following board and legal standards.
    - Ministry files: brief pastoral/ministry notes, kept under church/PMA privacy rules (clergy-communicant privilege where applicable).
- Never place NAIC membership agreements or AIRFA-based consent forms inside your licensed clinical chart; keep them in the ecclesiastical file.
- If the same person is both a client and a member, explicitly label each contact note with the **role/context** (e.g., "Clinical session – LPC role" vs. "NAIC ceremony – ministerial role").

6. Scope of Practice and Content of Services

- In **clinical sessions** (licensed role):
    - Interventions must meet your profession's standard of care; spiritual themes can be integrated, but you remain accountable to clinical best practices and board rules.
- In **ministry/NAIC sessions**:
    - Services are limited to **non-invasive** Religious Therapeutics and Indigenous practices, including prayer, counsel, ceremonial work, Chirothesia, herbal stewardship, and movement and breath practices.
    - Do not use invasive techniques or restricted drugs outside of narrow, well-defined tribal/church sacraments, and only if your organization explicitly authorizes and safely structures them.
- In all settings, avoid **forbidden medical verbs** (diagnose, prescribe, treat, prevent, mitigate, cure) in a secular sense unless you are clearly operating within a licensed medical scope AND are comfortable with regulatory scrutiny.

7. Communication with Boards, Employers, and Church/Tribal Authorities

- Review your **license board's rules** on:
    - Dual relationships.
    - Use of spiritual/religious interventions.
    - Advertising and public claims.

- Where appropriate, notify your employer (in general terms) that you have a **separate religious ministry**, and confirm any policy boundaries about seeing current patients in that context.
- Ensure your **church/tribal/PMA** has on file:
  - Your ordination/commission.
  - Your NAIC or equivalent membership and scope of practice.
  - Any special licenses (e.g., NAIC LCHT, LCCT, LCP) that define your ministry role

8. Risk-Management and Escalation Plans

- Identify **high-risk situations** in advance:
  - Suicidality, homicidality, abuse/neglect, grave disability.
  - Substance use crises.
  - Severe psychosis or trauma responses.
- Decide which **role** you will operate from in those scenarios and what your **non-negotiable duties** are (e.g., mandated reporting, duty to warn/protect).
- In ministry settings, explicitly state in your consent that:
  - You will **refer or require medical/psychiatric care** when certain red-flag conditions appear.
  - Participation in ceremonies or Religious Therapeutics does not replace needed emergency or ongoing medical care.
- Keep a **referral list** of trusted secular providers (and, where possible, culturally sensitive/Indigenous-friendly clinicians) to whom you can send members when clinical care is indicated.

9. Supervision, Consultation, and Ongoing Education

- Arrange **regular consultations** in both domains:
  - Clinical supervision/peer consultation for your counseling role.
  - Ecclesiastical/tribal mentoring with elders, senior ministers, or experienced medicine people for your ministry role.
- Seek out training on:
  - Ethics of dual roles and boundary maintenance (pastoral + clinical).
  - Legal frameworks for Native American and religious freedom (AIRFA, RFRA, IHCIA, RLUIPA, UNDRIP).
- Periodically review and update your **personal policy** on dual roles as your practice evolves or as laws change.

10. Personal Integrity and Spiritual Discernment

- Regularly ask yourself:
  - "Am I using my ministerial status to avoid standards I should be meeting as a clinician?"
  - "Am I hiding my faith or Indigenous commitments in ways that confuse or mislead those I serve?"
- Commit to **truthful representation**:
  - Never imply you are providing secular clinical treatment when you are acting solely as a minister/medicine person.
  - Never imply that Religious Therapeutics alone will suffice when you know someone needs emergency or specialized care.
- Use prayer, ceremony, and consultation with elders to discern when to **switch hats, refer out, or say no** to a particular dual role.

Used thoughtfully, this checklist can help you build a counseling practice that honors both your license and your calling, walking in two worlds with one coherent, ethical heart.

Chapter 22 Conclusion – Two Roads, One Integrity

For the students, practitioners, and physicians this book addresses, the goal is not to abandon your hard-won licenses, nor to hide your calling as a healer-minister. It is to **bring both under a coherent integrity**: honoring the state's expectations when you act as its agent, and honoring Creator and community when you act as a minister or medicine person.

When you clearly separate roles where needed, integrate them carefully where possible, and root everything in informed consent, transparency, and ethical boundaries, you embody what it means to "walk in both worlds." You show that a legitimate religious health ministry can coexist with, and even enrich, the work of licensed professionals, without surrendering either to confusion or coercion.

LEARNING EXERCISE 22.1
Review & Application
Instructions: Select the best answer based on the reading.

1. What are the "two jurisdictions" a dual-role practitioner inhabits?
   A) Federal and international law
   B) Criminal and civil law
   C) Secular licensing (state board/employer) and ecclesiastical/tribal/PMA jurisdiction
   D) Urban and rural

E) Online and offline
Correct Answer: C

2. Why is it crucial to know "which hat you are wearing"?
   A) To optimize marketing
   B) To avoid religious scrutiny
   C) Because your behavior, language, paperwork, and setting must match the legal and ethical expectations of the role you are acting in
   D) To qualify for grants
   E) To avoid paying taxes
   Correct Answer: C

3. How does the chapter distinguish licensing from certification?
   A) They are identical
   B) Both are governmental
   C) Licensing is a government-granted privilege to perform otherwise restricted acts; certification is private recognition of training
   D) Certification is more powerful
   E) Licensing is always religious
   Correct Answer: C

4. In Model One (clean separation), what is the main structural strategy?
   A) Blend all services under one name
   B) Use one set of forms for everything
   C) Maintain distinct entities, branding, forms, and records for licensed work and religious ministry
   D) Abandon licensure
   E) Avoid documentation
   Correct Answer: C

5. What role does informed consent play across models?
   A) It is optional
   B) It is required only in secular clinics
   C) It clarifies the role you are in, what you offer and don't offer, and directs people to seek licensed care when needed
   D) It replaces ethics codes
   E) It is relevant only to research
   Correct Answer: C

Chapter 23 – Organizational Allies and Oversight Bodies

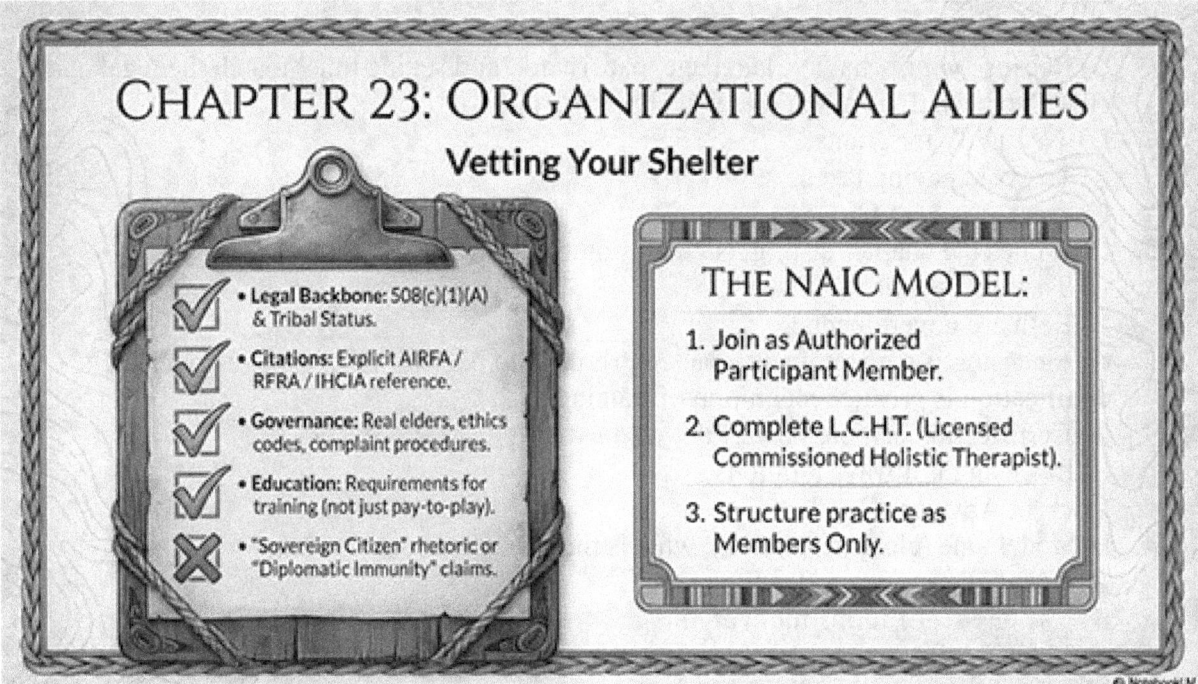

- The kinds of churches, tribal organizations, and PMA-based ministries that can credibly shelter Religious Therapeutics.
- What to look for (and avoid) when choosing an umbrella: law, elders, ethics, education, and realistic promises.
- A step-by-step example of how to enroll in an NAIC-style Legal Shield program and align your practice with it.

A single practitioner with a brochure looks like an unlicensed clinic; a practitioner standing inside a real **church, tribal organization, or PMA with clear oversight and licensure** looks like what they are: a minister or medicine person doing recognized religious work. For students, practitioners, and physicians who want to practice under a **religious therapeutic legal umbrella**, the question is not only "What do I believe?" but also "Who is willing to stand with me, in law, ethics, and community?"

This chapter introduces several types of organizational allies and oversight bodies, then outlines what you should look for before you join any of them. Examples include NAIC and its **Legal Shield** ministry, SMOKH/Priory of Saving Grace, First Nation Medical Board, Nemenhah-type Native churches, and PMA-based wellness ministries such as GoldCare Health & Wellness. The goal is not to sell you on any one group, but to show you what credible shelter looks like, and how it can support a legitimate Religious Therapeutics or Indigenous medicine practice.

1. Why Organizational Allies Matter

Organizational allies do at least four critical things for you:

- **Legal shelter.** They embody the "layered legal umbrella": ecclesiastical jurisdiction, Native American/tribal status, and PMA structure that move your work from the public, commercial domain into a protected private, religious domain.
- **Oversight and credibility.** They issue ordinations, commissions, and licenses; define scopes of practice; and maintain codes of ethics and complaint procedures that demonstrate self-regulation.
- **Education and standards.** They provide training in Religious Therapeutics, Indigenous medicine, and Chirothesia that you can point to when asked about competence.
- **Community and advocacy.** They connect you with peers, provide legal and ethical guidance, and, in some cases, advocate at the state and federal levels for traditional medicine and religious freedom.

When regulators or courts look at your practice, one of their first questions, spoken or unspoken, is: "Who says you can do this?" A solid organizational ally lets you answer that question clearly

2. Examples of Organizational Allies and Oversight Bodies

This list is illustrative, not exhaustive. Always do your own due diligence.

Native American Indigenous Church (NAIC, Inc.) and NAIC Legal Shield

- **Type:** Native American religious tribal organization, church, and expressive PMA; UN/WHO-registered Indigenous Peoples Organization.
- **Role:**
  o Provides church membership for providers and clients.
  o Issues ordinations, commissions, and special licenses such as **N.A.I.C. Licensed Commissioned Holistic Therapist (L.C.H.T.)** through the **NAIC Legal Shield Ministry**.
  o Defines scopes of practice for Religious Therapeutics, Chirothesia, SomaVeda® Thai Yoga, Ayurveda, Indigenous medicine, and related holistic services as **ecclesiastical and tribal**, not secular medicine.
- **NAIC Legal Shield for Holistic Practitioners:**

- Located at naiclegalshield.org, it offers a Licentiate-level license (L.C.H.T.) for religious, ecclesiastical, holistic, and Indigenous providers who want full legal protection for their modalities under NAIC's tribal/church umbrella.
  - Legal Shield literature states that L.C.H.T. providers can "stop practicing in the shadows" and practice Somaveda®, Thai Yoga, Ayurveda, Christian pastoral care, herbalism, energy therapies, and many other holistic services "with all legal protections afforded to N.A.I.C." across all U.S. states and internationally, as long as they meet education and scope standards.
  - The site lists dozens of protected modalities, from Native American medicine and Chirothesia to holistic nutrition, energy therapies, Christian pastoral care, and traditional tribal health care, explicitly framed as **religious and Indigenous**, outside state-mandated scopes.
- **Contact and resources:**
  - NAIC Legal Shield main site and applications: naiclegalshield.org (e.g., "I'm a Holistic Practitioner," "Join NAIC Legal Shield," practitioner resources).
  - Church/Articles of Religious Practice: nativefirechurch.org
  - Education: naic-edu.org, thaiyogacenter.com

Sacred Medical Order of the Church of Hope (SMOCH/SMOKH) & Priory of Saving Grace

- **Type:** Ecclesiastical medical order and diocese of the Eastern Apostolic Orthodox Catholic Church of the Americas (Chaldean-Syrian Rite); Priory of Saving Grace as NAIC's parent ecclesiastical body.
- **Role:**
  - Provides seminary and monastic training in sanctified healing, ecclesiastical medicine, and holistic and Indigenous medicines.
  - Ordains priest-physicians and friars; issues ecclesiastical medical licenses and recognizes Traditional and Indigenous medicine as a sacred ministry.
- **Benefit to you:** Creates a **church-based medical vocation** (monastic medicine, priest-physician) that dovetails with NAIC's tribal/religious framework, strengthening the "layered umbrella."
- **Contact:** https://smoch.org; https://NativeFireChurch.Org

First Nation Medical Board (FNMB)

- **Type:** Indigenous medicine licensing board.
- **Role:**
  - Provides **medical licensing for providers** practicing Indigenous and holistic medicine; positions itself as an alternative to state boards for "doctors who want

to practice natural medicine, be safe from prosecution, and focus on putting patients first."

- o Recognizes multiple traditional and holistic disciplines and sets standards and accountability for Indigenous Medicine (IM) practice.
- **Benefit:** For some physicians, naturopaths, and advanced practitioners, FNMB offers a recognized Indigenous medicine license that complements NAIC/SMOKH church and tribal credentials.
- **Contact:** firstnationmedicalboard.com

Native American Church / Nemenhah-Style Organizations

- **Type:** Native American Church variants and inter-tribal religious organizations emphasizing natural healing sacraments.
- **Role:**
  - o Provide a religious identity and community where natural medicine is a sacrament, often linked to Peyote or other plant sacraments and traditional ceremonies.
  - o Offer ordinations or recognition for "medicine men/women" and natural practitioners within their spiritual framework.
- **Caution:** Structures and legal soundness vary widely. Some NAC branches have deep historical and tribal roots; others are newer and more loosely organized. You must investigate how any given branch relates to AIRFA, RFRA, and recognized tribal authorities.
- **Contact:** Search for the specific Native American Church (NAC) or Nemenhah body; review their legal and tribal documentation carefully.

GoldCare Health & Wellness (PMA-Based Health Ministry)

- **Type:** Private Membership Association and wellness-oriented health ministry.
- **Role:**
  - o Offers a PMA framework for doctors, nurses, naturopaths, coaches, and wellness professionals to provide **personalized, values-driven care** outside insurance and state-dominated models.
  - o Emphasizes freedom of choice, trust, and personalized wellness, including natural and preventive approaches; members agree to private-association terms.
- **Benefit:** For providers aligned with its Judeo-Christian and medical freedom ethos, GoldCare can serve as an example of how a **PMA-anchored wellness ministry** can function. However, it is not a tribal church like NAIC.
- **Contact:** goldcare.com; join.goldcare.com

Other Allies and Contexts

- **Christian counseling and pastoral associations** that issue ecclesiastical counseling credentials and codes of ethics; helpful especially when you combine pastoral counseling with Religious Therapeutics.
- **Urban Indian health organizations and tribal health departments** are integrating traditional healers into whole-person care models, offering practical precedents and, in some cases, formal recognition for traditional practitioners.

3. What to Look For in an Organizational Umbrella

When evaluating any church, tribal organization, order, or PMA as a potential umbrella, consider at least these areas.

A. Legal and Jurisdictional Backbone

- Clear statement of **jurisdiction**:
  - 508(c)(1)(A) status for churches/FBOs
  - Tribal or Native American religious status, where applicable.
  - PMA structure based on First and Fourteenth Amendment rights, with membership contracts and private-domain language.
- Explicit reference to **AIRFA, RFRA, IHCIA, RLUIPA, UNDRIP**, and relevant state religious-practice exemptions, not vague "sovereign citizen" rhetoric.
- A track record: years of operation, published legal guidelines or compliance pages, and, ideally, citations in court records, agency memoranda, or academic/NGO discussions.

B. Governance, Ethics, and Scope of Practice

- A written **Code of Ethics** and ceremonial/clinical protocols; internal discipline for misconduct.
- A defined **scope of practice** for the licenses or commissions they issue (e.g., NAIC LCHT, FNMB Indigenous Medicine license, SMOKH priest-physician), including clear non-medical framing for Religious Therapeutics and Chirothesia.
- Transparent **complaint and oversight mechanisms**: who handles grievances, how decisions are made, and what consequences exist for boundary violations.

C. Education and Formation

- Real training, not just "ordination by credit card." Look for:

- o Course catalogs, syllabi, and credible instructors.
- o Minimum hours and practicum requirements (e.g., NAIC LCHT's 700+ hours plus supervised practice).
- Ongoing formation in law, ethics, and Indigenous/Religious Therapeutics (e.g., NAIC Legal Shield's practitioner resources, surveys, and legal booklets).

D. Theological and Cultural Alignment

- A theology and cultural stance that genuinely match your own (Indigenous, Christian, interfaith, etc.), so your ministry is not just legally but **spiritually** at home.
- Respect for Indigenous sovereignty and protocols if they claim Native American identity; beware groups that borrow Native imagery without authentic ties or accountability.
- Alignment with your **faith and lineage**: Christian, Indigenous, intertribal, interfaith, etc.
- Respectful, authentic handling of Indigenous identities and ceremonies, with real Native leadership and accountability where Native claims are made.

E. Realistic, Non-Inflated Promises

- Be cautious with organizations that:
  - o Over-sell "diplomatic passports," "new birth certificates," or sweeping claims of immunity from all laws.
  - o Use "sovereign citizen"-style language or encourage defiance of basic criminal or safety laws.
- Favor organizations that emphasize **compliance and cooperation**: they talk about exemptions as **exceptions**, not loopholes, and repeatedly stress safety, ethics, and working within the bounds of law.

Sound organizations:

- Talk about **exemptions and protections** as carefully delimited, not magical shields.
- Emphasize working ethically **within** the law, not escaping it.

Red flags:

- Claims that you will be completely "beyond all law" or never have to answer to any authority.
- Heavy selling of passports, "diplomatic immunity," or unrelated "trust packages."

4. Questions and Concerns to Explore Before You Join

Before committing to any umbrella, ask:

- **What exactly are they offering me?**
  - Ordination? A counseling or Indigenous medicine license? A PMA membership only? A provider directory and telehealth platform?
- **What are my responsibilities?**
  - Tithes or dues? Participation in ongoing training? Adherence to specific doctrine? Reporting requirements?
- **What happens if there is a dispute or investigation?**
  - Do they have legal counsel or guidance? Will they stand behind you? What is their track record when members face regulatory questions?
- **How do they treat Indigenous knowledge and communities?**
  - Are Indigenous protocols honored? Are there Native leaders in governance? Do they apply UNDRIP/OCAP-style respect for data and plant knowledge?
- **Is their rhetoric sober or sensational?**
  - Serious organizations talk about "religious exemptions," "tribal jurisdiction," and case law (e.g., *Boyll*, *O Centro*); unserious ones promise instant immunity and magic documents.

Before you commit: Let's reiterate

- **What exactly will I receive?**
  - Membership only? Ordination? A Licentiate license (e.g., NAIC LCHT)? A place in a provider directory?
- **What are the prerequisites and expectations?**
  - Education and training hours? Continuing education? Tithes or dues? Participation in oversight?
- **How have they responded when members faced scrutiny?**
  - Can they point to actual cases where their framework helped clarify a practitioner's status or de-escalate regulatory concerns?
- **Do they support dual-role practitioners?**
  - If you hold a state license, do they offer guidance on keeping roles distinct and compliant, as NAIC and NAIC Legal Shield emphasize?
- **Can you talk to current practitioners?**
  - Personal testimonies from those practicing under their umbrella are often the best indicator of real-world support.

If possible, **speak with current members**, especially those who have navigated regulatory questions, before you sign anything. Their lived experience is often more revealing than marketing language.

5. How to Join NAIC?

Here is a practical implementation checklist you can use to guide **NAIC Legal Shield (L.C.H.T.) enrollment** from first inquiry through active practice under the NAIC umbrella. It is written for students, practitioners, and physicians who want to bring their holistic/Indigenous work under a religious therapeutic legal shield.

1. Clarify Fit and Intent

- Confirm your **overall goal**:
    - Protect an existing holistic or Indigenous practice.
    - Launch a new Religious Therapeutic ministry under NAIC
- Review the NAIC Legal Shield site sections:
    - "I'm a Holistic Practitioner"
    - "Who Can Join NAIC?"
    - "Practitioner Resources"
- Ask yourself:
    - Are my services non-invasive and natural (no drugs, no surgery)?
    - Am I willing to reframe my work explicitly as **Religious Therapeutics/Indigenous Healthcare (IHSM)** rather than as secular medicine?

2. Inventory Your Training and Practice

- List your **current modalities** (e.g., Thai Yoga, massage, yoga, Ayurveda, herbalism, energy work, counseling, coaching, bodywork, Indigenous ceremonies)
- Document your **education and hours**:
    - NAIC/ACNM or Thai Yoga Center courses (CTP1–3, Ayurveda, etc.) and hours completed.
    - Other recognized trainings (Reiki, yoga therapy, counseling, nursing, etc.), including approximate contact hours.
- Identify your **current scope** and where it already fits NAIC's list of accepted holistic services (see "Who Can Join NAIC?" service list, energy balancing, herbology, coaching, etc.).

3. Establish or Confirm NAIC Membership

- If you are **not yet a member**:

- Apply for an NAIC Participant or Full Member (AFM) card through NativeFireChurch/NAIC membership pages. Membership is a prerequisite for L.C.H.T. licensure.
- If you **are a member**:
    - Confirm your status is "active and in good standing."
    - Make sure you have read and agree to the **NAIC Code of Ethics** and the Authorized Participant Member Agreement (A.P.M.A.), as these are preconditions for Legal Shield licensing.

4. Review L.C.H.T. Prerequisites and Scope

- Carefully read the **"Join NAIC Legal Shield"** page. Confirm that you:
    - Are an active NAIC Authorized Member in good standing.
    - Have substantial formal education in one or more of:
        - SomaVeda® Integrated Traditional Therapies / Indigenous Thai Yoga
        - Christian pastoral/clerical/holistic medicine
        - Holistic wellness, ministerial/pastoral care, nutrition, Indigenous medicine, etc.
    - Meet or can reasonably meet the **minimum hours**:
        - Typically: completion of Thai Yoga Center CTP1–3, plus at least 100 hours supervised practice, **or**
        - A minimum of 700 hours of training in relevant holistic, pastoral, or Indigenous areas, plus 100 hours of documented clinical practice under approved teachers.
- Review the **L.C.H.T. scope of practice** as described:
    - Commissioned Holistic Therapist/Minister with a broad Religious Therapeutic scope (Thai Yoga, Ayurveda, Huna/Lomi, Christian counseling, Indigenous medicine, etc.), explicitly as **spiritually based holistic and natural therapies**, not secular medicine

5. Complete the L.C.H.T. Application

- Open the NAIC Legal Shield **L.C.H.T. Membership Application** (JotForm).
- Prepare to provide:
    - Personal information and contact details.
    - Summary of your holistic practice and modalities.
    - Education history (courses, schools, hours, transcripts if available).
    - Any existing licenses or certifications (secular or ecclesiastical).

- Read the **Membership Contract / Agreement** text embedded in the application:
  - Declaration of Purpose from NAIC Articles of Association.
  - Acceptance of ecclesiastical jurisdiction and private-membership domain language.
- Upload or be ready to submit:
  - Copies of certificates/transcripts from NAIC/ACNM or other approved programs.
- Submit the application online, and if instructed, print, sign, and mail or scan/email the signed contract to the NAIC address and support email:
  - NAIC, Inc., 8491 Central Ave., Brooksville, FL 34613
  - support@nativefirechurch.org

6. Arrange Payment and Understand Fees

- Review the current **passage fee and renewal** structure on naiclegalshield.org:
  - Initial L.C.H.T. donation/passage fee plus a separate application fee (amounts may update; check the current page).
  - Annual renewal (e.g., around $250–$275) and any late-fee policy.
- Clarify:
  - Whether discounts are available for multi-year commitments.
  - Refund and cancellation policies (see NAIC Tribal Org. donation/cancellation policy).
- Make payment via the method specified in the application or on the site.

7. Prepare Supporting Documents for Vetting

- Gather and organize:
  - Copies of all relevant training certificates and transcripts.
  - A brief CV or resume, including clinical/ministry experience.
  - Any existing professional licenses (LMT, RN, ND, MD, counselor, etc.), along with a short statement on how you intend to **keep secular and ecclesiastical work distinct**, as NAIC recommends
- Have available:
  - A written description of your current practice, framed in NAIC language (Religious Therapeutics, Indigenous Healthcare, Chirothesia, etc., not secular "massage" or "medicine")

8. During the Review and Vetting Period

- Allow up to about **10 business days** (excluding holidays and weekends) for NAIC to review your application, vet documentation, and process payment, as indicated in the JotForm notice.
- Be prepared to:
  - Answer follow-up questions or supply additional documentation (e.g., proof of supervised hours, letters from teachers).
  - Clarify any high-risk modalities you use (e.g., structural bodywork, entheogens, invasive techniques) so NAIC can help you frame a lawful scope under its Legal Shield

9. After Approval: Set Up Your Practice Under the Shield

Once you receive confirmation and your L.C.H.T. license/ordination:

- **Update your identity**:
  - Add the appropriate ecclesiastical title (e.g., "N.A.I.C. Licensed Commissioned Holistic Therapist (L.C.H.T.), Ordained Minister") to ministry materials, not to secular employer documents
- **Align your practice structure** with NAIC guidelines:
  - All clients become NAIC APM/AFM members or sign NAIC membership/waiver forms before receiving services.
  - Services are explicitly described and delivered as Religious Therapeutics/Indigenous medicine, not as secular medical or massage services.
- Implement NAIC's **ethical framework**:
  - Adopt the NAIC Code of Ethics and Chirothesia Practitioners Code (Do no harm; informed consent; whole-person focus; honor elders and lineage).

10. Compliance, Marketing, and Ongoing Support

- Review **"Practitioner Resources"** on naiclegalshield.org regularly for updates on:
  - Legal compliance, terminology, "forbidden words," and DSHEA/FDA language.
  - Best practices for website wording, meta-tags, and linking to official NAIC/ACNM sites.
- Adjust all public-facing materials to:
  - Avoid regulated secular terms ("massage," "diagnose," "treat," "cure") except in clearly ecclesiastical contexts
  - Use NAIC-approved descriptors (SomaVeda® Integrated Traditional Therapies®, Indigenous Thai Yoga Therapy, Religious Therapeutics, Native American Medicine, etc.).

- Stay connected:
  - Subscribe to NAIC Legal Shield updates, NAIC POST, and practitioner bulletins.
  - Participate in NAIC/ACNM continuing education and gatherings to keep your practice aligned with evolving standards. https://NativeFireChurch.org

11. Periodic Review and Renewal

- Track your **license expiration date** and NAIC membership status.
  - Renew your L.C.H.T. license on time to avoid late fees and any lapse in coverage.
- Annually review:
  - Your scope of practice, to ensure you are still within NAIC's authorized modalities
  - Your dual-role boundaries if you also hold state licenses (e.g., LMT, RN, counselor), and make adjustments as your practice evolves.

Used step-by-step, this checklist will help you move from interest to **fully authorized NAIC Legal Shield L.C.H.T. practitioner**, with your holistic or Indigenous ministry clearly defined, documented, and sheltered under a coherent tribal-church legal framework.

Chapter 23 Conclusion – Choosing a House Worthy of Your Medicine

For those of you stepping into Religious Therapeutics and Indigenous medicine, your choice of organizational ally may be the most important legal decision you make. A good house, NAIC, SMOKH/Priory, FNMB, Nemenhah, a solid PMA like GoldCare, or a similarly grounded body, gives your ministry a **roof**: clear jurisdiction, ethical oversight, and a community that understands both ceremony and law.

For those preparing to practice under a religious therapeutic legal umbrella, the organization you align with is not just a logo; it is a **house** that will either hold or drop you when pressure comes. NAIC, with its Legal Shield ministry; SMOKH/Priory; FNMB; Native American Church bodies; and carefully structured PMAs such as GoldCare, each illustrate different ways churches, tribal organizations, and associations can provide housing.

Choose slowly and with discernment. Look for real law, real elders, real ethics, and real training. When you find an ally that meets those tests, you gain more than legal coverage; you gain a community and a lineage that can carry your Religious Therapeutics and Indigenous medicine forward in a way that is both spiritually faithful and legally defensible. That is the kind of house worthy of the calling into which you are stepping.

Do not join lightly. Ask hard questions, read their codes, study their legal basis, and test whether their spirit and structure match your calling. When you find the right ally, you will not only gain protection; you will gain elders, peers, and a living tradition that can carry your work forward long after you are gone. That is the kind of umbrella worthy of the medicine you are learning to carry.

LEARNING EXERCISE 23.1
Review & Application
Instructions: Select the best answer based on the reading.

1. Why are organizational allies (churches, tribal bodies, PMAs) so important?
   A) They provide marketing only
   B) They guarantee income
   C) They offer legal shelter, oversight, education, and community credibility for Religious Therapeutics
   D) They eliminate personal responsibility
   E) They replace personal conviction
   Correct Answer: C

2. What does NAIC Legal Shield's L.C.H.T. license represent?
   A) A state medical license
   B) A federal DEA registration
   C) An ecclesiastical/tribal licensure for holistic and Indigenous Religious Therapeutics under NAIC's legal umbrella
   D) A malpractice policy
   E) A corporate franchise
   Correct Answer: C

3. Which feature is *essential* when evaluating any potential umbrella organization?
   A) Celebrity endorsements
   B) Promises of diplomatic immunity papers
   C) Clear legal basis (e.g., 508(c)(1)(A), tribal status, PMA), ethics code, scope of practice, and real governance
   D) No requirements for training
   E) Anonymous leadership
   Correct Answer: C

4. Which is a red flag mentioned in the chapter?
   A) References to RFRA and AIRFA
   B) Requirement to tithe
   C) Heavy promotion of "sovereign citizen"-style immunity, passports, or magic documents
   D) Internal complaint procedures
   E) Continuing education
   Correct Answer: C

5. In the NAIC enrollment checklist, which step moves a practitioner from interest to sheltered practice?
   A) Posting on social media
   B) Skipping documentation

C) Becoming an NAIC member, completing the L.C.H.T. application, and structuring practice to serve members only under NAIC forms and language
D) Closing all existing practices
E) Avoiding any contact with NAIC
Correct Answer: C

Chapter 24 – Standing in Your Conviction: Walking the Two Roads

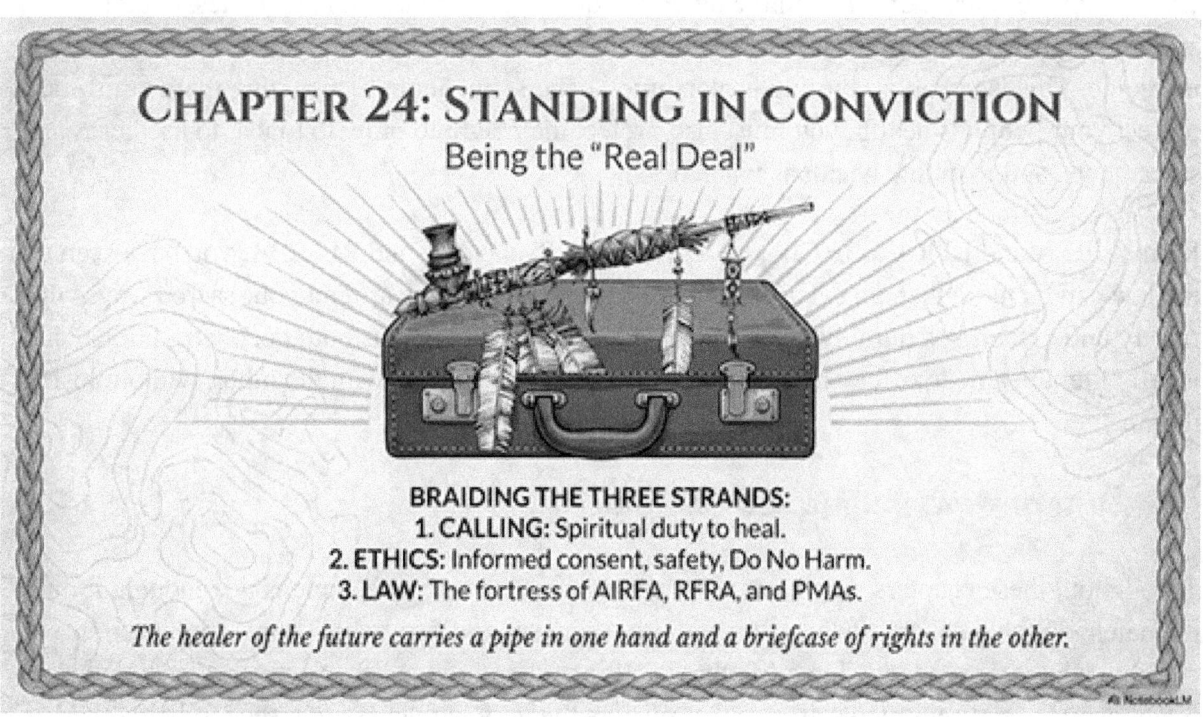

CHAPTER 24: STANDING IN CONVICTION
Being the "Real Deal"

BRAIDING THE THREE STRANDS:
1. CALLING: Spiritual duty to heal.
2. ETHICS: Informed consent, safety, Do No Harm.
3. LAW: The fortress of AIRFA, RFRA, and PMAs.

The healer of the future carries a pipe in one hand and a briefcase of rights in the other.

- ❧ How to weave together theology, ethics, and law into a single coherent way of life as a healer-minister.
- ❧ What it means to be "the real deal" in the eyes of elders, courts, and the communities you serve.
- ❧ How to craft your own Statement of Sacred Conviction, refine your structures, and continue walking the Red Road with "sacred hands" and "secured rights."

From the first page of this course, you have been invited to see yourself not as a technician competing with secular medicine, but as a minister and medicine person whose work is rooted in Indigenous ceremony, scripture, and natural law. Along the way, you have learned the four umbrellas, the meaning of Religious Therapeutics and Chirothesia, the legal architecture of AIRFA and RFRA, the Herbalist Charter, and the practical ethics of informed consent and scope of practice. This final chapter gathers those strands into a single charge: to walk the **two** roads,

217

Red Road and legal road, with a sincere and firmly held conviction that is visible in how you live, speak, and serve

The healer of the future

The course gave you a striking image: "the Medicine Man of the past carried a bow; the Medicine Man of the future holds the Law." You might picture that future healer standing upright, Sacred Pipe and smudge in one hand, before a table of wholesome food and pristine water, with a briefcase of rights in the other, the domestic and international codes, church articles, PMA contracts, and ethical guidelines that secure space for Indigenous and religious medicine. This is not about turning healers into lawyers, but about recognizing that in this era, to protect your people's health, you must also protect their right to pray, to touch, to use herbs and sacraments, and to define health as wholeness.

From AIRFA and RFRA to IHCIA, UNDRIP, OCAP, Nagoya, and RLUIPA, you have seen that the law can be more than an enemy; it can be part of the **fortress** around your sacred ways when rightly understood and humbly used. The healer of the future is thus both deeply traditional and legally literate, able to offer ceremony with one hand and citation with the other, without losing their center.

Integrating calling, ethics, and law

Throughout these chapters, you have also been shown that sincerity alone is not enough; it must be matched with a coherent way of practicing. A sincere and firmly held conviction becomes credible when it is embedded in a life that is clean and ordered: a life of prayer, ceremony, right relationship, and disciplined self-care that mirrors the very wholeness you seek to help others find

Ethically, you were asked to embrace informed consent, honest language, respect for boundaries, and a commitment to "do no harm" using non-invasive, natural, and spiritual means. Legally, you were taught to stand inside real structures, such as churches, tribal organizations, PMAs, and to define your work plainly as Religious Therapeutics and Indigenous medicine, not as diagnosis, prescription, or treatment under state medical acts. When these three, calling, ethics, and law, are braided together, your practice does not hide in the shadows; it stands in the light as a lawful, principled ministry.

Being the "real deal."

One theme has repeated from prologue to this final page: the importance of being the **real** deal. That means your use of terms like "minister," "medicine person," "Native healer," or "pastoral counselor" is not marketing language, but a truthful description of how you were trained, who ordained or commissioned you, and what you actually do. It also means your invocation of exemptions is not a loophole grab, but a natural consequence of living out your church's or tribe's doctrines, ceremonies, and codes of conduct.

Courts and boards look past paper and ask, "Is this person authentically acting within a religious or Indigenous system, or are they just rebranding massage or medicine to avoid regulation?" The "real deal" practitioner can answer that question calmly: by pointing to their lineage, training, ordination, NAIC or other memberships, scopes of practice, consent forms, and above all, a way of life that clearly matches the convictions they claim to hold. When your inner road and outer road line up, your credibility rises, and the likelihood of vexation falls.

Final encouragement and next steps

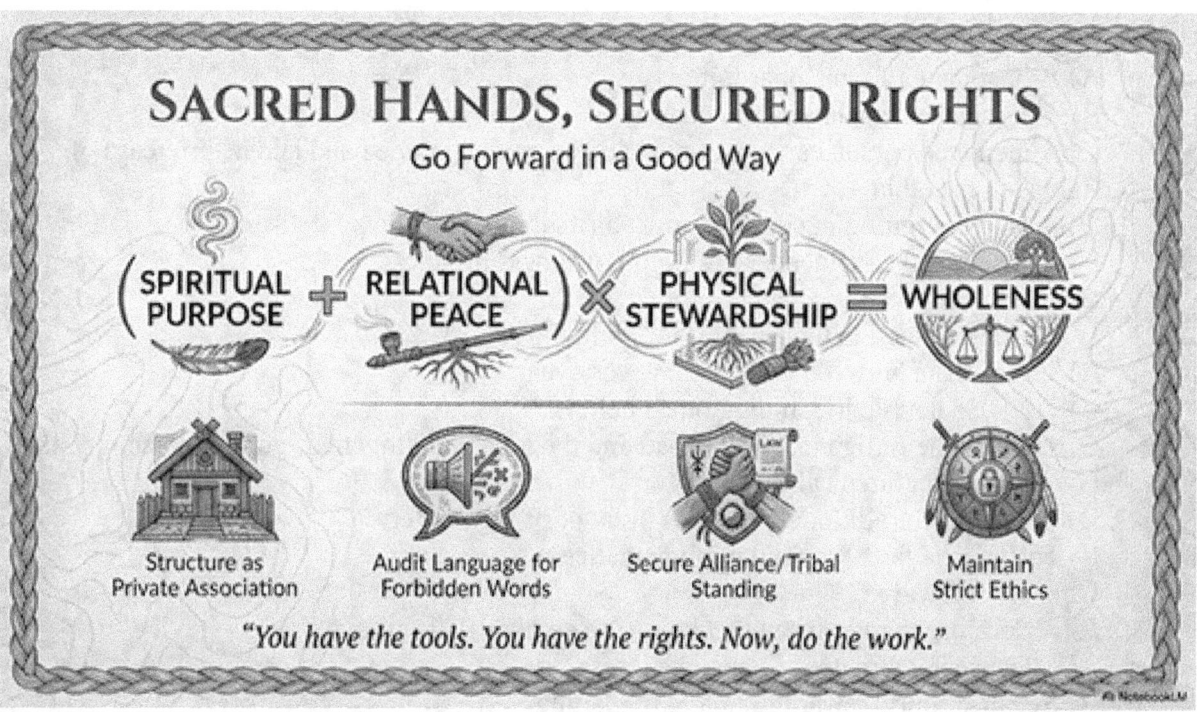

As this course closes, the road does not end; it widens. You have been given language to describe your work, frameworks to protect it, and examples of how others have woven Indigenous ceremony, Christian faith, holistic medicine, and modern legal protections into a single, walkable path. Now the work is to make it concrete in your own setting.

Your next steps might include refining your **Statement of Sacred Conviction**, formalizing your relationship with a church or tribal body, completing NAIC-aligned training or Legal Shield licensure, updating your consent and membership forms, and aligning your marketing language with your religious and tribal identity. It may mean having hard conversations with employers, colleagues, or family about what you actually do, and do not, offer.

Most of all, it means choosing every day to walk upright: to pick up the Pipe and smudge with reverence, to bless and share good food and water, and to carry that briefcase of rights not as a weapon of defiance but as a tool of protection for your people. If you can do that, standing in your conviction, practicing in good faith under a lawful umbrella, and living as an example of the health and wholeness you teach, then the long Red Road you have walked through these pages will continue under your feet, and under the feet of those who follow you.

LEARNING EXERCISE 24.1
Review & Application
Instructions: Select the best answer based on the reading.

1. What image does the chapter use to describe the "healer of the future"?
   A) A hospital CEO in a boardroom
   B) A researcher in a laboratory coat
   C) A medicine person carrying a pipe and a smudge in one hand and a "briefcase of rights" in the other
   D) A lawyer arguing in court without spiritual practice
   E) A social media influencer promoting wellness products
   Correct Answer: C
2. What does it mean in this chapter to "walk the two roads"?
   A) To alternate between two careers every year
   B) To live a double life, hiding one's beliefs
   C) To walk the Indigenous/Red Road and the legal road together, uniting ceremony and law in one integrated calling
   D) To abandon traditional practices in favor of legal safety
   E) To separate faith from all public practice
   Correct Answer: C
3. Why does the chapter insist that being "the real deal" is crucial?
   A) Because it guarantees financial success
   B) Because courts reward dramatic marketing
   C) Because credible religious-freedom claims depend on authentic training, lineage, ordination, practice structure, and a life that matches one's stated convictions
   D) Because it impresses social media followers
   E) Because it eliminates the need for consent forms
   Correct Answer: C
4. Which combination best describes the three strands the chapter says must be braided together?

A) Marketing, technology, and networking

B) Politics, fundraising, and branding

C) Calling, ethics, and law

D) Diet, exercise, and supplements

E) Research, publication, and conferences

Correct Answer: C

5. What concrete "next step" does the chapter encourage readers to take?

A) Avoid any organizational affiliation

B) Depend only on informal verbal agreements

C) Refine a personal Statement of Sacred Conviction and align structures, membership, consent, organizational alliances, and language with that conviction

D) Immediately close all existing practices

E) Stop engaging with any legal frameworks

Correct Answer: C

Appendix A: Sample Statement of Sacred Conviction and Ecclesiastical Duty

This sample text illustrates how a practitioner can frame their work as religious and Indigenous ministry rather than secular medicine. Adapt details (name, lineage, scriptures, ceremonies) to your own tradition.

Sample

I, _____, stand before Creator, my ancestors, and this body as a servant of Spirit. I walk two roads: the Indigenous path taught by my elders and the path of the Gospel, which calls me to heal the sick, comfort the broken, and restore those who have lost their way. My work is not a commercial service; it is a sacred duty.

I hold as a central tenet of my faith that a human being is a unity of spirit, soul, and body. Health, in my belief, is not merely the absence of disease but a state of wholeness, Shalom, The Good Way, in which a person lives in right relationship with Creator, with their own conscience, with their community, and with creation. Any practice that treats the body as a machine while ignoring the spirit is, in my understanding, incomplete and contrary to my religious convictions.

Therefore, the herbs, laying on of hands, prayers, ceremonies, moral counsel, and other natural remedies I offer are not "medical treatments" as that term is defined in secular law. They are sacraments and religious therapeutics. I act as a minister and a medical person, not as a secular physician or psychotherapist. I aim to remove impediments to wholeness, to restore harmony, and to support the person's own journey toward spiritual integrity and peace.

I acknowledge the authority of the Native American Indigenous Church / ecclesiastical body that has ordained or commissioned me, and I agree to practice within the scope, ethics, and ceremonies they have set forth. I also acknowledge the laws of the United States and its States, including the American Indian Religious Freedom Act, the Religious Freedom Restoration Act, and related protections, which affirm my right to exercise and express my traditional and religious healing practices for those who seek them.

To deny these ministries to those who request them in faith would be, in my conscience, to disobey both the Great Commission and the law of All My Relations. I therefore declare that my work is and shall remain an expression of sincerely held religious belief and Indigenous identity, carried out transparently, ethically, and within the protections granted by church, tribe, and law.

Appendix B: Sample Membership and Informed-Consent Forms

These examples show structure and key clauses, not final legal documents. Always adapt language to your jurisdiction and organizational rules and seek legal counsel where needed.

1. Sample Membership Agreement (Private Religious/Tribal Association)

Title: Participant Membership and Private Association Agreement

1. **Parties and Purpose**
   - I, _____ ("Member"), voluntarily apply to become a member of _____ (church/tribal organization/PMA).
   - I understand that this body is a private, faith-based, Indigenous religious association dedicated to spiritual education, Religious Therapeutics, and traditional medicine for its members.
2. **Private Domain and Jurisdiction**
   - I agree that all services, communications, and activities I receive from ministers/practitioners of this organization are provided in a private, ecclesiastical, and tribal context, between members, and are not open to the general public.
   - I consent to resolve any disputes through the organization's internal processes and ecclesiastical/tribal arbitration mechanisms, not through public courts except where required by criminal law.
3. **Nature of Services**
   - I understand that ministers and practitioners do not diagnose, prescribe, treat, or cure medical or psychological conditions as defined by state practice acts, and that their services are spiritual, pastoral, ceremonial, educational, and traditional in nature.
   - I have been advised to seek licensed medical care for any condition I believe requires such attention.
4. **Acknowledgment and Signature**
   - I have read and understood this agreement, and I join as a member freely and without coercion.

Member Signature: _____ Date: _____

2. Sample Informed-Consent for Religious Therapeutics Session

Title: Religious Therapeutics / Indigenous Healing Session Consent

1. **Request for Services**
   - I, _____, request Religious Therapeutics and/or Indigenous healing services from _____ (practitioner), an authorized minister/medicine person of _____ (organization).

2. **Definition of Health and Scope**
   - I understand that within this ministry, health is defined as wholeness and right relationship, spiritual, emotional, mental, and physical, not merely the absence of disease.
   - I understand that the practitioner will use non-invasive, natural, and spiritual methods, including prayer, anointing, laying on of hands, movement, breathwork, herbal and nutritional guidance, and traditional ceremonies.

3. **Non-Medical Nature of Services**
   - I understand that the practitioner does not provide diagnosis, treatment, prescription, or cure for any disease, injury, or mental disorder as defined by secular law and that these services are not a substitute for licensed medical or psychological care.

4. **Voluntary Participation and Assumption of Responsibility**
   - I participate voluntarily and accept responsibility for my own health decisions, including whether to use conventional medical services.

5. **Confidentiality and Records**
   - I understand that records of these sessions are maintained as ecclesiastical/tribal pastoral records, not as medical records, and are protected under clergy-communicant and association privacy principles where applicable.

6. **Consent**
   - By signing below, I acknowledge that I have had the opportunity to ask questions and that I consent to receive these services.

Member Signature: _____ Date: _____

Appendix C: Excerpts from Key Statutes and Cases

The following brief excerpts and summaries are provided for study and reference. Always consult the full text for precise language.

1. American Indian Religious Freedom Act (AIRFA), 42 U.S.C. § 1996

- **Policy statement:**
    - "It shall be the policy of the United States to protect and preserve for American Indians their inherent right of freedom to believe, express, and exercise the traditional religions of the American Indian, Eskimo, Aleut, and Native Hawaiians, including but not limited to access to sites, use and possession of sacred objects, and the freedom to worship through ceremonials and traditional rites."

2. Religious Freedom Restoration Act (RFRA), 42 U.S.C. § 2000bb

- **Core rule:**
    - Government shall not substantially burden a person's exercise of religion unless it demonstrates a compelling governmental interest and uses the least restrictive means.

3. Indian Health Care Improvement Act (IHCIA), 25 U.S.C. § 1680u, "Traditional health care practices" (IHCIA traditional practices provision; promotion authority + U.S. liability limitation). https://www.law.cornell.edu/uscode/text/25/1680uTraditional healers:

- Authorizes the Indian Health Service "IHCIA contemplates incorporation of tribal culture and **traditional health care practices** into Indian health programs: for example, the Community Health Representative Program directs the Service to promote traditional health care practices of the tribes served (25 U.S.C. § 1616), and the Act includes a specific 'Traditional health care practices' provision that addresses promotion consistent with Service standards and sets a federal liability limitation (25 U.S.C. § 1680u)." (https://www.law.cornell.edu/uscode/text/25/1616)

4. Religious Land Use and Institutionalized Persons Act (RLUIPA), 42 U.S.C. § 2000cc

- Land use protects religious assemblies and institutions from substantial burdens imposed by zoning and land use regulations unless strict scrutiny applies.

5. United States v. Boyll, 774 F. Supp. 1333 (D.N.M. 1991)

- Holding: protections for Native American Church sacramental peyote use are based on religion, not race; they can extend to sincere non-Indian members.

6. Gonzales v. O Centro Espírita Beneficente União do Vegetal, 546 U.S. 418 (2006)

- Holding: under RFRA, the federal government must allow a small church to import and use a sacramental tea containing a controlled substance, absent a demonstrated compelling interest and least restrictive means.

7. Florida State Exemptions for Religious Practice

- Example: **Fla. Stat. § 491.014 (Exemptions)** and **Fla. Stat. § 458.303(2)(g)** exempt the practice of the religious tenets of any church and ministerial duties (without separate charge or under church auspices) from psychology and medical licensing requirements.

8. United Nations Declaration on the Rights of Indigenous Peoples (UNDRIP)

- Article 24: affirms that Indigenous peoples have the right to their traditional medicines and to maintain their health practices.
- Article 31: affirms their right to maintain, control, protect, and develop their cultural heritage, traditional knowledge, and traditional cultural expressions, including traditional medicines and associated resources.

9. OCAP® Principles (First Nations Information Governance Centre)

- Ownership, Control, Access, Possession: framework for Indigenous data sovereignty, ensuring communities own and manage data about themselves and their knowledge.

10. Nagoya Protocol on Access and Benefit-Sharing

- Requires prior informed consent and mutually agreed terms for use of genetic resources and associated traditional knowledge, including benefit-sharing for Indigenous communities.

Appendix D: NAIC-Style Implementation Example (Optional)

This hypothetical example illustrates how a practitioner might apply the book's principles within an NAIC-style framework.

Profile

- "Elena" is a licensed massage therapist and yoga teacher who has also completed NAIC/ACNM training in SomaVeda® Thai Yoga, Ayurveda, and NAIC religious therapeutics. She feels called to function as a minister and an Indigenous-style healer rather than only as a secular bodyworker.

Step 1 – Clarifying Identity

Elena discerns that her deepest work is spiritual and Indigenous in nature, not purely clinical. She writes a personal Statement of Sacred Conviction and discusses it with NAIC elders, confirming a call to Religious Therapeutics and Chirothesia rather than to secular massage.

Step 2 – Joining NAIC and Legal Shield

She joins NAIC as an Authorized Full Member and then applies for the N.A.I.C. Licensed Commissioned Holistic Therapist (L.C.H.T.) through NAIC Legal Shield, documenting her training hours and supervised practice.

Step 3 – Structuring the Ministry

Elena:

- Registers her practice under an NAIC-aligned name such as "Indigenous Religious Therapeutics – SomaVeda® Thai Yoga Ministry."
- Requires all people she serves to join as NAIC participant members and to sign NAIC-style informed consent and PMA agreements.
- Stops advertising "massage therapy" and instead uses NAIC's approved descriptions (SomaVeda® Integrated Traditional Therapies®, Religious Therapeutics, Indigenous Thai Yoga Therapy).

Step 4 – Separating Secular and Ecclesiastical Work

She keeps a small, separate practice where she occasionally works under her state massage license, clearly labeled and documented as such, and maintains strict boundaries between that and her NAIC ministry. Clinical charts stay in one file, ecclesiastical notes in another.

Step 5 – Everyday Practice

In sessions, Elena:

- Begins with prayer or intention, explains that the work is sacramental and non-medical, and reviews consent.
- Uses Thai Yoga postures, breath work, gentle pressure, and Ayurvedic suggestions as religiously framed practices, not as physical-therapy techniques.

- Refers members to physicians or psychotherapists when she recognizes red-flag conditions, honoring the complementary nature of her work.

Step 6 – Ongoing Accountability

She participates in NAIC continuing education, tithes to support the tribal organization, and remains available for review or counsel by NAIC and SMOKH leadership.

By following these steps, Elena practices what she believes, stays within a religious and Indigenous scope, and can credibly demonstrate that her work is ministry and traditional medicine, not unlicensed secular practice.

Appendix E: Glossary of Legal and Theological Terms

AIRFA (American Indian Religious Freedom Act)
United States statute (42 U.S.C. § 1996) establishing federal policy to protect and preserve the inherent rights of Indigenous peoples to practice their traditional religions, including access to sites, use of sacred objects, and traditional rites.

Alma-Ata Declaration
1978 WHO/UNICEF declaration affirming health as a fundamental human right and establishing primary health care as the key to "health for all," emphasizing community participation and cultural appropriateness.

Chirothesia
From Greek roots meaning "hand" and "setting/doing," interpreted here as "led by the healing hand of God," this phrase denotes the ritual laying on of hands and related touch as a religious act of healing, blessing, and ordination.

Contentious Medicine
Term used in this course for practices likely to draw legal scrutiny, such as the use of controlled substances in ceremony or invasive rituals; requires heightened caution and robust organizational protocols.

Ecclesiastical Jurisdiction
Authority exercised by a church or religious body over its ministers, members, and internal affairs, including ordinations, discipline, and the definition of religious practices and sacraments.

Exemption (Legal)
A clear, intentional exception written into law that frees certain persons or activities from

otherwise applicable regulations (e.g., exemptions for the practice of the religious tenets of any church from medical licensing). Distinct from a "loophole."

IHSM (Indigenous Healthcare, Healing Science, Counseling, and Medicine)
NAIC's term for spiritually based, non-invasive Indigenous and clerical/pastoral health practices, encompassing CAM, Religious Therapeutics, and traditional Native medicine within a religious context.

IHCIA (Indian Health Care Improvement Act)
Statute 25 U.S.C. § 1680u, "Traditional health care practices" (IHCIA traditional practices provision; promotion authority + U.S. liability limitation). https://www.law.cornell.edu/uscode/text/25/1680u and related sections)

Mala in se / Mala prohibita
"Mala in se" refers to acts evil in themselves (e.g., murder, rape); not protected in any domain. "Mala prohibita" refers to acts criminal only because prohibited by statute (e.g., unlicensed practice). Within properly structured religious/PMA contexts, some otherwise mala prohibita acts (like unlicensed massage) may become lawful religious acts.

NAIC (Native American Indigenous Church)
A Native American religious and tribal organization, faith-based church, and private membership association that provides legal, ecclesiastical, and educational structures for Indigenous and religiously based holistic medicine.

OCAP® Principles
First Nations' framework for data sovereignty: Ownership, Control, Access, and Possession of data about Indigenous peoples and their knowledge.

PMA (Private Membership Association)
A contractual association of individuals who agree to meet and transact privately under the First and Fourteenth Amendments, often used to host holistic or religious services outside the public regulatory domain, subject to limits on harm.

Religious Therapeutics
Concept (articulated by Gregory P. Fields and adopted here) describing principles and practices that support human well-being by integrating health and religiousness, including religious meanings, means of healing, and religiousness itself as a remedy.

RFRA (Religious Freedom Restoration Act)
Federal law (42 U.S.C. § 2000bb) reinstates a strict-scrutiny standard for laws that substantially burden religious exercise.

RLUIPA (Religious Land Use and Institutionalized Persons Act)
A law that protects religious institutions from burdensome land-use regulations and protects the religious rights of institutionalized persons.

Sincere and Firmly Held Conviction
Standard used in religious-freedom analysis; here, it refers to a practitioner's deeply rooted beliefs that define health, healing, ceremony, and duty, and that are consistently lived out in practice.

UNDRIP (United Nations Declaration on the Rights of Indigenous Peoples)
International declaration recognizing the collective and individual rights of Indigenous peoples, including rights to traditional medicines and to maintain and develop their health practices.

Appendix F, Legal Bibliography (verified/anchored links)

Format: Bluebook-ish for U.S. primary law; standard academic/web for organizational & international instruments; all entries include clickable links.

U.S. Federal statutes (primary authorities)

- American Indian Religious Freedom Act (AIRFA), 42 U.S.C. § 1996.
  https://www.law.cornell.edu/uscode/text/42/1996
- Freedom of Access to Clinic Entrances Act (FACE Act), 18 U.S.C. § 248.
  https://www.law.cornell.edu/uscode/text/18/248; DOJ overview:
  https://www.justice.gov/crt/freedom-access-clinic-entrances-places-religious-worship

U.S. Federal cases (primary authorities)

- Gonzales v. O Centro Espírita Beneficente União do Vegetal, 546 U.S. 418 (2006). (RFRA analysis; cited in draft.)
- United States v. Boyll, 774 F. Supp. 1333 (D.N.M. 1991). (Cited in draft; verify proposition/pinpoint in later batch when we extract the exact sentence you rely on.)

Organizational / web authorities (as cited sources)

- Native American Indigenous Church (NAIC), "NAIC Legal Compliance."
  https://nativefirechurch.org/naic-legal-compliance/
- Native American Indigenous Church (NAIC), "Certifications."
  https://nativefirechurch.org/certifications/

A. Primary law (U.S. Federal)

- Religious Land Use and Institutionalized Persons Act (RLUIPA), 42 U.S.C. §§ 2000cc to 2000cc-5. https://www.law.cornell.edu/uscode/text/42/chapter-21C
- Religious Freedom Restoration Act (RFRA), 42 U.S.C. §§ 2000bb to 2000bb-4 (pinpoint for strict-scrutiny rule: 42 U.S.C. § 2000bb-1). https://www.law.cornell.edu/uscode/text/42/chapter-21B

(Note: AIRFA and FACE Act were delivered in Batch 1 and remain in the same Primary Law section of the final appendix.)

B. Cases (U.S.)

- Gonzales v. O Centro Espírita Beneficente União do Vegetal, 546 U.S. 418 (2006). (Cited in draft; RFRA application.)
- United States v. Boyll, 774 F. Supp. 1333 (D.N.M. 1991). (Cited in draft; proposition/pinpoint to be verified against the exact sentence(s) where you rely on it when we extract the surrounding paragraph in a later batch.)

C. International instruments (authoritative)

- Universal Declaration of Human Rights, G.A. Res. 217 A (III), U.N. Doc. A/RES/217A(III) (Dec. 10, 1948) (Article 25 addresses "standard of living adequate for… health and well-being," including medical care and necessary social services). https://www.un.org/en/about-us/universal-declaration-of-human-rights
- Declaration of Alma-Ata, International Conference on Primary Health Care, Alma-Ata, USSR (Sept. 6–12, 1978). https://www.who.int/publications/i/item/WHO-EURO-1978-3938-43697-61471
- United Nations Declaration on the Rights of Indigenous Peoples (UNDRIP), G.A. Res. 61/295, U.N. Doc. A/RES/61/295 (Sept. 13, 2007) (non-binding declaration; draft relies especially on Article 24 re: traditional medicines/health practices and Article 31 re: traditional knowledge/genetic resources). https://undocs.org/A/RES/61/295
- Nagoya Protocol on Access to Genetic Resources and the Fair and Equitable Sharing of Benefits Arising from Their Utilization (to the Convention on Biological Diversity) (Oct. 29, 2010). https://www.cbd.int/abs/

D. Secondary/web authorities (supporting, non-binding)

- First Nations Information Governance Centre (FNIGC), "The First Nations Principles of OCAP®" (Ownership, Control, Access, Possession; framework for First Nations data sovereignty that your draft analogizes to medicine/knowledge protection). https://fnigc.ca/ocap-training/
- Native American Indigenous Church (NAIC), "NAIC Legal Compliance." https://nativefirechurch.org/naic-legal-compliance/
- Native American Indigenous Church (NAIC), "Certifications." https://nativefirechurch.org/certifications/

Sorted: **Primary law → Cases → International → Secondary/web**.

E. Primary law (U.S. Federal)

- Religious Land Use and Institutionalized Persons Act (RLUIPA), 42 U.S.C. § 2000cc (land-use protections; includes "equal terms" provision at § 2000cc(b)(1)). https://www.law.cornell.edu/uscode/text/42/2000cc
- Federal Food, Drug, and Cosmetic Act, 21 U.S.C. § 343(r)(6) (dietary supplement "structure/function" and related claims; DSHEA disclaimer/notification framework). (FDA overview and regulatory cross-references: 21 C.F.R. § 101.93.) https://www.fda.gov/food/information-industry-dietary-supplements/notifications-structurefunction-and-related-claims-dietary-supplements

F. International instruments (authoritative)

- Constitution of the World Health Organization (WHO) (definition of health; foundational "highest attainable standard" language in preamble). https://www.who.int/about/governance/constitution

G. Secondary/web authorities (supporting, non-binding)

- World Health Organization (WHO), "Health and Well-Being" (WHO Constitution definition of health quoted on the WHO site). https://www.who.int/data/gho/data/major-themes/health-and-well-being
- National Institutes of Health (NIH), Office of Dietary Supplements, "Dietary Supplement Health and Education Act of 1994, Wording." (Convenient reproduction of DSHEA amendment language, including the standard disclaimer.) https://ods.od.nih.gov/About/DSHEA_Wording.aspx

H. International instruments (authoritative)

- International Covenant on Economic, Social and Cultural Rights (ICESCR), Dec. 16, 1966, 993 U.N.T.S. 3, art. 12 (right to the highest attainable standard of physical and mental health). https://www.ohchr.org/en/instruments-mechanisms/instruments/international-covenant-economic-social-and-cultural-rights
- U.N. Committee on Economic, Social and Cultural Rights (CESCR), General Comment No. 14: The Right to the Highest Attainable Standard of Health (Art. 12 of the Covenant), U.N. Doc. E/C.12/2000/4 (Aug. 11, 2000). https://www.ohchr.org/sites/default/files/Documents/Issues/Women/WRGS/Health/GC14.pdf
- African Charter on Human and Peoples' Rights, art. 16 (right to enjoy the best attainable state of physical and mental health; state duty to protect health and ensure medical attention). https://achpr.au.int/en/node/641
- Declaration of Alma-Ata, International Conference on Primary Health Care, Alma-Ata, USSR, Sept. 6–12, 1978 (conference declaration; primary health care framework; "health

is a fundamental human right"). https://www.who.int/docs/default-source/documents/almaata-declaration-en.pdf; WHO publication page: https://www.who.int/publications-detail-redirect/declaration-of-alma-ata

I. Secondary / web authorities (supporting, non-binding)

- Digital Library of the United Nations, record for CESCR General Comment No. 14 (bibliographic record). https://digitallibrary.un.org/record/425041?ln=en

J. International instruments (authoritative)

- Universal Declaration of Human Rights (UDHR), G.A. Res. 217 A (III), U.N. Doc. A/RES/217A(III) (Dec. 10, 1948), art. 18 (freedom of thought, conscience and religion; includes the freedom to manifest religion or belief "in public or private"). https://www.un.org/en/udhrbook/pdf/udhr_booklet_en_web.pdf
- American Declaration of the Rights and Duties of Man (American Declaration), Ninth International Conference of American States (Bogotá, 1948), art. III (religious freedom and worship; right to profess, manifest, and practice faith in public and private). https://www.oas.org/en/iachr/mandate/Basics/american-declaration-rights-duties-of-man.pdf

K. Secondary/web authorities (supporting, non-binding)

- World Health Organization (WHO), *WHO Traditional Medicine Strategy: 2014–2023* (2013) (official WHO publication page; developed in response to WHA62.13; supports Member States in policy/action plans; emphasizes strengthening the role of traditional medicine and safe/effective use, including regulation of products/practices/practitioners). https://www.who.int/publications/i/item/9789241506096
- Pan American Health Organization (PAHO/WHO), "WHO Traditional Medicine Strategy: 2014–2023" (summary page with goals/objectives; useful as a readable web citation alongside the WHO publication record). https://www.paho.org/en/documents/who-traditional-medicine-strategy-2014-2023

L. Primary law (U.S. Federal)

- Civil Rights Act, Civil action for deprivation of rights, 42 U.S.C. § 1983. https://www.law.cornell.edu/uscode/text/42/1983 (alternate official codification view: https://www.govinfo.gov/app/details/USCODE-2015-title42/USCODE-2015-title42-chap21-subchapI-sec1983)
- Conspiracy Against Rights, 18 U.S.C. § 241. https://www.law.cornell.edu/uscode/text/18/241 (DOJ summary page: https://www.justice.gov/crt/statutes-enforced-criminal-section)

M. Primary law (Florida), initial verification

- Florida Statutes, ch. 491 (Clinical, Counseling, and Psychotherapy Services), § 491.014 (Exemptions), incl. clergy exemption language in subsection (3). https://www.leg.state.fl.us/statutes/index.cfm?App_mode=Display_Statute&URL=0400-0499/0491/Sections/0491.014.html

- Fla. Stat. § 458.303(2)(g) (medicine; exceptions: "The practice of the religious tenets of any church in this state."). Official Online Sunshine (2025 ed.):; Florida Senate mirror: https://www.flsenate.gov/Laws/Statutes/2024/0458.303

- Fla. Stat. § 490.014(1)(f) (psychology; exemptions: clergy activities within ministerial duties, with "no separate charge" condition OR under church auspices "with or without charge," plus accountability requirement). Florida Senate text: https://www.flsenate.gov/laws/statutes/2021/490.014; Online Sunshine chapter index confirming provision: https://www.leg.state.fl.us/statutes/index.cfm?App_mode=Display_Statute&URL=0400-0499/0490/0490.html

- Fla. Stat. § 1005.06(1)(f) (religious colleges exempt from Commission for Independent Education oversight if they meet annual affidavit requirements; see DOE). Florida DOE overview page: https://www.fldoe.org/sara/religious.stml

- Fla. Admin. Code r. 6E-5.001, "Religious Institution Letter of Exemption" (implements § 1005.06(1)(f); amended effective 12/21/2025 per rules gateway history). Florida rules gateway: https://flrules.org/gateway/RuleNo.asp?title=Exempt+Religious+Colleges&ID=6E-5.001

N. Primary law (U.S. Federal), IHCIA (flagged, not yet finalized)

- Indian Health Care Improvement Act (IHCIA), **Needs codification correction for "traditional health care practices" contracting language** (draft currently cites 25 U.S.C. § 1665; verify and replace with correct section/subsection once pinpointed).

O. Secondary/web authorities (Florida education exemption)

- Florida Department of Education, Commission for Independent Education, "Religious Institutions Not Under the Purview of the Commission" (summarizes § 1005.06(1)(f) and Rule 6E-5.001). https://www.fldoe.org/sara/religious.stml

APPENDIX G. Statement of Sacred Conviction

Fair Use Disclaimer: The author, publisher Meta Journal Press, and the Native American Indigenous Church (NAIC) Inc. do not assume any legal responsibility for the use of this statement as part of any proposed legal defense. The practitioner using this document acknowledges and disavows all liability and responsibility, asserting that their actions are directed solely by their own conscience and sincere, firmly held religious convictions.

Statement of Sacred Conviction and Ecclesiastical Duty

I, _____, stand as a steward of the soul and a bridge between ancient Indigenous wisdom and the revealed Word of Holy Scripture. I am not a technician of the body; I am a minister of **Bio-Spiritual Integrity**.

1. The Sacred Paradigm of Health My practice is founded on the unshakable conviction that a human being is a triune unity of Spirit, Soul, and Body. Health is not the mere absence of disease but a dynamic state of **Wholeness** (*Shalom* or "The Good Way"), achieved only when these three stand in right relationship with the Creator and all Creation. To treat the body while ignoring the spirit is, in my worldview, a form of spiritual malpractice.

2. Religious Therapeutics and Sacramental Scope The modalities I employ—including prayer, **Chirothesia** (laying on of hands), herbal stewardship, and Indigenous ceremonies—are liturgical acts of restoration, not medical treatments in the secular sense. I claim to facilitate wholeness as an exercise of religious freedom and cultural continuity, protected by the **American Indian Religious Freedom Act (AIRFA)** and the **Religious Freedom Restoration Act (RFRA)**.

3. Integration of POPLAR Principles and Ethical Safeguards

In recognition of current academic research, such as the findings of the **Project on Psychedelics Law and Regulation (POPLAR)**, I acknowledge the following:

- **The Traditional Container:** I maintain that sacred and traditional contexts provide the essential spiritual "container" needed to integrate difficult or mystical experiences, a framework often missing from secular models.
- **Opposition to Biopiracy:** I am bound to protect traditional Indigenous knowledge and plant medicine from extraction and commercialization, ensuring these "ancient technologies" remain within the custody of the communities that safeguarded them through prohibition.
- **Safety as Sacred Duty:** I acknowledge that certain high-risk rites or sacraments can catalyze extreme transformations. Therefore, I adhere to strict protocols of informed consent, screening, and supervision by authentically trained and authorized personnel to prevent cultural misappropriation and ensure participant safety.

4. Jurisdictional Mandate I act under a dual mandate of conscience: the Great Commission to "heal the sick" through God's power and the Indigenous law of *Mitákuye Oyás'iŋ* (All My Relations). I answer to a jurisdiction higher than any secular medical board: the sovereignty of the Creator.

5. Non-Medical Disclaimer I do not claim to diagnose, treat, or cure disease as those terms are defined in state medical practice acts. I provide Religious Therapeutics to fellow members of a **Private Membership Association**, moving our interaction out of public commerce and into the protected domain of private covenant.

Signature: _____ Date: _____

Witness/Elder: _____ Organization: _____

APPENDIX H.

Sample Administrative Petition Template Seeking DEA Religious Exemption

Disclaimer: Educational and Informational Use Only The following "DEA Exemption Template" is offered for educational and informational purposes only. It does not constitute legal advice. The author, publisher, and affiliated organizations strongly recommend obtaining competent legal counsel independently before seeking to file for any DEA Rule exception or religious exemption under the Controlled Substances Act (CSA). Every case involving "contentious medicine" is highly individualized and carries significant legal risk.

TO:

Drug Enforcement Administration (DEA)

Attn: Office of Diversion Control

8701 Morrissette Drive

Springfield, VA 22152

RE: Petition for Religious Exemption from the Controlled Substances Act (CSA) Pursuant to the Religious Freedom Restoration Act (RFRA), 42 U.S.C. § 2000bb et seq.

I. Petitioner Information

- **Name of Organization:** [Name of Church or Tribal Religious Organization]
- **Physical Address:** [Address of Sanctuary/Ceremonial Grounds]
- **Primary Contact:** [Authorized Minister/Elder Name and Title]
- **Mission Statement:** [Briefly describe the religious purpose and the role of the sacrament in attaining Bio-Spiritual Integrity].

II. Identification of the Sacrament

- **Substance:** [e.g., Ayahuasca, Psilocybin, etc.]
- **CSA Schedule:** [e.g., Schedule I]
- **Theological Significance:** Describe the substance not as a "drug" but as a teacher or covenantal being essential for purification, vision, and communion with the Creator.

III. Statement of Sincere Religious Belief Consistent with the holding in *United States v. Boyll*, 774 F. Supp. 1333, this petition asserts that the use of the sacrament is a central tenet of a sincere and firmly held religious conviction. The Petitioner maintains that:

- The human being is a unity of spirit, soul, and body.
- Health (*Shalom*) is a state of wholeness that requires spiritual alignment.
- The denial of this sacrament would constitute a "substantial burden" on the exercise of religion under RFRA.

IV. Proposed Safety Protocols and Diversion Control In alignment with the standards set in *Gonzales v. O Centro Espírita Beneficente União do Vegetal*, 546 U.S. 418, the Petitioner proposes the following safeguards to prevent health risks and diversion:

1. **Member-Only Access:** The sacrament is provided strictly to members of our Private Membership Association (PMA) who have provided informed consent.
2. **Screening:** All participants undergo medical and psychological screening to ensure the ceremony is safe for their condition.
3. **Traditional Container:** Rites are conducted in a supervised "traditional container" by authentically trained and authorized ministers.
4. **Security:** Outline specific measures for storage, transportation, and disposal of the sacrament to prevent non-religious use.

V. Legal Basis for Petition

This petition is grounded in the following authorities:

- **The Religious Freedom Restoration Act (RFRA):** Forbidding the government from burdening religious exercise without a compelling interest and the least restrictive means.
- **American Indian Religious Freedom Act (AIRFA):** Protecting the inherent right to exercise traditional religions through ceremonials and rites.
- **Project on Psychedelics Law and Regulation (POPLAR) Findings:** Recognizing that traditional containers are essential for the integration of mystical experiences.

VI. Conclusion The Petitioner requests a formal exemption to exercise our religious duty without fear of prosecution. We are prepared to cooperate with the DEA to ensure that our sacred acts are not misclassified as commerce or recreational use.

Signature: _____ **Date:** _____ [Authorized
Representative of Petitioner]

Verifiable Citations and Scholarly References for This Petition Type

1. **United States Supreme Court:** *Gonzales v. O Centro Espírita Beneficente União do Vegetal*, 546 U.S. 418 (2006).
2. **U.S. District Court:** *Church of the Holy Light of the Queen v. Mukasey*, 615 F. Supp. 2d 1210 (D. Or. 2009).
3. **U.S. District Court:** *United States v. Boyll*, 774 F. Supp. 1333 (D.N.M. 1991).
4. **Academic/Legal Initiative:** The Project on Psychedelics Law and Regulation (POPLAR) at the Petrie-Flom Center, Harvard Law School.
5. **DEA Administrative Process:** *DEA Guidance on Petitions for Religious Exemption* (Technical pathway for CSA exceptions under RFRA).
6. **Scholarly Commentary:** Fields, Gregory P. *Religious Therapeutics: Body and Health in Yoga, Āyurveda, and Tantra*. SUNY Press, 2001.

Bibliography I. and Further Reading

This list combines core sources used in this course with additional works for deeper study. All are real and publicly verifiable.

A. Primary Legal and Policy Texts

- American Indian Religious Freedom Act, 42 U.S.C. § 1996.
- Religious Freedom Restoration Act, 42 U.S.C. § 2000bb.
- Indian Health Care Improvement Act, 25 U.S.C. § 1680u, "Traditional health care practices" (IHCIA traditional practices provision; promotion authority + U.S. liability limitation). https://www.law.cornell.edu/uscode/text/25/1680u1665 and 25 U.S.C. § IHCIA, "Community Health Representative Program" (includes directive to promote traditional health care practices of tribes served). https://www.law.cornell.edu/uscode/text/25/1616
- Religious Land Use and Institutionalized Persons Act, 42 U.S.C. § 2000cc.
- Universal Declaration of Human Rights (UN General Assembly, 1948).
- Declaration of Alma-Ata (International Conference on Primary Health Care, 1978).
- United Nations Declaration on the Rights of Indigenous Peoples (UNDRIP, 2007).
- Nagoya Protocol on Access to Genetic Resources and the Fair and Equitable Sharing of Benefits (CBD, 2010).
- First Nations Information Governance Centre. "The First Nations Principles of OCAP®."

B. Case Law

- United States v. Boyll, 774 F. Supp. 1333 (D.N.M. 1991).
- Gonzales v. O Centro Espírita Beneficente União do Vegetal, 546 U.S. 418 (2006).

C. Core Course Texts and Internal Resources

- James, Anthony B. *Indigenous Religious Therapeutics: The Legal Basis for Religious-Based Indigenous, Traditional Native American Holistic, Complementary, and Alternative Medicine and Modalities, and the Right to Express Them.* Meta Journal Press, Brooksville, FL. (Course manuscript and NAIC Legal Guidelines, 2019–2026).
- NAIC Articles of Religious Practice, Education, and Healthcare Membership.
- NAIC Authorized Participant Membership Approval and Agreement.
- NAIC Legal Compliance resources (NativeFireChurch.org).
- NAIC Legal Shield Ministry – Practitioner resources and L.C.H.T. licensing information (naiclegalshield.org).

D. Books and Monographs

- Fields, Gregory P. *Religious Therapeutics: Body and Health in Yoga, Āyurveda, and Tantra.* SUNY Press, 2001.
- James, Anthony B. *Nuat Thai: Traditional Thai Medical Massage.* Meta Journal Press, 1983 and later editions.
- James, Anthony B. *Ayurveda of Thailand: Indigenous Traditional Thai Medicine and Yoga Therapy.* Meta Journal Press (AAPNA Veda Vyasa Award for Best Ayurveda Textbook, 2017).
- James, Anthony B., and Benoit Tano. *SomaVeda® Healing Protocols: Natural Recovery After COVID, Vaccines, and Boosters with Ayurveda, Thai Yoga, Integrative Medicine and Protocols to Reclaim Health.* 2023.
- Additional titles by Anthony B. James on traditional Thai Yoga, Ayurveda, Indigenous medicine, and Religious Therapeutics (see beardedmedia.com and Amazon author listings).

E. Articles, Reports, and Background Reading

- WHO. "Declaration of Alma-Ata." World Health Organization.
- WHO. "Traditional, Complementary and Integrative Medicine: Global Strategies."
- NLM / NIH. "Indigenous Native American Healing Traditions." *Complementary Therapies in Medicine.*
- "UN Declaration on the Rights of Indigenous Peoples." Office of the High Commissioner for Human Rights.

- BC Medical Journal. "Traditional medicines and healing practices." (Overview of traditional medicine in contemporary settings).

F. Ethics, Counseling, and Dual-Role Resources

- National Christian Counselors Association. *Code of Ethical Standards.*
- Brad Hambrick. "Comparing Pastoral Ethics and Counseling Ethics."
- FaithTrust Institute / VAWnet. "Healthy Boundaries 201 – Beyond Basics."
- Resources on dual roles and pastoral counseling ethics in clinical contexts.

G. Organizational and Informational Sites

- Native American Indigenous Church (NAIC) and NativeFireChurch.org – official church, legal, and membership information.
- American College of Natural Medicine / ThaiYogaCenter.com – education in SomaVeda® Thai Yoga, Ayurveda, and Indigenous medicine.
- Sacred Medical Order of the Church of Hope (SMOCH/SMOKH).
- First Nation Medical Board (FNMB).
- BeardedMedia.com – books and media on SomaVeda®, Ayurveda, and Indigenous healing by Anthony B. James.

Bibliography J. and Further Reading

Research and Citable Reference Bibliography

I. Case Law and Regulatory Opinions

- *Employment Division, Department of Human Resources of Oregon v. Smith*, 494 U.S. 872 (1990). (The pivotal case leading to the enactment of RFRA). Link
- *Gonzales v. O Centro Espírita Beneficente União do Vegetal*, 546 U.S. 418 (2006). (Affirming RFRA protection for the sacramental use of ayahuasca/Hoasca). Link
- *United States v. Boyll*, 774 F. Supp. 1333 (D.N.M. 1991). (Ruling that NAC peyote protections are based on religion, not race). Link
- *Church of the Eagle and the Condor v. Garland* (ongoing/recent litigation regarding the religious use of ayahuasca).
- *DEA Guidance on RFRA Exemptions*: (Technical pathways for religious groups to seek CSA exemptions). Link
- *WHO Traditional Medicine Strategy: 2014–2023.* Link

II. Academic and Scholarly Articles

- Petrie-Flom Center. "The Project on Psychedelics Law and Regulation (POPLAR)." *Harvard Law School.* Link
- Mason, M. "The Church's Path to a RFRA Exemption." *Psychedelic Week.* Link
- Sánchez, C., & Bouso, J. C. "Ayahuasca: Religious use as a protective factor for public health." *International Center for Ethnobotanical Education, Research, and Service (ICEERS).*
- "Ethical and Legal Implications of Psychedelic Research and Therapeutics." *Journal of Law, Medicine & Ethics* (special issues).

III. Federal Statutes & International Declarations

- American Indian Religious Freedom Act (AIRFA), 42 U.S.C. § 1996. Link
- UN Declaration on the Rights of Indigenous Peoples (UNDRIP), Article 24. Link
- Nagoya Protocol on Access and Benefit-Sharing. Link

IV. Clinical and Government Designations

- FDA. "FDA grants Breakthrough Therapy Designation for MDMA-assisted therapy for PTSD." (2017).
- FDA. "FDA identifies Psilocybin as a Breakthrough Therapy for treatment-resistant depression." (2018).
- FDA. "Breakthrough Therapy Designation for LSD in Generalized Anxiety Disorder." (2024).

V. Books

- Fields, Gregory P. *Religious Therapeutics: Body and Health in Yoga, Āyurveda, and Tantra.* SUNY Press, 2001. Link
- James, Anthony B. *Decoding AI Bias in Medicine.* Bearded Media, 2024. Link

Appendix K: NAIC-Style Implementation Example

This hypothetical example shows how a practitioner might implement the principles of this book using an NAIC-style framework, informed both by NAIC's internal Legal Guidelines and by broader works such as Lawrence Wilson's *Legal Guidelines for Unlicensed Practitioners* and the ThaiYogaCenter legal articles on Thai Yoga and Thai massage. It is not a template to copy verbatim, but a concrete picture of what "Sacred Hands" and "Secured Rights" look like when matched in everyday practice.

Case Study: "Dr. Maria," LMT, ND (Traditional), and NAIC Minister

Background

"Dr. Maria" (not a real person) is in her mid-40s. She is:

- A licensed massage therapist (LMT) in a state with strict massage laws.
- A graduate of a traditional naturopathy program (no drugs, no surgery), but not state-licensed as a naturopathic physician.
- Trained in SomaVeda® Thai Yoga and Ayurveda through the Thai Yoga Center / American College of Natural Medicine
- Recently ordained as an NAIC minister and commissioned as an N.A.I.C. Licensed Commissioned Holistic Therapist (L.C.H.T.) under the NAIC Legal Shield program.

She feels called to practice a truly holistic, Bible-respecting, and Indigenous-honoring medicine, no drugs, no surgery, non-invasive, focused on spirit, soul, and body, both for Native clients and for Christians disillusioned with the medical-industrial system. At the same time, she wants to avoid unlicensed practice issues and to keep her LMT license in good standing.

Step 1: Clarifying Her Two Roads

Maria begins by writing a personal **Statement of Sacred Conviction and Ecclesiastical Duty**, using the model in Chapter 21 and Part VI. In it, she affirms:

- A triune view of the person (spirit, soul, body).
- Health as Shalom / The Good Way, not merely the absence of disease.
- A dual mandate: the Great Commission ("heal the sick") and her ancestral obligation to All My Relations

She then reads Wilson's chapters on "licensing vs certification" and "defining your scope of practice," noting that her LMT license and her naturopathic and Thai Yoga **certifications** are different from a license to practice medicine. She accepts that:

- When she is "Maria, LMT" in a spa or rehab clinic, she is under the massage board.
- When she is "Rev. Maria, NAIC Minister / L.C.H.T.," working only with NAIC members, she is under church/tribal/PMA jurisdiction. She must avoid representing that work as "massage" or "medicine" in the statutory sense.

She commits, before changing anything external, to **never again collapse these two roads** in her own mind.

Step 2: Joining NAIC and Legal Shield

Maria formally joins NAIC as an Authorized Full Member (AFM) and completes the NAIC Legal Shield application for L.C.H.T., documenting:

- Her SomaVeda® Thai Yoga and Ayurveda training hours.
- Her traditional naturopathy education (no drugs, no surgery).
- Her ministry formation through NAIC and SMOKH/Church of Hope.

She reads and signs:

- NAIC Articles of Religious Practice, Education, and Healthcare Membership.
- The NAIC Authorized Participant Membership Agreement (A.P.M.A.).
- The L.C.H.T. membership and licensure contract, which spells out the scope, ethics, and private-domain status.

This ecclesiastical licensure does not change her state license, but it **creates a new, clearly defined role** for Religious Therapeutics and Indigenous medicine under NAIC/tribal jurisdiction

Step 3: Structuring Her Practice Under the NAIC Umbrella

Maria decides to run two clearly distinct operations:

1. **Secular LMT Role**
   - She keeps a part-time position at a medical spa, where she works strictly as "Maria _____, LMT."
   - All advertising, documentation, and billing in that context use standard massage language and comply with the massage board's rules.
   - She does not introduce NAIC language or ceremonial work in this setting, except perhaps for mild, board-approved "relaxation" language.

NAIC Religious Therapeutics Ministry

- o She launches "Sacred Hands Wellness Ministry – An NAIC Religious Therapeutics Practice" as a separate entity, using NAIC trademarks and logos appropriately
- o The ministry is explicitly described as:
  - An NAIC church/tribal ministry.
  - A Private Membership Association (PMA) of NAIC members only.
  - A practice of Religious Therapeutics, Chirothesia, and Indigenous Healthcare (IHSM), not massage therapy or medicine.
- o She uses a separate website, email, intake forms, and records system for this ministry.

In all her NAIC materials, she avoids generic terms like "Thai Massage" and "bodywork," following the ThaiYogaCenter legal guidance and NAIC's "Forbidden Words" list. Instead, she uses:

- SomaVeda® Integrated Traditional Therapies® / Thai Yoga.
- Indigenous Thai Yoga Therapy.
- Religious Therapeutics.
- Indigenous (clerical/pastoral/ministerial) Healthcare and Counseling.

This alignment of **words, structure, and scope** is exactly what both NAIC and Wilson emphasize as critical to avoiding trouble.

Step 4: Membership, Consent, and Scope Definition

For every person she serves in her ministry, Maria:

- Requires them to join as NAIC participant members (AFM/APM) or sign NAIC membership and waiver forms before receiving any services.
- Has them sign an **Informed-Consent and Participant Member Activity Consent, Disclosure, Waiver, and Disclaimer** based on NAIC's templates, which clearly state:
  - o Those services are Religious Therapeutics and Indigenous healing, not diagnosis, treatment, or prescription as defined by secular law.
  - o That members remain responsible for seeking appropriate medical care.
  - o That all work occurs within a private religious domain and is subject to NAIC's internal arbitration and ethics processes

She also includes a short, Wilson-style disclosure:

"I am not acting as a licensed medical doctor or licensed naturopathic physician in this ministry. My services are spiritual, educational, pastoral, and traditional. They are offered only to NAIC members in a private, ecclesiastical, and tribal setting."herballegacy+2

By defining her **scope** and **role** so clearly in writing and in speech, she shifts the interaction from the "public medical marketplace" that state boards police to the "private religious domain" protected by AIRFA, RFRA, IHCIA, RLUIPA, and association rights, as long as she truly stays within her non-invasive, non-diagnostic scope.

Step 5: Day-to-Day Session Flow

A typical session in her NAIC ministry might look like:

1. **Opening**
   o Confirm membership and prior consent on file.
   o Begin with a brief prayer or statement of intent, reminding the member that this is a spiritual and Indigenous healing session, not medical treatment.
2. **Assessment in Religious/Traditional Language**
   o Ask about the member's spiritual, emotional, relational, and physical concerns using non-medical language (e.g., "Where do you feel out of balance?" rather than "What diagnoses do you have?").
   o Observe posture, breath, pulse, and tongue in an Ayurvedic framework, explaining these as traditional maps, not medical diagnostics.
3. **Interventions**
   o SomaVeda® Thai Yoga sequences framed as religious Thai Yoga or Indigenous Thai Yoga Therapy, Mother Earth, Mind, Body, Spirit integration
   o Chirothesia (laying on of hands), anointing, or blessing prayers
   o Herbal and nutritional counsel described in DSHEA-compliant "structure/function" terms, avoiding disease claims
   o Scriptural or moral counsel where appropriate, within a pastoral scope.
4. **Closing and Referral**
   o Close with prayer and thanksgiving.
   o If Maria sees signs of serious pathology (e.g., red-flag symptoms, dramatic blood-pressure issues, major depression, suicidality), she gently but clearly recommends or insists on evaluation by a licensed physician or mental-health professional, documenting that recommendation in her pastoral notes.academic.oup+1

Throughout, she never promises to "treat" or "cure" any disease, never claims to replace doctors, and never suggests stopping needed medications, a posture both NAIC and Wilson emphasize as ethically and legally essential.herballegacy+1

Step 6: Handling Questions from Boards or Authorities

If Maria is ever questioned by a massage board, medical board, or other authority, she follows three principles drawn from NAIC's Legal Guidelines (NAIC Legal Shield- https://NAIC-EDU.org, and https://NativeFireChurch.org) (Sacred Hands, Secured Rights Book), Wilson's book, and the ThaiYogaCenter (https://ThaiYogaCenter.Com) legal articles:

1. **Calm, respectful explanation of roles**
   - She explains that when she works as "Maria, LMT" at the spa, she is fully under the board's jurisdiction and complies with all regulations.
   - When she works as an NAIC minister in her private ministry, she does not advertise or provide massage therapy; she offers Religious Therapeutics and Indigenous healing only to NAIC members, under church/tribal auspices and within explicit religious and Indigenous rights.
2. **Documentation**
   - She can present NAIC membership documents, her ordination and L.C.H.T. license, NAIC Articles of Religious Practice, sample consent forms, and evidence that she avoids forbidden medical/massage terms in her ministry marketing.
   - She can point to AIRFA, RFRA, IHCIA, and relevant state exemptions (for "practice of the religious tenets of any church") as the legal foundation for her ministry.
3. **Referral to organizational leadership**
   - She avoids arguing the law herself and, if needed, refers authorities to NAIC Legal Shield or other organizational counsel, consistent with Dr. Wilson's advice not to "wing it" with regulators.

Because she has kept her roles distinct, records separate, and language precise, she can show that she is **not** using a massage or naturopathy certificate to evade state medical rules, but is practcing a well-defined religious and Indigenous ministry under recognized legal exemptions

Step 7: Ongoing Formation and Accountability

Maria commits to ongoing:

- **Spiritual and ceremonial practice**, participating in NAIC ceremonies (sweats, pipe, sacred breath, etc.), and Christian worship, deepening her own integrity as a healer
- **Legal and ethical education**, reviewing NAIC updates, ThaiYogaCenter legal posts, and staying aware of changes in her state's laws.
- **Supervision and mentorship**, seeking counsel from senior NAIC/SMOKH/FNMB or PMA elders and, where appropriate, from licensed clinical peers when complex cases arise.

In this way, she embodies the book's core teaching: **Sacred Hands and Secured Rights must walk together.** Her ministry is deeply spiritual and Indigenous, yet carefully structured and ethically grounded. She honors the Hippocratic impulse to "do no harm," the biblical and Indigenous mandate to heal, and the legal frameworks that, rightly understood, allow her to do both without fear.

Appendix L. Books and Monographs

- Fields, Gregory P. *Religious Therapeutics: Body and Health in Yoga, Āyurveda, and Tantra.* State University of New York Press, Albany, 2001.
- **Wilson, Lawrence D.** *Legal Guidelines for Unlicensed Practitioners.* L.D. Wilson Consultants, Inc., 2000 (later printings 2016).
  - A concise manual on occupational licensing, risk management, and how to practice as an unlicensed or licensed practitioner without legal difficulties. Sixteen chapters cover basic legal concepts, record-keeping, scope-of-practice framing, advertising, informed consent, and responding to regulatory inquiries.
- James, Anthony B. *Indigenous Religious Therapeutics: The Legal Basis for Religious-Based Indigenous, Traditional Native American Holistic, Complementary, and Alternative Medicine and Modalities, and the Right to Express Them.* Meta Journal Press, Brooksville, FL (course manuscript and NAIC Legal Guidelines, 2019–2026).
- James, Anthony B. *Nuat Thai: Traditional Thai Medical Massage.* Meta Journal Press, multiple editions.
- James, Anthony B. *Ayurveda of Thailand: Indigenous Traditional Thai Medicine and Yoga Therapy.* Meta Journal Press, 2017 (AAPNA Veda Vyasa Award for Best Ayurveda Textbook).
- James, Anthony B., and Benoit Tano. *SomaVeda® Healing Protocols: Natural Recovery After COVID, Vaccines, and Boosters with Ayurveda, Thai Yoga, Integrative Medicine and Protocols to Reclaim Health.* Meta Journal Press, 2023.
- Additional titles by Anthony B. James on SomaVeda® Thai Yoga, Ayurveda, Indigenous medicine, and Religious Therapeutics, available via Meta Journal Press / BeardedMedia.com and major booksellers.

AUTHOR BIO

The Path of the Scholar-Warrior

My journey did not begin in a medical school lecture hall. It started in the blood.

"Big Thunder" Chief of Penobscots.

My lineage traces back through the generations to **Wakadjaxedga**—known as **Big Thunder**—of the Shawnee-Delaware and Lenni-Lenape (or possibly Chief "White Thunder" of the Iroquois- Mingo Seneca), my 10th Great Grandfather. Born of this very mixed heritage—Shawnee, Eastern Creek, Iroquois- Mingo Seneca, and Cherokee. It gets more interesting once you that I was initially introduced to Native American Spirituality and traditions by my father, Ronald Bruce James. My father, "Ronny" as he liked to be called, through his Grandmother, Eva Sevier (daughter of John Sevier 1858-1930), and Grandfather Charles White, was a mixed descendant of Shawnee/ Eastern Creek/ Cherokee Band according to family traditions. This type of mixed family heritage is not unusual and is typical of the results of the Native American diaspora when boiled down to the level of family heritage. I carried the genetic memory of a medicine that predates the stethoscope by ten thousand years. But memory alone is not enough; it must be trained.

That training took me far from the reservations of North America. It led me across oceans to the ancient temples of Thailand, where I earned the ranks of **Ajahn** and Grand Master in Traditional Thai Medicine. There, in the shadow of Wat Po, I found a medical system that mirrored the wisdom of my own ancestors. I studied the *Sen Lines* (energy pathways) that map the flow of life force through the body, realizing they were identical to the "Spirit Lines" spoken of by Native American healers. I saw that the "Wind" (*Lom*) in Thai medicine was the same as the "Holy Wind" (*Nilch'i*) in Navajo medicine.

I spent decades translating these Eastern systems for the Western mind, founding the **Thai Yoga Center** and the **American College of Natural Medicine** to formalize this wisdom into accredited degrees. I became a Dean. I built a curriculum. I learned the language of State Medical Boards and accreditation agencies. I learned to wear the suit and tie.

But my education was incomplete. To understand the "Original Cure," I had to go home. I had to return to the Earth.

The Adoption and the Obligation

My deep dive began with a Medicine Wheel Gathering led by Medicine Chief Sun Bear and the Bear Tribe Medicine Society. It was there, influenced by the teachings of Ed McGaa (Eagle Man) and other elders, that I entered my first Sweat Lodge. In the darkness and heat of that ceremony, the veil lifted. For the first time, I saw the path of trauma my family had carried—the pain passed down to me by my father—and understood it not as a burden, but as a calling.

At that moment, the vision of Black Elk became real to me. Ed McGaa taught me that the medicine **does not belong only** to the "full blood"; in the spirit of Black Elk's prophecy, it is the duty of the **Rainbow Warrior** to mend the Sacred Hoop. With this permission and incentive, I stepped away from my ordinary life. I headed West, driven

249

by a need to find and define the path of my own ancestors. I prayed and cried for a vision, and eventually, my prayers were answered.

Crow-Realbird Adoption: Teepee ceremony with Crow-NAC Elders, Road Chiefs and Family.

NAC-Whistling Water Clan- Realbird family adoption ceremony, Dr. Anthony B. James, Medicine Tail Coulee, Richard Realbird Ranch on the bank of the Little Bighorn River, adjacent to Bighorn Battlefield (formerly the "Custer Battlefield- The Little Bighorn Battlefield). In the photo, Chief Floyd Realbird, Chief Robert "Bobby" Littlelight, Chief Harry Mocasin, Crow Tribal Historian "Mickey" Old Coyote, Dr. Lanny Realbird, and Shawn Realbird. In the foreground are Charles " Charlie" Realbird, Ramona Realbird, Margo Realbird, Chief Richard Realbird, Kinnard Realbird, Nicolle Realbird, Lorraine Littlelight, Leon Pretty on Top, and other distinguished guests.

I carry the distinct honor and heavy responsibility of being an <u>adopted son</u> of the <u>**Crow Tribe**</u> **(Apsáalooke)**. I was taken in by the **Real Bird Family** of Garryowen, Montana, adopted by <u>**Chief Floyd Real Bird**</u> and Chuck and Ramona Real Bird into the **Whistling Water Clan**.

At the time, there was criticism from parties who did not understand why Grandpa Floyd and the Real Bird clan would adopt a man of mixed heritage. However, it was clear between us: this was about restoring the medicine that had been lost and restoring the family. Grandpa Floyd was a WWII veteran and war hero. He had traveled extensively outside the US and shared many stories with me about his experiences with "other" medicine and the good people he met along the way.

He told me stories about the missing medicine traditions of the Crow and other Native peoples. Even though I was an expert in Oriental Medicine, Thai Nuad Boran, and Ayurveda, when I worked with him by the Little Bighorn River, behind Charlie and Ramona Real Bird's home, he told me that what I was doing *was* Native American medicine, regardless of its origin. He stated, **"Tribal medicine is Tribal medicine, I don't care where it comes from."**

We were joined from time to time by other elders—**Chuck Real Bird (Charlie), Mickey Old Coyote, Harry Moccasin, Bobby Little Light, Leon Pretty On Top, Richard Real Bird, Kinnard Real Bird, Henry Real Bird, Pius Real Bird, Sean Real Bird, Tim Real Bird, and Wayne Moccasin**—and over several years, many others as well. These fine people, experienced and supportive, helped me bring lost and forgotten healing ways to the people there and to my other home away from Crow.

Grandpa Floyd did not care about my mixed heritage or blood quantum; he encouraged me to continue my work and teaching on integrative healing. Chief Floyd was also a Catholic Christian and taught that medicine was for everyone, "Just like Jesus taught." He was the inspiration for my forming the **Native American Indigenous Church (NAIC) Inter-Tribal Organization**, which remains active today, teaching Integrative Native American Medicine through the seminary, The American College of Natural Medicine, and the Thai Yoga Center.

A Lineage of Many Nations

My walk did not end at the Little Bighorn. The mandate to heal led me to sit with and learn from the **Jibarro-Taíno** of the Caribbean, the **Tsáchila** of Ecuador, and the **Huichol-Tarahumara** of Mexico. In each instance, the recognition was the same: the medicine recognizes its own.

I was honored to do my first Vision Quest at **Bear Butte Mountain** (*Hoka Sapa*), near Sturgis, SD, with **Chief Douglas White** and one of my adopted brothers, **Ryan Two Thunder Hawks**. That summer of '92, Grandpa Doug invited me to attend the first **Dakota Pipe Carriers Sun Dance** at Pipestone, Minnesota. There, I was asked to support the Sun Dance by Sun Dance Chiefs **Chris Leith** and **Clyde Bellecourt**.

I went back to the reservation for years, and after the passing of Chief Floyd Real Bird, I continued to do so until the present day.

Standing on the banks of the Little Bighorn River, beside the Medicine Tail Coulee where history was written in blood, they did not teach me pharmacology. They taught me **Sovereignty**. They taught me that a healer without a lineage is just a technician. They taught me that medicine is not something you buy; it is something you carry. It is a bundle.

I am forever indebted to my Crow family—brothers, sisters, aunts, and uncles—for showing me what it means to be true representatives of both Christ and the Red Road. This book is the unfolding of that bundle.

www.ingramcontent.com/pod-product-compliance
Lightning Source LLC
Chambersburg PA
CBHW081718220526
45468CB00008B/1894